PC DOS User's Guide

Chris DeVoney

Que Corporation
Indianapolis

Library of Congress Catalog No.: 83-62485
ISBN 0-88022-040-6

88 87 86 85   14 13 12 11 10 9 8

Interpretation of the printing code: the rightmost double-digit number is the year of the book's printing; the rightmost single-digit number, the number of the book's printing. For example, a printing code of 83-4 shows that the fourth printing of the book occurred in 1983.

Editorial Director
David F. Noble, Ph.D.

Editors
Diane F. Brown, M.A.
Virginia D. Noble, M.L.S.

About the Author

Chris DeVoney is vice president, Technology, for Que Corporation and editor of Que's monthly newsletter, /c. He received his B.S. degree from the University of Gloucester. Mr. DeVoney has been employed in the microcomputer industry since it began in 1975. He founded Marcum Consulting and served as technical consultant to two retail computer stores. Mr. DeVoney has conducted workshops for multinational operating systems and microcomputers. Mr. DeVoney is author of *IBM's Personal Computer*, first and second editions, and *MS-DOS User's Guide*, and coauthor of *Introducing IBM PC*jr, all published by Que Corporation.

Acknowledgments

The author of this book wishes to thank the following people:

George Eberhardt of Computer Innovations, Inc., Red Bank, New Jersey

Joe Hancock, Rex Hancock, Marlene Hilligoss, and the staff of ComputerLand of Indianapolis, Indiana

William McAllister of the IBM Product Center, Indianapolis, Indiana

Mark Tyson of IBM Entry Systems Division, Boca Raton, Florida

Tom Fenwick of Manx Software Systems, Inc., Shrewsbury, New Jersey

Chris Larson and Don Immerwahr of Microsoft, Inc., Bellevue, Washington, for their invaluable assistance

John Freeland and the staff of Microsonics, Inc., Indianapolis, Indiana

Foreword

I received my first copy of the DOS V2.0 documentation in late 1982. After reading it for several hours, I was both excited and confused. I like the UNIX operating system. It has several features I wish were on more microcomputer systems. The prospect of an operating system that combined the friendliness and performance of Microsoft's MS-DOS Version 1 with some of the powerful features of Bell Laboratories' UNIX operating system was tantalizing. The idea of using hierarchical directories, I/O redirection, and piping on my Personal Computer was awesome. I pored through the manuals, imagining what it would be like to have DOS Version 2.

At first, I could not understand all the concepts and materials in the documentation. Not having a working copy of DOS V2.0 made my usual learning technique—understanding by trying—impossible. IBM did not announce PC DOS V2.0 until March, 1983. I had to wait until April before I could use DOS V2.0.

In April, 1983, I was writing the second edition of *IBM's Personal Computer*. I thought it would be appropriate to use the XT while I wrote the book because a major part of the book covered the XT and the differences between it and the PC. That XT still resides on a table in my office.

In the second edition, I tried to explain all about DOS V2.0 in less than 30 pages, a feat I did not feel I accomplished. Although the book is excellent, I felt that someone needed to cover DOS V2.0 in more detail.

After I finished the book, I took a short break. While on that vacation, I walked into a book store and counted more than 35 titles on the IBM Personal Computer. Several books covered PC DOS, Version 1. Having gone through the experience of learning a new version of an operating system, I felt that others should not have to suffer through the experience the same way—the hard way.

This book is the result.

DOS V2 is not very hard to learn, but more time is needed to learn how to use its new features and functions. I made several "near fatal" mistakes while becoming familiar with DOS V2. Most of them were unimportant, but two almost wiped out all the information on my 10-megabyte hard disk.

That is why I wrote this book. One of Murphy's sayings is, "Experience is directly proportional to the amount of equipment ruined." I changed that saying to, "Computer experience is directly proportional to the number of disk files ruined." I am a very experienced DOS V2 user!

This book is a user's guide to DOS V2 for the novice-to-intermediate computer user. The book discusses the philosophy and concepts behind DOS V2, the way the computer operates, and examples of all the commands. Often, you see on the page exactly what happens on the video screen.

But this book is more than just a user's guide. It is also an excellent DOS V2 reference book. That is why the Command Summary section was created. Every command has sections on its purpose, syntax, rules, and exit codes. Many commands also have examples or sample sessions as well as additional background notes. The commands are alphabetized for easy reference. This feature allows anyone, including the advanced user, to locate a command quickly, find the information needed to make it work, and continue working.

Throughout this book hints, suggestions, and occasional warnings appear, stemming from my experience with DOS V2. As I wrote this book, I attempted to exercise DOS to its limits. What would DOS allow? What would it find objectionable? Occasionally, DOS would accept an improperly phrased command and do the completely unexpected. Actually, DOS did exactly what it was instructed to do, which was not always what I wanted. Sometimes I ran into genuine bugs with DOS. The known bugs (only two real bugs for DOS V2.0) are listed in Appendix A. Fortunately, these bugs are fixed by DOS V2.1.

Don't be intimidated by DOS V2. I have never met a person who learned how to ride a bicycle just by reading a book. The same is true for computers. Try the examples. Experiment. Be daring occasionally. However, be sure to experiment with practice disks (diskettes that do not contain valuable information) until you get the hang of DOS. There

vi

are very few "dangerous" commands in DOS. (FDISK, FORMAT, ERASE, and DISKCOPY are the major ones.) If you make a mistake, look at what you typed. Most often, you simply mistyped a word. Try to find out what you did wrong and try the command again. The Commands Section of the book will help you determine what might be wrong. DOS is friendly once you get to know it.

Introduction

What You Should Know

Before you start reading this book, you should familiarize yourself with three things: the control and editing keys, the FDISK program (if you own an XT), and the EDLIN line-editing program. The DOS V2.0 manual provided with your computer is the best source of information about these topics.

The control keys and DOS editing keys are covered on pages 2-21 through 2-40. The most important section is pages 2-21 through 2-28. Be sure to read this section before proceeding with this book. The DOS editing keys, on the other hand, may be learned at any time. They make typing mistakes easier to correct.

The FDISK program configures the hard disk for IBM Personal Computer XTs. Your dealer might have already configured your hard disk for you. If not, either contact your dealer for this service (possibly for a fee) or read Chapter 4 of your DOS manual on the hard disk. Follow the instructions on pages 4-6 through 4-12. These well-illustrated instructions are easy to understand.

The EDLIN program is a *text editor*. It allows you to record and edit text into a disk file, but is only half of a word-processing program. (The other half is the printing process.) As a limited, line-oriented text editor, EDLIN is not as good as many other programs, such as VEDIT, WordStar, IBM's Personal or Professional Editor, etc.

You will need a text editor later in this book, starting with the discussion of batch files in Chapter 9. If you decide to use EDLIN, read the brief tutorial on pages 2-41 through 2-52 in your DOS manual. A full explanation of EDLIN appears in Chapter 7 of the manual.

You may use a different text editor or word-processing program. If you choose a word-processing program, use its programming or nondocument mode. With some word processors, such as WordStar, the characters are manipulated and stored differently by the document and nondocument modes. Text to be used by DOS should always be created under the word processor's nondocument mode.

What You Should Have

Starting in Chapter 2, you will need the following items:

- Your computer system, connected and working

- The diskettes provided with DOS V2.0, your DOS master diskettes

- Several blank diskettes, with the accompanying protective envelopes and blank labels

Throughout this book you will be asked to try a command or sequence of commands on your computer system. To work these exercises, you will need your working computer, the DOS diskettes, and several blank diskettes.

What Will Be Covered

Chapter 1 presents the basic history of DOS and its role in the computer system. Chapter 2 is a hands-on session during which you prepare blank diskettes, copy diskettes and files, and learn basic DOS concepts. The inner workings of DOS and DOS' major sections are discussed in Chapter 3.

Chapter 4 offers facts about disk drives and diskettes as well as some useful tips, and Chapter 5 contains information about disk files and disk file names. It also introduces some of the conventions used in this book.

Chapter 6, which discusses devices and device names, leads into the new features of DOS V2. Two important DOS V2 features— I/O redirection and piping—are covered in Chapter 7, and Chapter 8 treats the hierarchical directory system of DOS V2.

Chapter 9 introduces batch files and their new and unique sub-commands, and Chapter 10 covers the new CONFIG.SYS file that allows you to tailor DOS to your needs with little effort.

Old and new DOS commands that have changed from Version 1 to Version 2 are presented in Chapter 11. Chapter 12 offers advice and tips for hard disk users on the BACKUP and RESTORE programs and other related topics. RECOVER is also covered in this chapter. A Final Thoughts section in Chapter 13 provides more facts about DOS V2.0 and suggests additional sources of information.

Some of the known bugs of DOS V2.0 are listed in Appendix A. This list may be outdated by the time you read this book as IBM corrects the problems of DOS V2.0 with DOS V2.1. Appendix B is an example of a disk showing the hierarchical directory structure, and Appendix C is an ASCII character chart. A detailed index completes the book.

What Is Not Covered

No book can cover DOS completely. There are so many aspects of this operating system that no book can be at the same time a tutorial on learning DOS, a DOS reference guide, a system programmer's guide, etc. For this reason, several subjects were omitted from this book:

- Control and DOS editing keys

- The FDISK program, for XT owners

- The EDLIN (line editor), DEBUG (assembly language debugger), and LINK (program linker) programs

- The ANSI terminal control codes

- The DOS function calls

- Writing device drivers

- Similar technical details about DOS

Most of this information is important to programmers. If you do not program, or program only in Disk or Advanced BASIC, the lack of this information will not matter to you. If you'd like more information on the programming aspects of DOS, read your DOS manual.

The Case for PC DOS V2

PC DOS 2 offers many important new features. In addition to the UNIX-like features and the ability to handle the hard disk, several other

xi

features make PC DOS V2 particularly attractive. The strongest of these is the 12-percent increase in minifloppy disk storage. What was a 320K minifloppy disk drive is now a 360K drive, a 40K improvement. Nine V2.0 diskettes can hold the equivalent of ten V1 diskettes. Also, a little known bug in the random write function of DOS V1.1 was fixed. Disk operations are faster (16 percent or more) with DOS V2-formatted diskettes than with V1.1 diskettes. For these reasons, I recommend that Personal Computer owners switch to DOS V2. Once you are comfortable with the UNIX-like features of DOS V2, you may never want to use V1.1 again.

I can think of only two reasons why you might not want to use DOS V2. The first is that your computer may have only 64K of RAM memory. DOS V2 requires at least 96K of memory, and 128K or more to take full advantage of some of DOS' features. However, because RAM memory is inexpensive and many programs run better with 128K or more, there is no reason why you shouldn't increase the RAM capacity of your computer to use DOS V2.

The second reason is especially valid. Some programs do not work with DOS V2.0 because they are copy-protected or constructed in such a way that they will simply not work with DOS V2. I understand your, the user's, plight, but I have no sympathy for the program publishing houses that have locked you into an old version of an operating system.

Can you use both versions of DOS, V1 and V2, on the same computer? You can, but with two serious warnings. First, don't ever use DOS V1.1 utilities while your computer is running DOS V2. Likewise, don't use DOS V2 utilities while your computer is running DOS V1.1! You can actually lose disk files if you do. Second, using DOS V1.1-formatted diskettes with DOS V2 is perfectly safe. However, DOS V2-formatted diskettes (diskettes formatted at the new higher capacities) cannot be used with DOS V1.1. If you can operate with these two limitations, you can use two versions of DOS on the same computer.

Read, try, learn, and enjoy. After all, the computer is just a servant. All you have to do is be comfortable in your role as user.

Table of Contents

1
DOS and You

DOS is the acronym for disk operating system. An operating system is a collection of programs that direct and aid in the management of the computer's resources. A *disk* operating system also controls the use of disk drives for the storing and loading of programs and data.

Anyone who uses a personal computer with one or more disk drives should have some knowledge of DOS. What you need to know depends on what you want to do with your computer. You may want to know only how to turn on the computer, start DOS, and issue one or two commands. On the other hand, you may use your computer so much that you need to know all the commands and how they work. Most people fall somewhere in between.

What should you know about DOS? There is no exact answer to this question, but you must know some commands and facts. The most basic commands cover how to format a disk, place a copy of the operating system on the diskette, copy and erase disk files, get a list of the files on a disk, and perform other fundamental operations of DOS. Everyone who operates a computer should know these commands.

If you use your computer extensively, you will need to know even more. Knowing how disk files are actually stored, finding the amount of free space on a disk, establishing and using the hierarchical directories, or using redirected I/O will be important to you. If you fall into this "heavy-user" category, be sure to read about all the features and commands.

DOS has many useful functions and features. You don't have to use all of them, nor are you obligated to learn everything about each command you use. The first time through, just try to remember the basic functions of each command. Later, you can return to this book or your DOS reference manual and learn more about the commands and functions of DOS.

At times, learning about DOS can be a circular process. You may need to know one thing before you can go on to something else. When this problem occurs, you do not need to be alarmed, because DOS is not really complicated.

The Origin of MS-DOS

The following is a "fairy tale" description of the origin and evolution of MS-DOS.

In the beginning (1972), there were microprocessors, a computer on a silicon chip. This chip had replaced many different chips, but the microprocessors were without software, the instructions that told these computers-on-a-chip what to do.

So engineers from such companies as Intel™ Corporation began to write software. But they found that writing software was difficult. Each instruction had to be entered by hand as a number, not an English-like word or phrase. So the engineers designed assemblers, programs that took pidgin English-like commands (*mnemonics*) and transformed them into instructions the microprocessors could understand. After assemblers came debuggers, programs that helped engineers find problems in other programs.

A convenient way to get the programs into the microprocessors was still needed. In those early days, the mighty paper tape punch and reader were the standard. They were slow, however, and handling paper tape was difficult.

The engineers then began to write new operating systems that used a new device called a disk drive. One was partially developed at IBM. A circular piece of flexible plastic, eight inches in diameter and coated with iron ferrite, was placed in a cardboard jacket. This *floppy diskette* was inserted into the disk drive, and a special board placed into the computer controlled the actions of the disk drive. The floppy disk drive was exciting because it could hold 246,784 bytes of information, the equivalent of over a mile of paper tape. The new operating system that handled the placing, reading, and organizing of information on the diskette was called a *disk operating system*.

In 1975, in front of a computer club, a new company displayed its new board that used floppy disk drives and floppy diskettes. The software used to "control" the new board was called Control Program for Microcomputers, or CP/M™. Dr. Gary Kildall was the co-author of this early disk operating system.

And so CP/M became a standard for the microcomputers that used microprocessors from Intel (the 8080 and later 8085 CPU) and a new company called Zilog Corporation (the Z80 CPU). As time passed, CP/M was improved and continued to grow.

Soon (1978) Intel Corporation announced a new and improved version of its microprocessor, the 8086 CPU. It worked faster and could immediately use more RAM memory than its predecessors. Because of some differences between the systems, the software that worked with the older Intel microprocessors would not work with the new 8086 CPU.

Later, Intel developed a sister microprocessor to the 8086 CPU, the 8088 CPU. It worked like the 8086, and both could use the same software, but the 8088 "talked" only half as well to memory and the outside world as the 8086. The 8086 could communicate in units of 16 bits at a time. (A *bit* is a *b*inary dig*it,* the smallest unit of storage in the computer. Eight bits make up one *byte,* the basic unit of storage that holds one character.) The 8088, though, could talk to memory or the outside world in units of only 8 bits at a time.

After the 8086, but before the 8088, a small company in Seattle, Washington, wrote a new disk operating system for the 8086 CPU. The author was Tim Paterson, a co-owner of Seattle Computer Products. The firm had developed a computer that used the 8086 CPU and needed a disk operating system for it. In 1979, Tim Paterson wrote 86-DOS. It was patterned after the CP/M operating system. However, Paterson added some changes to 86-DOS. He wanted the operating system to work quickly and take advantage of the new features offered by disk drives and other computer equipment. He also wanted the operating system to be friendly to a newcomer and its internal workings to be different from CP/M and better.

Meanwhile, the world's largest computer maker, International Business Machines, was considering making a personal computer. IBM decided that it was important to have a BASIC programming language available for its computer. The logical choice was to use BASIC from Microsoft, Inc., a company located in Bellevue, Washington. Microsoft had written the most popular version of the BASIC programming language. At that time, Microsoft BASIC was running on more than 500,000 computers.

Bill Gates, then president of the company and one of the two authors of Microsoft BASIC, met with IBM. Microsoft began to work on a special version of its 8086 BASIC language. (Microsoft's BASIC-86 made its debut in 1979.)

At the same time, IBM began talking to Digital Research, Inc., the Pacific Grove, California, company that wrote CP/M. IBM and Digital Research did not come to an agreement. IBM began to look elsewhere for an operating system for its new personal computer.

Microsoft quickly acquired the rights to distribute Tim Paterson's 86-DOS and began talking to IBM about using this new operating system. An agreement was made, and Microsoft's MS-DOS became one of the operating systems for the new IBM Personal Computer.

Just before this, Microsoft acquired the rights to rewrite and distribute Bell Laboratories' UNIX™ operating system. Microsoft called its version of UNIX, XENIX™, believing that XENIX would be the best operating system for the new generation of microcomputers that used the new, more powerful microprocessors. The impact of this decision will become apparent later in this story.

In April, 1981, IBM announced the IBM Personal Computer, which uses the 8088 CPU and the IBM Personal Computer Disk Operating System. The microcomputer industry nicknamed the new operating system PC DOS. It is really MS-DOS with some program additions from IBM. PC DOS quickly became the most popular operating system for the Personal Computer. Soon many other companies began marketing computers that used MS-DOS, the foundation for PC DOS. Companies such as Zenith Data Systems, Wang Laboratories, Digital Equipment Corporation, Texas Instruments, and Victor Technology made computers with the 8088 or 8086 CPU that ran the MS-DOS operating system.

Microsoft began to work on a new version of its operating system. This version would be a hybrid. It would combine many of the features of the current MS-DOS with some of the features of the XENIX operating system. Microsoft felt that the current version of MS-DOS was well suited for one person doing one thing at a time on one computer. However, the new computers allowed more than one person at a time (multiple users) to run more than one program at a time (multiple tasks). MS-DOS Version 2 was written to start the transition.

Microsoft took some of the features of its XENIX operating system and incorporated them into MS-DOS Version 2. As a result, features that had not been available before on microcomputers became available through MS-DOS V2. One of the biggest changes was the use of hierarchical directories. (This concept is discussed in Chapter 8.) This change was necessary as larger, faster hard disk drives became popular. The hard disk drive could hold twenty to forty times more information than a floppy disk. In addition, the XENIX method of organizing information on the disks was more attractive than the old method.

Almost two years after IBM announced the Personal Computer, the Personal Computer XT made its debut. The XT came with a ten-million-byte hard disk drive. Although IBM could modify DOS Version 1 to handle the hard disk, the need to organize information on the hard disk with the new XENIX method was important. IBM announced PC DOS Version 2.0, the IBM/Microsoft implementation of MS-DOS V2, for the Personal Computer XT.

Today, every IBM XT owner uses PC DOS V2. Old and new Personal Computer owners are also buying and using DOS V2.

What Did This Story Tell You?

The origin of MS-DOS is closely linked to Tim Paterson of Seattle Computer Products and IBM. Microsoft acquired 86-DOS because of

IBM. Initially, the only difference between 86-DOS and MS-DOS was the name. MS-DOS is a trademark of Microsoft. Microsoft has improved MS-DOS since the first version. Tim Paterson worked for Microsoft for a year to help perfect MS-DOS. The first published version of PC DOS was V1.0, which was MS-DOS V1.10. Microsoft corrected several problems with MS-DOS, and it finally evolved into MS-DOS V1.25. This version became PC DOS V1.1, which also incorporated the routines for handling the new double-sided floppy disk drives. In the latter part of 1982, Microsoft wrote MS-DOS V2.0. It was adopted by IBM and became PC DOS V2.0.

MS-/PC DOS V2 represents a transition in operating systems: a directory on the disk is used to store the list of the files on that disk. The old Version-1 method for handling the directory (covered in Chapter 5) worked well for floppy diskettes, but hard disk drives posed a new problem. A different method was needed to handle the directory. Microsoft used the UNIX-style hierarchical directories to solve the directory problem. This method allowed many more files to be stored and retrieved. In addition to incorporating this UNIX feature, Microsoft added the UNIX abilities to redirect I/O and pipe information between programs, along with the necessary DOS system calls. It is not important to know all the terms that were just mentioned. They are discussed in detail in later chapters. The point to remember is that MS-DOS V2 deliberately resembles the UNIX operating system.

Chapter 2 is a hands-on session. If you have just started using your computer, go through this chapter step by step. If you have already used your computer and are comfortable with it, skip to Chapter 3 for a discussion of how DOS works.

2

Starting Out

I am a firm believer in learning by doing. In this chapter, you will use several DOS commands to copy a diskette, format a diskette, copy some files, and get a listing of the files on a disk.

I am an anxious person. I like to try new things as soon as I can. If you are like me and, in addition, are a newcomer to DOS, please read carefully each complete step before you try it. If you don't, you may miss some small detail that could make things not work the way they should.

Before you start, take a moment to become familiar with the notation used throughout this book. It will help you distinguish what you type from what the computer displays. What you type on the computer appears **like this**. Anything the computer displays looks like this. For example, in the following line:

A>**DIR**

DOS printed the A>. You would type the **DIR**. There is one more "symbol" that you can't see. After you type **DIR**, you must hit the Enter key. The Personal Computer uses the ← symbol to mark the Enter

7

key. In almost every case, you should hit the ◄─┘ key after you have finished typing a line.

For this session, you will need the following:

1. Your Personal Computer or Personal Computer XT, plugged in and ready to go

2. The two diskettes that come with DOS V2.0

3. Three blank diskettes, plus labels and write-protect tabs (These normally come in the box with the blank diskettes.)

If you have a Personal Computer XT and have not yet set up the hard disk, do so now. Follow the instructions in Chapter 4 of the DOS V2.0 manual. When you format the hard disk, use the **/S** option. It will put DOS on your hard disk so that you can start your computer without using a floppy diskette.

Three Important Keys

Before you start, make certain that you know by now three important keys: Enter, Backspace, and Escape.

The Enter key is the "go" key. When you press Enter, you signal DOS that you have finished typing, and that DOS should act on your answer. The first two examples below show the Enter key as the last character on the line to remind you to hit Enter after you type a line. After a few times, you should find yourself typing Enter automatically.

The Enter key can also be "the point of no Return." In many cases, once you have tapped Enter, you cannot re-enter your answer to the computer's request. Before you hit the Enter key, take a moment to check that your typing is correct. After you become acquainted with DOS, you will know when typing mistakes are harmless and when they can cause trouble.

Several programs or DOS commands need only a one-letter answer, such as a "Y" for yes or "N" for no. In some cases, you don't need to hit Enter after you type your response. For now, *always* finish what you type by tapping the Enter key.

The backspace key, ◄─, can be used after you make a mistake. Each time you tap this key, the cursor will back up one character and erase it.

The *cursor* is the flashing underscore character that shows you where the next character you type will be placed on the screen. After you back up the cursor and erase the mistake, you can retype the rest of the line.

If you have made some major typing mistakes, tap the Escape key before you hit the Enter key. This will put a backslash (\) on the screen and drop the cursor to the next line. DOS will ignore what you typed on the previous line and let you retype the entire line. The Escape key, Esc, is located on the upper left-hand part of the keyboard. Occasionally, you may overshoot the 1 key and hit the Esc key instead. If this happens, just retype your line.

The Boot

Put your DOS master diskette (the diskette that does not say "Supplemental Programs") in the left-hand floppy disk drive and close the door.

If your computer is turned off, turn it on. If your computer is on, press these three keys at once:

    Ctrl Alt Del

The Ctrl key is a tan key located next to the A key. The Alt key is a tan key located to the left of the space bar, the longest key on the keyboard. The Del key is on the lower right part of the keypad, on the right side of the keyboard. Del shares the key with the period (.).

When you simultaneously type these three keys, the Personal Computer does a *system reset*. This restarts the computer from scratch. Any information still in the computer is lost. A system reset is slightly different from turning off and on again the power to your computer. When you power up your computer, the system does a self-test to check whether the computer is working properly. When you do a system reset, the Personal Computer skips the self-test.

The red light on the left-hand minifloppy disk drive should come on. DOS will then ask you for the current date and time. I wrote this chapter at 3:45 p.m. on August 27, 1983. I answered both questions in the following manner:

```
Current date is Tue  1-01-1980
Enter new date: 8-27-83◄─┘
Current time is  0:00:13.47
Enter new time: 15:45:27◄─┘
```

Notice how the current date and time were entered. The date is entered as numbers in the form **mm-dd-yy**, where **mm** is for the month; **dd,** the day; and **yy,** the year. I used hyphens between the numbers, but I could have used slashes instead.

DOS is a little fussier about the time. You enter the time as **hh:mm:ss.xx**, where **hh** is for the hour; **mm,** the minutes; **ss** , the seconds; and **xx,** the hundredths of a second. You must use a colon (:) between the hours, minutes, and seconds but a period (.) between the seconds and hundredths of a second.

DOS uses a 24-hour clock, similar to military or universal clocks. You add 12 to the afternoon hours. For example, 3:00 p.m. becomes 15:00.

Enter the current date and the time now. Don't bother entering the hundredths of a second (xx), and don't forget to hit the Enter key after you finish typing.

```
Current date is Tue  1-01-1980
Enter new date: 8-27-83
Current time is  0:00:13.47
Enter new time: 15:45:27

The IBM Personal Computer DOS
Version 2.00 (C) Copyright IBM Corp 1981, 1982, 1983
```

Does your screen look something like the above? If its says something else or nothing at all, there is a problem. If you have the message Invalid Date or Invalid time on your screen, then you did not enter the number correctly. You might have typed a nonsense date or time, incorrectly punctuated the date or time, or used the numeric keypad on the right side of the keyboard. When DOS reboots, the keypad is set in the "cursor control/editing" mode. To use the numbers on this pad, you must either hold the shift key down as you type the numbers or hit the Num Lock key once. Then you can re-enter the date or time.

If the video screen looks like the example, DOS has successfully started and is in control of your computer system. This process is called *booting*. Now everything you type will be handled by DOS.

If the numbers after the decimal point are different from the example, don't worry. You have a later revision of DOS, which does not matter for now.

Copying a Diskette

Now that DOS is started, let's copy the DOS system diskette, which is the diskette in drive A.

If you are using a Personal Computer XT or a Personal Computer with only one minifloppy disk drive, read the next section and try the first example. Because you have only one disk drive, your instructions will be different from those for users with two drives.

If you have a Personal Computer, place the new blank diskette into drive B, the right-hand drive. Close the door and type:

A>DISKCOPY A: B:

Then hit Enter. Always press Enter after you finish typing a command. For now, type your commands in capital letters. In most cases, DOS does not care if you use upper- or lower-case letters, but there are some instances where the distinction between them is important.

The red light on the left-hand drive should come on briefly. Then the following message will appear:

```
    Insert source diskette in drive A:
    Insert target diskette in drive B:
    Strike any key when ready.
    _
```

If you have a one-minifloppy drive system like the XT, you will see:

```
Insert the source diskette in drive A:

Strike any key when ready.
```

DOS is now waiting for you to hit any key. Type either Ctrl-C or Ctrl-Break. (Break is the same key as the tan Scroll Lock key on the upper right-hand side of the keypad.) You do this by holding down the Ctrl key, then tapping either the C key or the Break key.

If you are using a two-minifloppy disk drive system, you should see the following message on your screen:

```
Insert source diskette in drive A:
Insert target diskette in drive B:
Strike any key when ready.
^C

A>_
```

If you have a one-minifloppy drive system, you won't see the "target diskette" line. Typing Ctrl-C or Ctrl-Break initiates the "stop what you are doing" command. Whether you type Ctrl-C or Ctrl-Break does not matter; both work the same way. This sequence is labeled either *Control-Break* or just Ctrl-Break. When you type it, you are telling DOS to stop immediately the program that is running, exit the program, and take control again. That's what the ^C on the screen means.

If you get into a situation where things are drastically wrong, such as the wrong diskette is in the drive, or you invoked the wrong command or used the wrong file, Ctrl-Break is one panic button you can use. You should be able to stop the program by typing Ctrl-Break or Ctrl-C. Note that this does not always work, and later in the book you will learn why.

You should keep in mind that when DOS says, Strike any key when ready, it really means, "Strike *almost* any key when ready." If you tap the Shift, Alt, Caps Lock, Num Lock, or Scroll Lock keys, DOS will ignore them and continue to wait. The system reset sequence, however, is guaranteed to reset your system, so don't type it unless you want to reset your computer. Generally, the Enter key and the space bar are two good, large targets to use when DOS wants any key struck.

Two-Floppy Disk Drive DISKCOPY

If you have a one-minifloppy drive system, including XT owners, read the rest of this section, but don't do the examples. The instructions for you follow this discussion.

For the copying process, the *source diskette* is the DOS master diskette that you put in drive A. The *target diskette* is the new, blank diskette that you place in drive B.

If you inserted the correct diskettes into the correct disk drives before you typed DISKCOPY, you may hit any key to start the copying process.

First, the light on the A drive will go on. You will see the message:

```
Copying 9 sectors per track, 1 side(s)
```

In three to eight seconds, the light on the A drive will go out, and the light on the B drive will go on. Then you will see the message:

```
Formatting while copying
```

This message tells you that DOS is setting your blank diskette in drive B to hold the information that will be transferred from the DOS master diskette in drive A.

You will probably notice that the lights on the drives will go on and off again several times. The number of times this occurs depends on the amount of RAM memory in your computer.

After DISKCOPY has finished copying the diskette, you will see the message:

```
    Copy another (Y/N)? _
```

DOS is asking if you want to copy another diskette. We don't, so you should answer **N** for no. The A> sign will reappear.

You have just made a copy of your DOS diskette. Find one of the labels for your diskettes and write "DOS V2.0 System Master" on the label. Put the label on the diskette. Always label a diskette after you perform a DISKCOPY. The label will remind you that the diskette has something useful on it.

Put your original DOS system diskette back in the envelope and place the copy you made into drive A.

One-Floppy Disk Drive DISKCOPY

If you have two floppy disk drives, skim this section, but don't try the example. If you are an XT owner, or have one floppy disk drive in your system, this section will show you how to DISKCOPY your DOS diskette.

Put your original DOS diskette in drive A, then type:

A>**DISKCOPY A: A:**

You will see the message:

```
Insert the source diskette into drive A:

Strike any key when ready
```

The source diskette is the DOS master diskette and is already in drive A. Hit the space bar. The light on your floppy disk drive will go on. In a few seconds, you will see the message:

```
Copying 9 sectors per track, 1 side(s)
```

After a few more seconds, you should see the message:

```
Insert the destination diskette into drive A:
Strike any key when ready.
```

Take your DOS diskette out of the floppy disk drive, put the blank diskette into the drive, close the door, and press a key. You will then see the message:

```
Formatting while copying
```

DOS is now setting up your diskette to hold the information from the DOS master diskette. After a few seconds, you will see the message:

```
Insert the source diskette into drive A:

Strike any key when ready.
```

Take out the second diskette and place your DOS diskette in the drive. Close the door and hit a key. After a few seconds, you will see:

```
Insert the destination diskette into drive A:

Strike any key when ready.
```

Change diskettes again, close the door, and hit a key. These messages may appear one or two more times. If they do, exchange diskettes each time and hit a key.

The message

```
Copy another (Y/N)? _
```

indicates that DISKCOPY has finished making the copy of the DOS master diskette. Answer **N** for no in response to this question. The A> sign should reappear.

Take out a label for the diskette and write "DOS V2.0 System Master Diskette" on the label. Take the diskette out of the drive and place the label on the diskette.

You can perform the same task by typing either

DISKCOPY

or

DISKCOPY A:

The result is the same because you are using the same floppy disk drive to make the copy.

Formatting and Copying a Diskette

Everyone should try this exercise. Get the diskette you made in the last exercise, the one with the label "DOS V2.0 System Master Diskette." Find one of the write-protect tabs that came with your diskettes. Put the tab over the slot on the upper left-hand edge of the diskette. Once you have done this, put the disk into drive A.

FORMAT is one of the few DOS commands that do not require you to hit ◄─┤ when answering yes or no to a question. As you do this example, always finish your answer by hitting the ◄─┤ key unless you can answer the question with a **Y** or **N**. I'll point out where this happens.

Now we will format a blank diskette and put the DOS operating system on it. Type:

FORMAT A: /S /V

Notice how this command line is phrased. First, you type the name of the command, **FORMAT**, then the name of the disk drive you are using to format the diskette. Next, enter two switches: **/S** and **/V**. The **/S** tell DOS to put the operating system on the diskette you are formatting. The **/V** tells DOS that you want to put a volume label on the diskette. (These switches are discussed in detail later.)

What is a *switch?* Most DOS commands have options that affect the way the command works. In the case of FORMAT, the two options copy the operating system to the newly formatted disk and place a volume label on it for identification. To use these options, you must "pull the switch" when you use the command. When you pull the switch, you tell the command to do extra work or handle things in a different way. Most DOS commands have switches. To use a switch, type the switch character (a slash [/]), followed by the character for the switch. A switch is typed on the same line as the DOS command and is usually the last item typed on that line.

After you type the FORMAT command line, the red light on the disk drive will come on for a while. You will then see the following message:

```
Insert the new diskette for drive A:

Strike any key when ready.
```

Take the DOS diskette out of drive A, put your blank diskette in the drive, then tap a key. The red light will come on again, and a message will appear:

```
Formatting . . .
```

After 20 to 40 seconds, you will see:

```
Formatting complete
```

The disk drive will keep spinning. After a few more seconds, you will see the message:

```
System transferred
```

Now DOS asks,

```
 Volume label (11 characters, ENTER for none)? _
```

Type **My DOS disk**, then hit Enter.

The diskette will whirl, then DOS will tell you how much total information the disk can hold, how much space is being taken by DOS, and the amount of free space. For my system, I saw

```
 362496  bytes total disk space
  40960  taken by system
 321536  bytes free
```

A total disk space of 362,496 bytes is the maximum user storage capacity of the disk or diskette. This space is equivalent to 354K. A K is 1,024 bytes. By dividing 362,496 by 1,024 you get 354. This number tells you that you are using double-sided disk drives. If you are using single-sided disk drives, the amount of total usable disk space is about 179K. The amount of free space shown on the screen should be 138,296 bytes.

Note that the actual storage capacity of the disk or diskette is higher. The total usable disk space numbers do not include three small sections recorded on the disk or diskette by DOS. The actual capacity of a single-sided disk drive is 180K, and a double-sided drive holds 360K, the numbers we'll use in this book. These "invisible" sections are discussed in Chapter 4 in a section on how DOS uses disks and diskettes.

If you have a line that says . . . bytes in bad sectors, DOS found some sectors on the diskette that are bad and cannot be used to hold information. Your total amount of free space will be reduced by the number at the front of this line. If you see this message, answer **Y** to the question

```
    Format another (Y/N)? _
```

but don't hit Enter. This is the only spot where you don't need to hit the Enter key. Take the disk partially out of the drive, reinsert the diskette, close the door, and tap a key. Some diskettes do not format correctly the first time but usually do so the second time. If the disk does not format properly the second time, something may be wrong with the disk drive or the diskette (most likely the diskette). If the diskette has some bad sectors, you can either take the diskette back to the dealer for another diskette or just live with the fact that you won't have all the storage space you should from this diskette.

FORMAT should now be asking:

```
    Format another (Y/N)? _
```

Answer **N** for no and don't hit the Enter key. This is the only question FORMAT asks for which you don't need to hit the Enter key. The A> should reappear.

You have formatted a diskette that holds a copy of the DOS operating system. Now type **DIR**. You should see:

```
A>DIR

Volume in drive A is MY DOS DISK
Directory of A:\

COMMAND   COM   17664 3-08-83 12:00p
1 File(s)321536 bytes free

A>_
```

You have just asked DOS to display a list of files on the diskette in drive A. That is the purpose of the DIR (directory) command. If you want to know what files are on a disk, use the DIR command.

The first line shown above is the *volume label* for the diskette. As indicated earlier, this label helps you to identify the diskette. DOS does not do anything with a volume label except show it with certain DOS commands.

The next line tells you what disk drive and directory path are being displayed. (These concepts are discussed in the next two chapters.)

You will see one line for every file on the disk. The only file here is COMMAND.COM. The line shows the root name of the file, the suffix, the length of the file in bytes, and the date and time that the file was first created or last updated (when the information in the file was changed).

The last line tells you the number of files displayed by the DIR command and the amount of free disk space. Again, the number of free bytes may vary because of bad sectors on the disk or the use of a single-sided disk drive.

But something is wrong. The only disk file on the list, COM-MAND.COM, is only 17,664 bytes. Didn't FORMAT tell us that more than 40,000 bytes were used by DOS?

The rest of the space is taken up by two additional files that you cannot see: IBMBIO.COM and IBMDOS.COM. These files are *system* files that hold the disk operating system. They do not show up when you ask for a directory (the DIR command). Although these files are on this disk, they are hidden from you.

If you have a two-floppy diskette drive system, take the diskette out of drive A and place it in drive B. Then put your copy of the DOS master diskette in drive A and type:

COPY A:*.* B: /V

Your disk lights will flash several times. The /V switch used here is different from FORMAT's /V switch. It tells DOS to verify the copy and make sure that the copied information has been recorded properly. Many DOS commands use the same switch, but it has a different meaning for each command. Watch out for this distinction.

Shortly, you will see the message:

```
   23 file(s) copied
```

then the A>. You may see a number other than 23, but don't worry. You just have a different version of DOS.

The message above indicates that you have just copied all the files from your copy of the DOS system diskette to the second diskette.

If you have double-sided disk drives, copy the files from the DOS Supplemental Program diskette to the second diskette. Put the DOS Supplemental diskette into drive A and type:

COPY A:*.* B: /V

The files from the DOS Supplemental diskette will then be transferred to the second diskette. You should see the message:

```
   14 file(s) copied
```

Don't worry if the number is different here also. The COPY process has finished. Take the diskette out of drive B. Get one of the floppy diskette labels and write a title on the label so that you can quickly identify this diskette as holding all of the DOS V2.0 programs. Put the label on the diskette. Then take your DOS Supplemental disk out of drive A, put it back in the envelope, and put this diskette aside.

If you have an XT, you will need to do a few extra steps to copy these files. If you already have a subdirectory called DOS, change to SOD (merely DOS spelled backwards) all the places in the directions where DOS is used.

Make sure that your hard disk is set up properly, then type:

MD C:\DOS

This creates a new subdirectory called DOS on the hard disk. If you already have a directory called DOS, type:

MD C:\SOD

instead. Don't forget to use SOD instead of DOS in the following instructions. (Subdirectories are discussed in Chapter 8.)

Now place your copy of the DOS master diskette in drive A and type:

COPY A:*.* C:\DOS /V

In less than one minute, you will see the message:

```
23 file(s) copied
```

Now take the copy of the DOS master diskette out of drive A and put the DOS Supplemental Program diskette in drive A. Type:

COPY A:*.* C:\DOS /V

All of the DOS programs are now transferred to the hard disk. Take the DOS Supplemental diskette out of drive A, put it back in the envelope, and put the diskette you formatted at the beginning of this session into drive A. Then type:

COPY C:\DOS*.* A: /V

This command copies all of the files in the DOS subdirectory (the DOS programs) onto the floppy diskette in drive A. Label this diskette accordingly.

The hard work is over. You have just created two diskettes. One diskette is an exact copy of the DOS master diskette that came with DOS V2.0, and the other is a diskette that holds the two DOS diskettes that came with V2.0. You also used the COPY, DIR, DISKCOPY, and FORMAT commands.

The next three chapters cover what you just did, how DOS works with the equipment in your computer system, and some uses of DOS.

Keep on hand the two diskettes you have just made. You will use them later. If you copied the DOS programs to your hard disk, leave them there. You will use that information later also.

3

A Brief Look inside DOS

DOS is composed of three major parts: the I/O system, the Command Processor, and utilities. The I/O System handles every character that is typed or displayed, printed, and received or sent through the communication adapters. It contains the disk filing system for DOS, which handles the storing and retrieving of programs and information from the disk drives.

The Command Processor has several built-in functions, or subprograms, that handle most common tasks for DOS, such as copying files, displaying a list of files on the disk, and running your programs.

The utilities, which are discussed throughout the book and appear in the Command Summary at the end, are used for housekeeping tasks, such as formatting diskettes, comparing files, finding the free space on a diskette, and background printing. All three parts of DOS were used in Chapter 2.

The I/O System

I/O is the abbreviation for input/output. This term refers to activities related to the computer's central processing unit, or CPU (the "brain" of the computer), and memory. When you type a character on the keyboard, the character moves from the keyboard inward to the CPU and memory. This is *input*. When the computer prints a line on the screen or printer, the line moves outward from the CPU and memory to the screen or printer. This is *output*.

Input and output take place between the computer and the computer's *peripherals*. These devices are used by the computer's CPU and memory but are not part of the CPU and memory itself. The screen, keyboard, printer, and disk drives are peripherals. They are important to the computer because without peripherals, the CPU and memory would have no way to communicate to the outside world.

Each peripheral has a different purpose and method of talking to the computer. Before a computer can use a peripheral, the computer must have a set of instructions that tell it how to talk with the peripheral and control the peripheral's actions.

The BIOS

The software that performs this function is called the *BIOS*, short for Basic Input/Output System. It has fundamental routines that control the keyboard, video display, disk drives, and other peripherals of the computer. Without the BIOS, your computer would not have a standard way to communicate and control these devices.

The BIOS of the Personal Computer is actually located in two places: the System Board and IO.SYS. In the System Board of the computer, the BIOS is contained in a read-only memory chip called a ROM. The nickname for these routines is ROM BIOS, or RIOS (pronounced RYE-ose). The ROM holds the basic routines for communicating with most of the devices used by the Personal Computer.

IBMBIO.COM

The disk file IO.SYS is the second location for these routines. For the Personal Computer, the file name is IBMBIO.COM. This file holds the next level of software routines for controlling and communicating with peripherals.

The IBMBIO.COM file is one of the two "system" files on the diskette you created in Chapter 2. You will recall that these files are hidden from you to prevent accidental erasure or alteration. If you unintentionally erased or altered IBMBIO.COM, you could not properly use the operating system from this diskette.

IBMDOS.COM

The next part of the I/O system is the MSDOS.SYS file. On the IBM PC, MSDOS.SYS is called IBMDOS.COM. This file contains the major part of the operating system and holds the routines for controlling the information passed between the computer and its peripherals. IBMDOS.COM has two separate filing systems: one for disk drives and one for all nondisk peripherals.

Every peripheral talks to the computer either one character at a time or in groups of characters called *blocks*. The keyboard, printer, and video screen are three common character-oriented devices. They talk to the computer one character at a time. Modems also fall into this category. Disk drives talk in blocks of characters and, therefore, are block-oriented devices.

Because the methods used to control these two sets of devices are so fundamentally different, DOS keeps two separate sets of management routines to handle the two classes of devices.

When it gets information from a character-oriented device, DOS checks whether the device has a character to send, then gets the character and puts it in the appropriate spot. When sending a character to the screen or printer, DOS checks whether the device is ready to receive another character, then sends it.

DOS tells the disk drive to move its recording head to the appropriate location on the disk and get, or put, a block of information at that location.

The filing system (IBMDOS) is the control center. IBMDOS communicates its directions to the BIOS. The BIOS, in turn, does the actual "talking" to the devices and transmits the filing system's directions.

There is a good reason for this. All the unique instructions for handling the various devices attached to the computer system are handled in one spot, the BIOS. If additional software routines are needed for new devices, the BIOS will get these new instructions. The filing system portion of DOS remains unchanged.

The two DOS filing systems—character-oriented and disk—perform different tasks. The character-oriented filing system:

>   Gets a character from a device
>   Sends a character to a device
>   Checks whether a device is ready to get or send a character
>   Gets a line of characters from the keyboard
>   Sends a line of characters to the screen
>   Gets or sets the date and the time

In most cases, the device can be the keyboard, screen, printer, or serial adapters.

The disk filing system:

>   Creates a file
>   Opens a file for reading or writing
>   Writes information to a file
>   Reads information from a file
>   Closes a file
>   Searches for a file name
>   Tells the names of files
>   Gives the size of a file
>   Changes the name or attributes of a file
>   Removes a file
>   Resets the disk system
>   Indicates the amount of free space on a disk
>   Tells which disk drives are being used
>   Loads and runs programs
>   Sets up (allocates) memory for programs
>   Frees allocated memory
>   Handles the hierarchical directory system

Although handling memory may not seem to be a block-oriented device function, it does belong here. Because DOS must load and run programs, it needs to be able to manage the memory of the computer.

Don't worry about new or "foreign" terms in this list. All of these functions are discussed at different points in this book. This list simply gives you a glimpse of all the tasks DOS handles.

Together, the BIOS and the filing system provide a unified set of routines—the I/O System—for controlling the computer's resources. It provides a standard way of controlling and directing the computer.

As you use the computer, you may not care how the information is handled, as long as it is done correctly. You do care, however, that a program you buy will work with your computer. If a program uses the standards established by DOS, the program will work with your computer.

For example, BASIC does not have its own routines for controlling the disk drives. It calls on the I/O System to do the hard work. Most programs operate this way. For example, most word-processing programs do not have the routines to grab information directly from the keyboard. Instead, such a program calls on the I/O System to get a character from the keyboard and give it to the program.

The Command Processor

The Command Processor, COMMAND.COM, is the second major part of DOS. COMMAND.COM is the program you communicate with, and it, in turn, tells the rest of DOS what to do.

COMMAND.COM prints the A> on the video screen when you start DOS. A> is called the *system prompt*. It indicates that you are talking to COMMAND.COM. When you type a command, COMMAND.COM will interpret it and take the appropriate action.

COMMAND.COM is made up of several parts. The first area is *critical interrupts*. When a hardware device demands attention, COMMAND.COM will divert the computer's attention to the device. Once the device has received the necessary attention and the need for the critical interrupt is over, COMMAND.COM restores the computer's attention to whatever it was doing before. If the computer was executing one of your programs, it will continue to do so.

The second area is *critical errors,* which are usually disk problems or divide-by-zero errors. The computer gives control to COM-

MAND.COM to handle the error. If you leave a disk drive door open when DOS is trying to read the disk, you may see:

```
Disk error reading drive A
Retry, Ignore, Abort
```

COMMAND.COM displays this message and waits for you to take the appropriate action.

The end-of-program housekeeping utilities are the last part of COMMAND.COM. When a program ends, COMMAND.COM tells the filing system to free the program's RAM memory so that it can be used by other programs. COMMAND.COM also checks itself to see that it is intact. If the memory space normally occupied by COMMAND.COM has been used by the program, COMMAND.COM will reload itself from the disk.

There are also two portions to COMMAND.COM. One portion is *resident*; it always stays in the RAM memory. Most of the COMMAND.COM functions discussed above are in the resident part. The second portion is *transient*. It also stays in RAM memory but can be freed for use by your programs. If your program uses this part of memory, COMMAND.COM must reload itself from the disk when the program has finished.

The transient portion of COMMAND.COM has several commonly used DOS commands built in. These *internal* commands can be used when you are at the system prompt level, A>.

COPY	Copies files
DATE	Sets or shows the system date
ERASE or DEL	Erases disk files
RENAME	Changes the name of a disk file
TIME	Sets or shows the system time
TYPE	Displays on the screen the contents of a disk file

COMMAND.COM also handles:

> The batch files and subcommands ECHO, IF, FOR..IN..DO,
> GOTO, REM, and PAUSE

> The hierarchical directory commands CHDIR, MKDIR,
> and RMDIR

These commands are covered later in this book. For now, just remember that you can execute any DOS command listed above when you are at system level (A>). You don't have to load a program into memory to use these DOS functions.

The new I/O redirection functions are also built into COMMAND.COM. (I/O redirection is covered in Chapter 7.)

The last thing that COMMAND.COM does is direct DOS to load your programs into memory and give them control over the computer. When you type **BASIC**, COMMAND.COM goes down the list of internal commands it knows. BASIC is not one of these commands. COMMAND.COM then tells the filing system to go out to the current disk drive and look for a program called either BASIC.COM or BASIC.EXE. If the filing system finds this program, it is loaded into memory and COMMAND.COM gives the program control of the computer. This is the way you invoke the BASIC language.

The illustration above is also a good example of how the operating system works. You communicate to COMMAND.COM. It then communicates to the filing systems of DOS. They communicate to the BIOS, which talks to the devices. The information constantly passes up and down the line from each major section of the operating system to the devices and to you.

When a program is running, it fills the place between you and COMMAND.COM. You talk to the program. The program talks to portions of COMMAND.COM and the filing system, and the process continues as before.

The operating system, therefore, gives you, the computer user, a way to control the computer's resources. DOS does this job well.

How DOS Starts Up

The process of loading and starting the operating system is called *booting*. It comes from the term "bootstrap," as in pulling oneself up by the bootstraps.

When you do a system reset or turn on the computer, the CPU of the computer executes a small program in the read-only memory of your system. This program is the bootstrap loader. It reads the first part of the disk and brings in the bootstrap program, which starts the chain of events that will load and start DOS. This program starts the primary, or first, disk drive of the computer system. Then the first part of the diskette is read into the RAM memory.

The slightly more intelligent bootstrap program now takes control. It checks the list of files on the diskette for IBMBIO.COM and IBMDOS.COM. If it finds both names, it begins to load IBM-BIO.COM. Because of the limited intelligence of the bootstrap program, IBMBIO.COM must be the first file on the diskette and must be stored consecutively. If both conditions are not met, the entire process will fail. Once IBMBIO.COM is loaded, the bootstrap program also brings IBMDOS.COM into memory.

After IBMBIO.COM is in memory, the bootstrap loader gives control to IBMBIO.COM, the BIOS. It checks to see what equipment is attached to the system and sets up the equipment to be used. The term for this is *initialization*. If your printer is attached and turned on, you will hear a click as the printing head moves back to the first printing position. The BIOS does this as it initializes the printer adapter.

Once the equipment, including the keyboard, screen, and serial and parallel adapters, is initialized, IBMBIO.COM looks for the CON-FIG.SYS file in the primary directory of the disk called CONFIG.SYS. If CONFIG.SYS is found, IBMBIO.COM loads it and executes its instructions. (CONFIG.SYS is discussed later in this book.)

After IBMBIO.COM has finished its work, it moves IBMDOS.COM to the correct location in memory and gives control to IBMDOS.COM. IBMDOS.COM also does setup work. After the setup work is completed, IBMDOS.COM designates a portion of memory that will hold COMMAND.COM. COMMAND.COM is then loaded into memory and there receives control of the computer from IBM-DOS.COM.

DOS is now fully loaded and functioning. The boot of DOS is complete.

One more thing happens before DOS turns control over to you. DOS looks for a file called AUTOEXEC.BAT on the boot diskette. If DOS finds the file, DOS will start executing the file's DOS commands. (AUTOEXEC.BAT and batch files are also discussed later in this book.)

If you have an IBM XT, this process is slightly different. The bootstrap loader inside the ROM first looks for a diskette in drive A. If a diskette is not found, the bootstrap loader jumps to the hard disk to look for DOS. If DOS is found on the hard disk, the process is similar to booting DOS from the diskette.

Like many other processes of your computer system, the startup of DOS is based on one program building on the work of another. In essence, that is how your computer system works. The programs that you run, such as word-processing, accounting, or spreadsheet programs, all use the foundation established by DOS.

4

Disks and Diskettes

Disk drives are your computer system's most important peripherals. Keyboards and video screens are useful input and output devices. Printers and modems extend the capability of the system. But with disk drives the computer can store and retrieve large amounts of information. The first word in "Disk Operating System" says it all.

A computer uses RAM memory to hold temporarily your programs and data. Even DOS is loaded into the RAM memory and run from RAM. Most RAM memory, however, is *volatile*. If you turn off the power, whatever is in the RAM memory disappears.

Disk storage, though, is not volatile. When you turn off the power, whatever is on the floppy disk stays. That is why disks are so important.

Consider three popular uses for computers: accounting, spreadsheets, and word processing. For accounting, the disk holds your daily transactions. One stored set of information is used for invoicing, statements, trial balances, and reports. Information does not need to be re-entered or recalculated manually. For spreadsheets, developing a model is time-consuming. Spreadsheets would not be useful if the model could not be stored and recalled. For word processing, visual editing is only half the story. In writing this book, I first typed on the keyboard what I wanted to say. The computer captured my keystrokes as I typed and stored them on the disk. Then I revised this material until it was correct. Later, an electronic copy of the book was stored on hard disk, and editors worked with this copy.

If you have a spare diskette nearby, get it. The next part of this chapter is a tour of the floppy diskette.

Diskettes

Look at your diskette. Most diskettes come in a flimsy, black cardboard or PCB plastic jacket. The diskette and its jacket are placed inside a white protective envelope. Take the diskette out of the protective envelope. The diskette should slide right out. If it looks as if you need to cut something open to get at the diskette, you have confused the diskette with its envelope.

The floppy diskette got its name from the flexible jacket: the diskette "flops" when you shake it. Because the jacket does not provide much protection for your diskette, you must handle it with care.

The inside of the jacket usually has a felt-like, plastic material glued to it. This material traps small particles from the diskette as it whirls around. The felt-like material is usually lubricated with silicone so that the diskettes do not wear while rubbing against the material.

Inside the jacket is the diskette itself. It is usually made of mylar or polyurethane coated with metal oxide. Most diskettes are shiny and dark brown in color, but some new diskettes are red, gold, or even green. The diskette itself is circular with a diameter of 8 or 5 1/4 inches. Most IBM Personal Computers and MS-DOS computers use 5 1/4-inch diskettes.

Technically, 8-inch diskettes are called *floppy* diskettes, and the 5 1/4-inch version is a *minifloppy* diskette. Sloppy use has blurred the distinction between these terms. Many times the term "floppy" is used in referring to a 5 1/4-inch diskette, which is technically a minifloppy diskette. (I have used the terms floppy and minifloppy interchangeably in this book, to my chagrin.)

Returning to your diskette, make sure that the side with the printed label is facing you. This is the front of the diskette. In the center of the diskette is a large *centering hole*. The disk drive grabs the diskette by this hole. Sometimes a plastic ring is placed on the centering hole to provide extra strength and to help center the diskette when it is in the disk drive.

At the bottom of the diskette jacket on each side is an oblong opening through which the diskette can be seen. These openings are the *access holes,* where the recording heads of the disk drive make contact with the diskette.

Hold the diskette by the cardboard's edge. The top side of the diskette is the side with the printed label. Have this side facing you. Hold the diskette so that the access holes are at the bottom, in the 6-o'clock position.

Between the 12-o'clock and 2-o'clock positions on 8-inch diskettes, or the 3:30 position for minifloppies, you will notice a small hole in the cardboard jacket. This hole is the *index* or *timing hole*. Put two fingers in the center hole and gently rotate the diskette until you see a smaller hole in the diskette itself. Keep rotating for a couple of inches to check for other holes.

The disk drive uses the index hole to help determine where things are stored on the diskette. If you can find only one hole in the diskette, you have a *soft-sectored* diskette. If you rotate the diskette and find more than one timing hole, you have a *hard-sectored* diskette. Hard-sectored diskettes can have 11 to 17 holes for a 5 1/4-inch diskette and up to 33 holes for an 8-inch diskette.

Most computers use soft-sectored diskettes. You cannot use hard-sectored diskettes with computers designed for soft-sectored diskettes, nor can you use soft-sectored diskettes with computers designed for hard-sectored diskettes.

If you have an 8-inch diskette, look at the bottom right edge of the cardboard. (For 5 1/4-inch diskettes, look at the upper left-hand side.) You should see a small notch in the cardboard. This is the *write-protect notch*. Eight-inch and 5 1/4-inch disk drives handle the write-protect notch differently.

If you cover the notch for an 8-inch diskette, you can put information on the diskette. If the notch is uncovered, the diskette is write-protected, and no information can be placed on it. For 5 1/4-inch diskettes, you leave the notch uncovered when you want to put information on the diskette. When you cover the notch, the disk is write-protected. Technically, the notch on the 5 1/4-inch diskette is called the *write-enable* notch.

The write-protect notch provides an easy way of protecting diskettes. By covering a 5 1/4-inch diskette's write-protect notch, you stop anyone from putting information on the diskette, as well as from erasing files. Look at the diskettes provided with DOS V2. The IBM DOS diskettes do not have a write-protect notch. This permanently write-protects the information on the diskette from being altered or erased by the computer. The 8-inch DOS master diskettes usually have the write-protect notch uncovered, thus protecting the files. You can cover this notch, but that would not be advisable.

To protect the files on an 8-inch diskette from accidental erasure or unwelcome changes, keep the write-protect notch uncovered.

Floppy Disk Drives

A floppy disk drive has three major sections: one that holds and spins the floppy diskette, one that moves and controls the recording head (or heads) of the disk drive, and the electronics that communicate to the computer.

The parts that hold and spin the diskette are straightforward. When you close the door, two clutches, one on each side of the disk, grab the center hole of the diskette. The bottom clutch is connected by a belt to a motor that spins the diskette inside its cardboard jacket at 300 rpm. This motor is connected to the rest of the disk drive's electronics.

Inside the disk drive are two connected, mobile arms that hold the recording head (or heads). A disk-drive recording head is smaller than a tape-recorder head and is mainly ceramic, not metal.

Single-sided disk drives have one recording head at the end of the bottom arm. The end of the top arm holds a piece of felt. The felt piece and the recording head face each other.

Double-sided disk drives have a recording head at the end of each arm. As with single-sided disk drives, the ends of the arms face each other.

The arms may be mechanically connected to the door so that they clamp onto the diskette when the door is closed. Some disk drives use a magnetic relay to clamp the arms into place only when the disk drive is reading or writing information to the diskette.

As the arms clamp onto the diskette, it is trapped between the recording heads or the recording head and the felt piece. This positioning keeps the diskette from bouncing away from the recording head(s) and allows information to be written or read reliably.

The coordinated mobile arms move back and forth down the center of the drive. A small "stepper" motor connected to a cam or gear moves the arm. Look at the diskette's access holes and think about how you insert the diskette into the disk drive. From this you can imagine how the recording heads move.

The recording heads, the stepper motor, and the magnetic relay (if used) are also connected to the electronics of the disk drive.

The last part of the disk drive is the electronics for talking to the computer. The write-protect switch is also connected to these circuits. If the write-protect switch senses that the diskette is write-protected, the disk's electronics stop the disk drive from recording information on the diskette.

The small red light on the front of the disk drive comes on whenever the computer is using the disk drive. This light tells you that the disk drive is in use. You should not open the drive door until the light goes out.

The other electronics receive signals from the computer to start the motor that spins the diskette, clamp the recording arm on the diskette, move the recording arm, and get information from or put information on the diskette.

Most of the "intelligence" needed to control the disk drive is on a board inside the computer itself. The floppy disk drive is a fairly "dumb" peripheral. The intelligence needed to control the disk drive is located mainly in the computer on a *disk controller adapter* or *disk controller board*. This means that the BIOS of the operating system coordinates and governs the actions of the floppy disk drive.

Some 8-inch disk drives and most Winchester disks are "intelligent"; they are more electronically sophisticated and can handle more of the workload. In these cases, DOS issues a high-level command, and the disk drive itself figures out what DOS wants. Some intelligent disk drives work faster than their dumb counterparts.

The floppy disk drive is more reliable today than it was several years ago. More information can be packed into a 5 1/4-inch diskette than could be held in an 8-inch floppy diskette only five years ago.

Care and Maintenance

Diskettes

Floppy diskettes are fragile. It may be hard to believe that a minifloppy diskette can hold between 360,000 and 1,000,000 characters, or more. Eight-inch diskettes can hold over 2,400,000 characters. The cardboard or plastic jacket protects the diskette from about 80 percent of the dust, fingerprints, smoke, and other contaminants that can come in contact with your diskette. A little common sense is necessary to ensure a long life for your diskette. Treat your diskettes like your personal or business records. In some cases, the diskettes *are* your records.

Some diskette manufacturers have instructions on the back of the envelope about caring for your diskettes. You may want to read those instructions after you read this discussion.

Do's for Floppy Diskettes

Put diskettes into the disk drive carefully. "Easy does it" is the best term. The diskette should slide into the disk drive with very little resistance. You may even hear a soft click as the write-protect switch slides into place. The disk drive door should close with little resistance. In a short time, you will know by touch whether a diskette is properly inserted. If, in inserting the diskette or closing the disk drive door, you sense that there is a problem, take out the diskette and put it back in again. You can damage the diskette, disk drive, or both if you try to "force" a diskette into a disk drive and close the door.

When you're finished with a diskette, put it back in the envelope. The protective envelope's purpose is to protect the diskette when you are not using it. The envelope stops dust and most other contaminants from getting to the access hole of the diskette.

Label every diskette. Diskettes multiply like rabbits. Nothing is more frustrating than trying to find one diskette in a group of 50 identical diskettes without labels. This is time-consuming and frustrating. After you format a diskette, put a label on it. You might put down the date you formatted the diskette, the version, or similar information. Write on the label something you will be able to remember later.

A diskette without a label is fair game and also less useful. Treat each diskette with care and protect it with a label.

Once the label is on the diskette, use a felt-tipped pen to write on the label. Don't press down hard or use a pen or pencil. Undue pressure can damage the diskette under the cardboard jacket.

If a label becomes loose, remove it and put on a new one. I learned the importance of this the hard way while writing this book. A diskette that held several chapters of the book had a label that was beginning to peel away from the diskette. As I removed the diskette from the disk drive, I didn't notice that the label fell off inside the drive and became lodged on the bottom of the drive.

Later that day, I was looking for a diskette to format and grabbed a diskette from the top of a pile of unlabeled diskettes. After several hours, I looked for the diskette that held part of this book. I searched for 20 minutes, then had a sickening thought. I carefully reached inside the disk drive and found the diskette label on the bottom of the drive. I had formatted the wrong diskette and lost my chapters! Fortunately, I had a one-day-old backup copy of the diskette. All I had lost was one day's work. As I said before, "I am an experienced computer user."

To avoid costly loss of information, always check the diskette you're about to format. Make sure that it is blank or has no useful information on it.

Back up diskettes frequently. What saved me from having to re-enter several weeks of work was the fact that I had a backup diskette. Diskettes have a finite life. In the past (1978-1981), diskettes had a *spin life* (the amount of time that a disk drive actually reads or writes information on the diskette) of 40 to 80 hours. The newer diskettes can be used much longer. Exactly how much longer is hard to determine, but a good estimate is well over 1,000 hours of spin life. Diskettes, however, do eventually wear out. Computer malfunctions or inadvertent operations (such as erasing the wrong file) can also destroy information on the diskette.

Very important information should be backed up daily, or every two days when the information is changed, such as with accounting records. Important information should be backed up every two days, or at least once a week. Backing up diskettes is a very cheap form of insurance.

Keep infrequently used diskettes and backup copies of diskettes away from your computer. Why clutter the place where you work? Why dig through many diskettes to find the one you need? Keep the number of diskettes at your computer to a minimum; have at hand just the ones you constantly need. When you need a different diskette, get it, use it, and put it back. It's much easier to manage diskettes this way.

Keep your diskettes "comfortable." Like phonograph records, diskettes can bend or warp if they are not stored perfectly flat or vertical. It takes several weeks to warp a diskette, but why risk this kind of damage? There are several diskette holders that do a good job of storing diskettes. Some hold 10 diskettes, whereas others hold up to 50. These cases are not too expensive (usually $20 to $40 for the 50-diskette holders) and can also help you organize your diskettes.

Keeping diskettes comfortable also means watching the temperature. Maintain the temperature between 50 and 125 degrees Fahrenheit (10 and 52 degrees Celsius). If your diskettes get cold, let them warm up before you use them. Cold diskettes become rigid and shrink slightly. Information can be misplaced (not recorded at the correct position) on a shrunken diskette. Disk drives do not work reliably with cold diskettes.

Be especially careful about excessive heat. On warm summer days, if you leave your diskettes in your car, keep them out of direct sunlight. The hot summer sun has made roller coaster rides out of diskettes I have left on the back seat of my car. Your car's trunk can also get hot. Needless to say, when diskettes turn into hot frisbees, the information stored on them is lost.

Buy the right diskettes. Diskette prices are very competitive. There are some good buys on quality diskettes. Unfortunately, there are also some "bargain" brands. These are cheap because they are not *certified* (checked to see that the diskette will properly hold information). In addition, there are a few brands I won't touch at all.

You can tell if you have a poor diskette when you format it. DOS will report that a large amount of disk space has been lost to bad sectors. Format your diskettes even if you use the diskette for DISKCOPY (DISKCOPY will format a diskette "on-the-fly"). Formatting the diskette will show you right away if you have a problem diskette.

If you have a double-sided disk drive, buy double-sided diskettes. Both sides of the diskette are certified. Single-sided diskettes are certified on only one side. Although both sides may be good, why take a chance? You don't trust important personal or business records to scrap paper; so why trust your important information to "scrap" diskettes?

When you turn off your computer or move it, take the diskettes out of the drive. In the past, a disk drive might write garbage on the diskette when the computer was turned on or off. As a result, diskettes were always removed before the computer was turned off, and the computer was turned on before the diskettes were placed into the disk drives.

Today, disk drives are usually manufactured to prevent this problem. However, there is a very small chance, about one in several million, that the disk drive would write garbage on your diskette. If you are in doubt, open the drive door before you turn your computer on or off.

Moving your computer is another story. When the disk drive door is closed, the recording heads are in contact with the diskette's surface. If the disk drive gets bounced around, the heads can scrape the diskette and damage it. When you move your computer, particularly if it is portable, take the diskettes out of the disk drives.

Some Don'ts for Diskettes

Don't touch the diskette's magnetic surface, particularly the area under the access holes. The oil from your fingers can interfere with the recording heads' ability to read and write information on the diskette. Hold the diskette by the black jacket. If you need to spin the diskette, put your fingers in the centering hole and turn your hand.

Keep your diskettes away from magnetic fields. This one can be tricky. You may not keep a magnet by your diskette, but what about the video monitor, a fan, or even your telephone? Each of these generates a magnetic field that has the potential to "clean" your diskettes and ruin precious information.

Generally, most appliances will not affect your diskettes, unless you keep the diskette near the appliance for a long time. As a rule, keep your diskettes one foot away from the possible offender. However, keep your diskettes farther away from appliances with heavy or strong electric motors, such as a pencil sharpener. The heavier the motor, the farther away you should keep your diskettes.

Plastic holders do not stop magnetic fields. Metal boxes do a better job.

Airport security systems are the new problem for the traveling diskette in the 1980s. Generally, the X-ray machines used at airports do not generate a strong enough field to erase diskettes. Also, the distance between the X-ray source and your luggage is more than a foot. However, ask the security people to hand inspect any carry-on diskettes. Don't let them be put on top of the X-ray machine or scanned by a hand scanner. The diskettes would be too close to damaging magnetic sources. I have found that airport security people are usually happy to cooperate with such requests.

If you are mailing diskettes and want extra protection, or just want extra protection when carrying diskettes in the airport, wrap them in aluminum foil. This will reduce the possibility of magnetic fields reaching your diskettes.

Don't let your diskettes take the "Pepsi™ *Challenge" or the "Sanka*™ *Break."* Be careful about having any liquids near diskettes. That also goes for cigarette, cigar, or pipe smoke and ashes, food, and other similar contaminants. If any of these things gets on your diskette and leaves a residue, the recording heads may not be able to retrieve information from the diskette. Also, this residue can lodge on the recording head, making it a menace to other diskettes.

A friend of mine once spilled some sweet dessert wine on a diskette. That diskette gummed up the disk drive's recording head and ruined several other diskettes. The repair bill for the disk drive was minor compared to the loss of information on the diskettes.

Don't bend the diskette. The information on a diskette is tightly packed. If you put a crease in the diskette, the recording head will "jump" over the crease, and you will lose information. Remember the saying for the old punch cards: "Do not fold, spindle, or mutilate."

Don't let your diskette get too full. Some programs generate temporary files for your data. If your diskette gets full, you might lose what you're working on. WordStar, the word-processing program I use, hates full diskettes. If you can't free up some room on the diskette, you will lose the last revision of your work. I don't blame WordStar; I curse myself when I let this happen.

Periodically, run CHKDSK on your diskettes to see how much room is left on a diskette or hard disk. Erase or copy and erase files to make room.

Floppy Disk Drives

Floppy disk drives are fairly rugged pieces of equipment, but they can be damaged. The following general rules about disk drives will help you minimize damage.

When you insert a diskette, close the drive door carefully. As mentioned earlier, if you jam a diskette into the disk drive and try to close the door, you may damage the clutches that clamp down on the diskette, the diskette itself, or both. After a while, you will be able to tell when a diskette is jammed.

Clean the recording heads infrequently. The recording head of a disk drive is ceramic and requires only infrequent cleaning, perhaps once every three months or a year. Overcleaning a disk drive head can cause problems. The cleaning diskettes and solutions can be more abrasive on the recording heads than normal diskettes. Alcohol-based cleaning solutions, if overused, can erode the glue that holds the recording head on the arm. If this happens, the recording head will fall off the arm. Generally, the felt-like material inside the diskette jacket will catch and hold most dust and dirt.

If you get floppy disk errors, run the diagnostics that came with your computer. First, format some blank diskettes on a "known" good disk drive. Then run the diagnostics. If you get disk errors, clean the disk heads with a cleaning diskette and rerun the diagnostics. If there is still a problem, the disk drive may have problems, or the diskette with the errors is bad.

Don't shock your disk drives. In other words, don't give them a strong bump or jar. The arm with the recording heads can get out of place. The belt that makes the diskette spin can fall off. The door to the disk drive can break. A floppy disk drive is made of metal and plastic. The plastic can break if you drop the disk drive or slam something into it.

When moving or shipping your disk drives over long distances, put the cardboard protector in the drive and close the door. With a double-sided disk drive, the recording heads face each other. When the door is closed, the faces of the recording heads are touching each other. If the disk drives receive a lot of bumps or jolts, the recording heads can clap against each other and become damaged. If you put the cardboard protector inside the disk drive and close the door, the cardboard piece will protect the recording heads.

Have your disk drives serviced periodically. Disk drives need a little preventative maintenance about every one to two years. For example, the belt that spins the diskette may stretch. The disk recording heads may move a little out of the track, or the arm mechanism may wear. The write-protect switch may also wear. The timing on the disk drives' motors may be off. Usually, a good service technician can test and shape up your disk drives at a very reasonable cost. This will prevent a small problem from getting bigger.

You can wait for a problem to surface with your disk drives. But at the first sign of problems, run your diagnostics. If the disk drive is malfunctioning, get it repaired before you ruin some information on good diskettes.

Hard Disks

The Winchester disk is the most popular hard disk for personal computers. Winchester disks were developed at IBM and have become a practical addition to personal computers.

There are several differences between a floppy disk drive and a Winchester. A Winchester disk drive has a sealed unit that contains the platters and the recording heads. The hard disk drive doesn't use diskettes, but rather rigid, circular platters coated with metal oxide.

These rigid platters give the "hard" disk drive its name. They are fixed on a spindle that rotates about 3600 rpm. Some Winchesters have a motor that is directly connected to the spindle. Others use a belt-and-spindle arrangement like the floppy disk drive.

A mobile arm holds the recording heads: one at the top and one at the bottom of each platter. The entire arm moves back and forth like the floppy disk drive's recording heads. The mobile arm also moves more precisely and in smaller increments than the floppy disk drive's arm. The recording heads are smaller than those of a floppy disk drive.

The smaller recording heads and more controlled movement allow more information to be placed on the platter's surface. Because the disk spins faster, the storing and retrieving of information are also faster. The Winchester can thus hold more information and store and retrieve it faster than most floppy disk drives.

Winchester disks for personal computers usually have 5 1/4-inch or 8-inch diameter platters. The most common is the 5 1/4-inch, although 3 1/2-inch drives are just starting to be made. Usually, the 5 1/4-inch platter holds 2 1/2 megabytes (million bytes) per side. The combination of two sides per platter and two platters in the drive gives you a 10M (megabyte) disk drive.

The Winchester is an "intelligent" peripheral. Most units have built-in electronics that allow automatic verification of information written to the hard disk and the use of sophisticated error-correcting techniques. Because of these capabilities, almost no additional time is needed to verify the writing of information to a Winchester disk.

Some problems are unique to hard disk drives. The air pressure generated by the spinning disk lifts the recording heads just thousandths of an inch off the surface. Should the heads hit any contamination (hair, cigarette smoke, a fingerprint, etc.), they will bounce over it and crash into the platters. The Winchester's sealed environment prevents contamination from getting to the platters.

Another danger is possible damage to the disk's surface if there is severe physical shock. Because the recording heads hover so close to the platter's surface, a strong blow to the disk drive while the unit is operating can cause the recording heads to crash into the disk surface. For this reason, you should not drop or bump a Winchester disk indiscriminately, nor should you strike the table or desk that holds the disk.

Winchester disks, however, can take a lot of punishment. When a drive is not in use, it can withstand a shock of up to 20 Gs (20 times the force of gravity). When in use, the drive can survive a shock of only 10 Gs. The maximum allowable shock is lower when the drive is operating because recording heads crashing into a moving platter can scrape off the disk's metal coating where information is stored. Newer Winchester disk drives have an extra coating on the platter to prevent such a loss of information, but the 20G and 10G restrictions remain.

The final problem with Winchester disks is disk failure. A hard disk drive will fail eventually, but its failure is difficult to predict. It can happen at any time during a broad span (usually between 8,000 and 20,000 hours of use). Since hard disk failure is so unpredictable, frequent backup of the information is essential. You cannot remove hard disk platters, so you must transfer information to separate media for backup. For most personal computers, floppy diskettes are used for backup. If you have an XT, read Chapter 12 on BACKUP and RESTORE.

When you install the disk drive, follow the manufacturer's directions. The disk drive that IBM uses does not require any physical setup. Some disk drives require that shipping bolts or screws be loosened before use. Usually, some programs must be run before you can use the drive. Follow your manufacturer's directions on this also. For IBM XTs, the programs involved are FDISK and FORMAT.

Prepare your Winchester disk before you move or ship it. The manufacturer provides instructions for moving or shipping your drive. The preparation procedure is usually the reverse of installing the disk drive. As a rule, Winchester drives are more fragile than floppy disk drives.

The IBM XT and similar Winchester disk drives have a program on the diagnostic diskette that you must run before moving or shipping the disk. This program moves the recording heads to the edge of the disk so that they cannot scrape the platters where information is stored. The program should be run whenever you move the hard disk more than a few feet.

Finally, you should learn about hierarchical directories because they can help you organize your files on a hard disk. (See Chapter 6.)

How DOS Divides the Diskette

To simplify the handling of a disk or diskette, DOS breaks the diskette down into smaller pieces. First, the diskette is broken down into a series of concentric circles called *tracks*. The number of tracks your diskette will have depends on the disk drive and is a function of the stepper motor that moves the recording heads. The smaller the step, the more tracks your diskette will have.

Most minifloppy disk drives have recording heads that record 48 tracks per inch (tpi is the standard abbreviation). This is the standard for most IBM-compatible minifloppy disk drives, but some minifloppy disk drives record 96 tracks per inch.

Note that the entire diskette cannot be used for recording. With 48-tpi drives, you can create only 40 tracks. The 96-tpi disk drives have only 80 tracks. This means that you use a circular band about 5/6 of an inch wide in the middle of the minifloppy diskette.

The tracks are sliced up into *sectors*. For the Personal Computer, DOS Version 1 sliced the tracks into 8 sectors. DOS V2 uses 9 sectors. The use of tracks and sectors allows the computer to move the disk drive recording head rapidly to the correct spot.

The single index hole of a soft-sectored diskette signals the computer when sector 0 passes under the recording head. DOS determines when the other sectors are below the recording head. Since these other sectors are located by software, the diskette is called "*soft*-sectored."

A hard-sectored diskette uses one hole on the diskette as the "master" hole but has other holes. These determine when each sector passes under the recording head. Because sectoring is determined by hardware, the diskette is labeled "*hard*-sectored."

How many sectors are on your diskette? IBM-compatible double-sided disk drives, using DOS V2, have

40 tracks * 9 sectors * 2 sides = 720 total sectors

Under DOS V1, only 8 sectors per track are recorded. Thus

    40 tracks * 8 sectors * 2 sides = 640 total sectors

These figures can also tell you how much information is stored on a diskette. Each sector on the minifloppy diskette (and hard disk) holds 512 bytes.

The number of bytes stored on a 9-sector, double-sided diskette is

    720 sectors * 512 bytes per sector = 368,640 bytes

You can determine the number of Kbytes by dividing this number by 1,024.

    368,640 bytes / 1,024 bytes per K = 360K

Hard disk drives use a similar scheme. The major difference is that the hard disk uses the concept of *cylinders.*

First, let's consider a double-sided diskette. Each side has 40 tracks. The first track on the top side is directly above the first track on the bottom side, and so on for each of the other 39 tracks. If you were to draw a vertical, three-dimensional figure that passed through both sides of the diskette at any track, you would have a cylinder.

For the hard disk, think about two platters stacked on top of each other on the spindle. The tracks for each side of each platter are in the same vertical plane. If you were to connect any one track through all four surfaces, you would again have a cylinder. The hard disk of the XT has 306 cylinders, which means that each surface on the four platters has 306 tracks. (One of these cylinders is used for internal purposes and is not available for storing information.)

One other difference between the minifloppy diskette and the hard disk is that each track on a hard disk platter has 17 sectors instead of 9.

DOS starts at the first track on side one of the diskette (the outermost track, or track 0), then uses sectors 0 through 8. If the diskette is double-sided, DOS then uses side two, track 0, sectors 0 through 8. DOS goes back to the first side to use track 1, sectors 0 through 8, then back to side two. This process continues until the entire diskette is full. If the diskette is single-sided, DOS does not switch sides. The hard disk works the same way, except that DOS uses each side of the platters (a cylinder) before moving to the next track.

Why does DOS work this way? The answer is speed. It takes less time for the disk drive to use the second side of a diskette than to move the recording heads. The same is true for the hard disk. Using a recording head for a different surface in the same location takes less time than moving the recording head to a new location.

What DOS Does with the Diskette

When you get a new diskette, it is not ready to be used. DOS must first record some dummy information on the diskette. This process is called *formatting*.

When you format a diskette or hard drive, DOS records dummy data in each sector. (Some additional housekeeping information that does not concern us is also recorded.)

Next DOS sets up three important areas on the disk. The first area is on the first side of the diskette in the first sector of the first track. This is called the *boot record*. It contains the bootstrap routine used by DOS to load itself.

FORMAT then sets up two copies of the *File Allocation Table,* or *FAT.* (FAT is discussed below.) If you have 8-sector diskettes, each copy of the FAT is one sector long. If you have 9-sector diskettes, each copy is two sectors long. The FAT also tells DOS what type of diskette you are using, 8- or 9-sector and single- or double-sided.

Next comes the directory, where DOS stores the name of each disk file, the date and time the file was created or last changed, the file attribute (the characteristics about the file), the starting cluster entry in the FAT, and the size of the file in bytes. The file attribute can be any combination of:

System	A file used by the operating system. This file is normally hidden from regular uses of DOS.
Hidden	A file that is also hidden from normal DOS operations.
Volume label	Not a disk file, but an 11-character label to help you identify the diskette. The volume label shows up when you execute some DOS commands like DIR, CHKDSK, or TREE.

Subdirectory Not a file, but a different directory that holds similar information about other files.

Archived Tells DOS that this file has not been BACKed UP. This attribute is turned on every time DOS creates a file, or you put new information into the file.

Every file you create or use has one directory entry. The entry is 32 bytes long. Single-sided diskettes use four sectors (2,048 bytes) for the directory. You can have 64 files listed in the directory on a single-sided diskette. Double-sided diskettes use seven sectors (3,584 bytes) for the directory. These directories can hold information on 112 files.

Unlike some other operating systems, in PC DOS the directory does not tell you where the file is on the diskette. Instead, the entry in the disk's directory for each file points to an entry in the FAT. The FAT tells DOS which sectors on the diskette actually hold the file. In other words, the FAT guides DOS in finding where information is stored on a diskette. The FAT also indicates what sectors are not being used by a file.

The FAT is a very important item to DOS. In fact, the FAT is so important that DOS keeps two copies of the FAT for every disk or diskette. DOS uses the directory entry to go to the correct part of the FAT for the file you use. It then uses the FAT to find where your file is stored on the diskette. When a file grows, DOS checks the FAT to see what sectors are not being used. When a free sector is found, DOS adds it to the chain for the file and uses the sector.

DOS uses a first-found, first-used routine for this process. In other words, DOS takes the first free sector it finds, and puts as much of the file in the sector as possible. DOS then looks for the next free sector and places more of the file in the new sector. After a while, a file can be scattered all over the diskette.

A *cluster* is the smallest unit of disk space that DOS will work with in the FAT. DOS does not actually look for a sector per se, but rather for a cluster.

For a single-sided diskette, a cluster is the same as a sector. When DOS searches for a free cluster on a single-sided diskette, DOS is looking for a free sector.

DOS assigns two sectors to a cluster, however, for double-sided diskettes. When DOS looks for a free cluster on a double-sided diskette, DOS is looking for a free pair of adjacent sectors.

If you use the **/S** switch, FORMAT will also place IBMBIO.COM, IBMDOS.COM, and COMMAND.COM on your diskette. If you use the **/V** switch, DOS will create a volume label. The volume label is placed in the directory, but has no entry in the FAT. This means that a volume label does not take up any disk space but does reduce by one the number of files a disk or diskette can hold.

Note that all DOS programs and utilities automatically deduct the disk space used by the boot record, the FAT, and the directory. Since you cannot use these areas to record your own information, DOS does not count these areas for your total disk space. This is why, when you figure the capacity of your disk based on the numbers DOS displays in the DIR, FORMAT, or CHKDSK programs, the number of K bytes is less. You get 354K instead of 360K, or 179K instead of 180K. The figures DOS gives you are total user space, not total disk space. There is no problem with this. Just think in terms of 180K or 360K for diskettes and remember that DOS gives you the actual user, not total, number of bytes for your disks or diskettes.

8 Inch Diskette

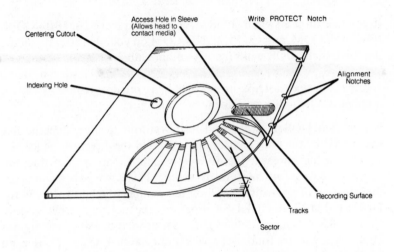

5-1/4 Inch Diskette

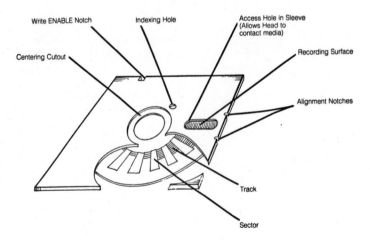

An anatomy of diskettes.

5
Files and Names

Files

In the last few chapters, we discussed and used disk files but never explained what files are. A *file* is a collection of similar items. To explain files as they relate to PC DOS, we can use a file cabinet as an analogy.

Disk storage is often compared to a file cabinet, which usually has several drawers. Inside each drawer are file folders. Each folder is for a particular subject and can contain facts about the subject, such as personnel records, charge card receipts, bank statements, invoices, appliance warranties, automobile repair records, etc.

A file folder can be empty or hold one or more papers related to the subject. For example, a folder for a checking account may hold your monthly bank statement and the checks returned from the bank.

The file folders inside the file cabinet may be sorted alphabetically or by some coding system. Such arrangement can help a person searching for a file about a particular subject. Files can also be organized by time, with new folders placed after older folders as new topics are filed. The files can even be completely disorganized. The person controlling the file cabinet decides how the files should be arranged.

The information inside each file folder can also be organized in some fashion or completely disorganized. As with the file folders, the person in control of the filing cabinet decides how the records should be arranged.

There's something to be said for filing systems. When the system is used properly, it works well. But when you don't file new items in their proper order in the cabinet or in the file folders, it takes a lot of work to straighten up the cabinet. The same is true if a drawer falls out of the cabinet, and the file folders fall out. The worst case is when a fire or theft permanently removes the information from the cabinet. The information is lost, unless another copy of the records is stored somewhere else.

This analogy closely fits disk storage. The file cabinet is the disk drive. The drawers are the diskettes or hard disk platters.

As indicated earlier, a file is a related series of items. A disk file is the equivalent of the file folder. Just as any information can be stored in a file folder, so can related data be placed in a disk file.

For example, the programs you use, the names and addresses of your customers or friends, or orders for your products can all be placed in a disk file. The electronic version of this chapter is in a disk file.

The only restriction on what you can place in a disk file is the computer's ability to handle the information. The computer must be able to process the information electronically.

The smallest allowable size for a file is 0—no information at all. The length of the longest disk file depends on the amount of available disk storage. You cannot create a file that is larger than the capacity of your diskette or hard disk drive. If a file is stored on two diskettes, it is physically two files, not one. Because of the way some programs handle disk storage, files may have further restrictions on file size.

DOS allows files of up to several gigabytes (billions of bytes). Today, no single hard disk drive can hold this much information. Disk drives can hold almost one gigabyte. As video disks are used for storage, DOS' ability to handle multigigabyte files will be appreciated.

As with the filing cabinet, what you put in each file is determined by your programs and you. The way the information is organized in the file is also determined that way. In other words, you and your programs have full control of the filing system.

To complete the analogy, each item inside the file folder is called a *record*. There are two types of records: physical and logical. From the physical standpoint of DOS, a record is a certain number of bytes, usually 512. This is the same as saying that each sheet of paper in the file folder is a record. From the "logical" or working view of how you use the file, a record is a related set of items. Each record in the file has the same basic organization, such as a person's name, address, city, state, and ZIP code. Each person occupies one record in the file. Most programs use this definition of a record. (For more information on both types of records, look at books on system or assembly language programming, other programming languages, and data management.)

Because anything can be in a disk file, how do you know what is in any one disk file? There are several ways to find out. First, every disk file has a name that is stored in the directory. Every file name must be unique; otherwise, DOS will be confused. If you can remember the file name, you should be able to remember what is in the file.

When you look at the file names in the directory, you may spot a familiar file name. You know that this file holds the names and addresses of your friends. How do you display this information? That will depend on what is really in the disk file.

Your computer uses the ASCII character set. *ASCII* is the acronym for American Standard Code for Information Interchange, the standard way your computer translates its binary ones and zeros into letters, numbers, punctuation, symbols, and special computer characters. Appendix C has the ASCII chart for characters.

If the names and addresses are stored on the disk as ASCII text, you can use DOS' TYPE command. "As ASCII text" means that the program you used took each character as you typed it and put it into the disk file with no changes. The TYPE command tells DOS to display on the video screen the information from a file. TYPE types on the screen the information from the file and provides a quick way to see the contents of a file without having to run another program.

If your program transforms information when it is stored on the disk, you will need a program that can undo this transformation to show the information on the screen. For example, if your program crunches or encrypts information so that a file takes less disk space, the information is not stored character by character as ASCII text. Should you try to TYPE this file, the information will look like gibberish because TYPE can display only bytes that are stored as ASCII characters. Generally, the program that stores the information can reverse any encoding.

Ask for a directory of a disk. Do you see any files that end with .COM or .EXE? Try to TYPE one of these files. At the DOS system prompt (A>), type **TYPE**, a space, and the complete name of the file. Don't be alarmed by what you see on the screen. The information is supposed to look like nonsense. There may be a few recognizable words or phrases, but most of them will be nonsense because you just asked DOS to type a program file.

To look at a program file, you must use another program. If the program is written in interpretive BASIC (Disk or Advanced BASIC), you need BASIC to load and list the program. If the program is in machine language (the native language of the computer's CPU), you need a *disassembler,* a program that transforms the binary language of the computer into humanly readable instructions. (This is one of the functions of the DEBUG program provided with DOS, but not covered in this book.)

Remember that DOS stores bytes on the diskette. Bytes can be humanly readable text, manipulated data, or program instructions. DOS does not care. It stores the bytes it was told to store. What these bytes represent is not DOS' concern. DOS is a somewhat mindless file clerk that follows your instructions. You and your programs tell DOS what to store.

When you want to use a file, give DOS the name of the file. DOS will go to the drawer (the diskette or hard disk), search for a file with the appropriate name, grab the file, and "open" it. If there is no file by this name, DOS will report that fact. You can also tell DOS to create a new file. If a file folder (file) by this name exists, the file folder will be emptied before DOS will put any new information in it. Otherwise, DOS types out a new file folder (puts the file name in the directory). You can even tell DOS to start at the beginning of the file or to go to a specific location (record) in the file. On your command, DOS will pull (read) information from the file or place (write) information in the file.

In all of these cases, DOS does the hard part of the work. DOS handles the mundane problems of expanding a file, creating a file, and retrieving information from or placing information in the file. You and your programs just tell DOS what to do.

The following are the key facts to remember about files:

1. A file holds a related set of information.

2. The information in a file can be humanly readable (ASCII text), usable only by programs, or a program.

3. You can display the contents of a file on the screen with the TYPE command. If the file holds only ASCII text, the display will be meaningful. If the file holds something else, the display will look like nonsense.

4. Every file you use has a name. The name must be unique for the directory that holds the file name.

5. DOS acts as a file clerk. It handles the storing and retrieving of files. You and your programs are responsible for what is placed in a file and how it is organized.

Names

We think in terms of names. A *name* is a word or phrase that we associate with a person, object, or action. When a name is understood and accepted, two or more people can use it to identify a person, an object, or an action.

When conversing with computers, we also use names. The preceding part of this chapter discussed how DOS knows about a disk file by its name. This name becomes the *handle,* the common phrase that we, our programs, and DOS use when working with a file.

Disk Drive Names

Disk drive names tell DOS which file drawer to use. In other words, the disk drive name tells DOS where to find the files you want.

A disk drive name is two characters long. The first character is usually a letter, and the second character must be a colon.

The common name for the starting disk drive is *A:*, the name of the first minifloppy or floppy disk drive. The name for each additional drive is the next letter of the alphabet. For example, the second disk drive would be B:, the third would be C:, and so on. Notice that the letters used here for the disk drive names are upper case.

MS-/PC DOS V1 allowed a maximum of sixteen disk drives, making the letters A through P legal names. In DOS V1, programs did not care if you used an upper- or a lower-case letter because DOS always translated the letter to upper case.

DOS V2 allows up to 63 device names. Because the alphabet has only 26 upper-case letters (allowing only 26 disk drives), DOS V2 starts with A and moves up the ASCII character set for drive names. After Z is used for the 26th disk drive, the disk drive names are very different. The thirtieth disk drive on the system would have ^: as the name; the fortieth, *i:*; and the fiftieth, }:. The last possible disk drive would have the name ~:.

Fortunately, most computer systems use only two to four disk drives. This means that most users will need only the drive names A:, B:, C:, and D:. DOS automatically translates lower-case letters into upper case if you have less than 27 disk drives on your computer system. This means that you can still use either upper- or lower-case characters when you type a disk drive name.

The rules for disk drive names are listed below.

Rules for Disk Drive Names

1. A disk drive must have a two-character name. The second character must be a colon (:).

2. The first disk drive is A:, the second disk drive is B:, etc.

3. The character for each additional disk drive is one character higher in the ASCII character set.

4. Only the letters A through P are valid for DOS V1. More characters are available for DOS V2.

> 5. When you use a disk drive name, the letter can be in upper or lower case if you have less than 27 disk drives.
> 6. When you tell DOS to run a program from disk, the program name may be preceded by a drive name.
> 7. Almost any time you give a file name, the disk drive name may precede the file name.
> 8. Don't use a nonexistent disk drive. DOS will display an error message if you do.

Notice rules 6 and 7. They explain how you tell DOS where to find your programs and other files.

You will recall the system prompt mentioned earlier. The A in the A> is not a coincidence. The letter in the system prompt tells you the current disk drive. The *current disk drive* is the drive DOS will use, *unless* you indicate otherwise. DOS always has one, and only one, current disk drive. When you run a program from the disk and don't give a drive name in front of the program name, DOS will get the program from the current disk drive.

To change the current disk drive (sometimes called the default or logged disk drive), type the full name of the new drive at the system prompt level and hit Enter. For example, to make drive C the current disk drive, you would type:

```
A>C:
C>
```

The system prompt will then change to C>, indicating that C: is the current disk drive. To change back to A:, type:

A:

The colon in the drive name is important. It tells DOS, "This is a disk drive name, not a file name."

To run a program from a different disk drive, enter the drive name before the program name. To run the CHKDSK program from a diskette in drive B, you would type:

A>B:CHKDSK

If you have a two-floppy disk system, put a diskette into both disk drives. Make sure that the CHKDSK program is on the diskette in drive B.

If you are using a hard disk, make sure that CHKDSK is on the hard disk. You should also make sure that a floppy diskette is in drive A, and the system prompt is A>. Use the letter for the hard disk drive instead of the **B:**. For XT owners, this would be **C:CHKDSK**.

Now type the command and watch what happens. Did you see what you expected?

Although DOS was directed to get the CHKDSK program from drive B: or C:, CHKDSK analyzed the diskette in A: because you did not tell CHKDSK which disk to analyze. Since CHKDSK did not find a disk drive name, the current disk drive, A:, was used. Unless you tell DOS otherwise, it will always use the current disk drive not only for running programs, but also as the object of the action. In this case, the action was analyzing the disk (CHKDSK). It is important to remember this concept.

To analyze the diskette in drive B or the hard disk (C:), you have two choices: you can make the disk holding CHKDSK the current disk drive, then run CHKDSK; or you can tell CHKDSK which disk drive to use. If you chose the former, you would enter:

Diskette	**Hard Disk**
A>**B:**	A>**C:**
B>**CHKDSK**	C>**CHKDSK**

If you chose the second method, you would enter:

Diskette	**Hard Disk**
A>**B:CHKDSK B:**	A>**C:CHKDSK C:**

Volume Labels

DOS V2 allows you to give a disk or diskette a volume name. The volume name appears when you ask for a directory of a disk, perform a CHKDSK (check disk), display the directory path (TREE command), or use a variety of other commands. This name is for your convenience

---

Rules for Volume Labels

1. A volume label can be 1 to 11 characters long.

2. Valid characters for file names are

   A. The letters A to Z and a to z

   B. The numbers 0 to 9

   C. The special characters and punctuation symbols

      $ # & @ ! & ( ) - { } ' _ ` ~

   D. The space (which is illegal for file names)

3. The following characters cannot be used in a volume label:

   A. Any control character, including escape (27d or 1Bh) and delete (127d or 7Fh).

   B. The characters

      ^ + = / [ ] " : ; , ? * \ < > | .

4. If DOS finds that an illegal character or the typed name is too long, DOS will ask you to enter the volume label again.

5. A drive name cannot precede the volume label.

6. FORMAT is the only DOS-supplied program that will make disk labels. You must use the **/V** switch when you make a disk label.

---

in grouping or identifying diskettes. Although the volume label has no significance to DOS, the label is relevant for both disk drives and files.

When you format a disk, using the FORMAT command with the **/V** option, DOS will ask you for an 11-character volume name after DOS has formatted the diskette. This is the only way to make a volume label with the provided DOS programs and utilities.

Some "outside programs" label or relabel a diskette after it has been formatted. One such program is provided with the *Norton Utilities* by Peter Norton.

The rules for volume labels are almost identical to the rules for file names (discussed in the next section).

There are three important things to remember about volume names. Each diskette or hard disk drive can have only one volume name. You can give a volume name to a diskette or disk that has been formatted for use by only DOS V2. DOS V1 knows nothing about volume names and treats the volume label as an empty disk file. Finally, the rules for volume names are a little less restrictive than for file names. A volume name is the only name that can have a space in it.

File Names

A file name has two parts: a *root name* and a *suffix*. The root name can have one to eight characters. The suffix, or *extension,* can be one to three characters long. If the suffix is used, it is separated from the root name by a period (.). The suffix can also be omitted if you prefer. There are some restrictions on the characters you can use in a file name. (These restrictions are discussed below.)

For example, the main part of the WordStar program is in a disk file called WS.COM.

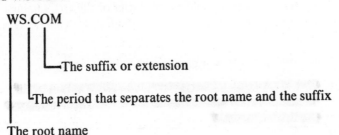

WS.COM

└──The suffix or extension

└The period that separates the root name and the suffix

The root name

In some cases, any name can be used for a file, subject to some restrictions. Some files don't need an extension (suffix), whereas others will because of program or DOS requirements for a specific root name or extension. Whether an extension is needed depends on what the file contains as well as its use.

When you create a file, you give it a name. If you use both a root name and an extension, the complete file name should appear as the root name, followed by a period and an extension. You should use this name whenever you copy, rename, or erase the file. If you do not use an extension, you can also omit the period.

Why use an extension? Usually DOS or your programs force you to use a certain extension. In other cases, your programs assume that you will use a certain extension, unless you indicate otherwise.

Program files are one example. If you want DOS to run a program stored on the disk, the program must have an extension of .COM or .EXE. COM is the abbreviation for a machine-language *command* file. The EXE stands for a DOS-*executable* file. DOS knows by the disk file's extension that it is a program, and from the file name what action to take to execute the program.

Batch files are covered in Chapter 9. A batch file must have the extension .BAT, or DOS will not recognize it.

If you look at the sample BASIC programs provided with DOS V2, you will see that each one has the .BAS extension. Unless you tell BASIC otherwise, it will store BASIC programs with the .BAS extension. This default extension is very convenient. To load and run the menu program from BASIC, you would type:

RUN"SAMPLES"

instead of

RUN"SAMPLES.BAS"

In this case, BASIC eliminates some of your work by automatically adding .BAS to the file name. When you load or save the program, BASIC will add the .BAS for you.

Table 5.1 lists some of the standard extensions. It reflects file name extensions that programs use automatically, extensions that files must have, and some common-sense file name extensions that will help you identify files. Usually the programs you use will determine the extensions you'll need.

Note the .TMP, .BAK, and .$$$ extensions. Don't create files with these extensions. Your programs may create files with these extensions that can erase useful files you want to keep.

The following notation often appears in this book.

d: **filename**.*ext*

The *d:* is the disk drive name. If the file you are using is not on the current disk drive, substitute the disk drive name for the *d:*. When the d:

appears as *d:*, the disk drive name is optional. When it looks like **d:**, you must give the disk drive name. There are also places where only a disk drive name is used. (This convention of showing you when the disk drive name is optional or mandatory is followed throughout this book.)

Table 5.1

Common File Name Extensions

Extension	What It Is
.ASM	Assembler source file
.BAK	Backup file
.BAS	BASIC program file
.BAT	Batch file
.BIN	Binary program file
.C	C source file
.COB	COBOL source file
.COM	Command (program) file
.DAT	Data file
.DOC	Document (text) file
.DTA	Data file
.EXE	Executable program file
.FOR	FORTRAN source file
.HLP	Help file
.INT	Intermediate program file
.LET	Letter
.LST	Listing of a program (in a file)
.LIB	Program library file
.MAP	Linker map file
.MSG	Program message file
.OBJ	Intermediate object code (program) file
.OVL	Program overlay file
.OVR	Program overlay file
.PAS	Pascal source file
.PRN	Listing of a program (in a file)
.SYS	System configuration or device drive file
.TMP	Temporary file
.TXT	Text file
.$$$	Temporary or incorrectly stored file

The **filename** represents the root name of a file. Because the root name is mandatory, it appears like **this** throughout this book.

The *.ext* represents the sometimes optional extension (or suffix) to the file name. If the extension looks like *.ext,* you should give the file name extension, if the file has one. Otherwise, skip the extension. If the extension appears like **.ext,** you must give the extension.

The rules for file names are presented below.

Rules for File Names

1. A file name has:

   A. A root name of one to eight characters

   B. An optional extension of one to three characters

   C. A period between the root name and the extension name, if one was used

2. The characters you may use in a file name are

   A. The letters A to Z (Lower-case letters are transformed automatically into upper case.)

   B. The numbers 0 to 9

   C. The special characters and punctuation symbols

      $ # & @ ! & ( ) - { } ' _ ` ~

   D. For DOS Version 1 only, the symbols

      | < > \

3. The following characters cannot be used in a file name:

   A. Any control character, including escape (27d or 1Bh) and delete (127d or 7Fh)

   B. The four characters mentioned in rule 2-D for DOS V2

   C. A space

   D. The characters

      ^ + = / [ ] " : ; , ? *

---

4. A device name can be part of a root name, but cannot be the entire root name. For example, CONT.TXT is okay, but AUX.TXT is not.

5. If DOS finds an illegal character in a file name, DOS stops at the character preceding the illegal one and uses the legal part of the name.

6. Each file name in a directory must be unique.

7. A drive name and path name usually precede a file name. (Device and path names are covered in the next few chapters.)

Note: Microsoft BASICs are famous for not translating lower-case, file-name letters into upper-case letters. Be careful of this.

Look at the following examples of valid file names. Each file name is correctly phrased and has no illegal characters.

MYTEST.TXT
COMMAND.COM
PRINTP.EXE
CHRIS
AUXILARY
@12PM
CINDY#2
(CARL)
PUT&GET
GO.COM
LETTER.BAK
AFILE
4-TO-GO
ABCDEFGH.IJK
2WAY.ST
$@#%&()

The file names below are not valid:

ABCDEFGHIJ.KLM	(Too many characters in the root name)
.TXT	(No root name)

TO:GO	(Cannot use a colon)
MY FILE	(Cannot have a space in the name)
PRN.TXT	(PRN is a device name)
THIS,WAY	(Cannot use a comma)
ABCD.EFGH	(Too may letters in the extension)
?ISIT.CAL	(Cannot use ? in a name)

When you use an improper (or illegal) file name, one of two things can happen, depending on what you typed and the program you are using: DOS may give you an error message and not perform the operation, or DOS may perform the operation and make a strange file name for it based on what you typed.

What DOS does depends on what illegal characters were used and where they were located in the file name. Generally, DOS will stop forming the root name or extension when it finds the first illegal character. The following shows what DOS will do if it encounters some of the files listed above:

Typed Name	What DOS Will Do
ABCDEFGHIJ.KLM	Use the file called ABCDEFGH.KLM
ABCD.EFGH	Use the file called ABCD.EFG

If you use too many characters, DOS will ignore the additional ones. This applies to both the root name and the extension; each is treated separately. DOS will recognize the first eight characters of the root name and the first three characters after the period. In the first case, DOS ignores the characters (IJ) after the eighth letter and before the period. In the second case, DOS ignores the character (H) in the extension after the letter G.

The following is true if you try to use just an extension as a file name:

.TXT	Displays an error message

DOS gives an error message because a file must always have a root name.

The following shows how DOS treats punctuated or separated file names:

TO:GO	Use two names, TO and GO
THIS,WAY	Use two names, THIS and WAY
MY FILE	Use two names, MY and FILE

DOS separates file names that contain a colon, semicolon, comma, quotation mark, equal sign, or a space. These punctuation marks and the space act as separators and are called *delimiters*. In each case, DOS sees two names: one before the delimiter and the other after it. The delimiter itself does not become part of the file name. What happens next depends on the program you are using. If you are using the COPY command and type:

COPY TO:GO MYFILE

COPY will display an error message, indicating that you have given too many parameters (three: the file names TO, GO, and MYFILE) when you should have given two.

If a program is expecting only one name, it may not check for more and simply use the file name TO. The file names GO and MYFILE will be ignored.

DOS handles the file name PRN.TXT in the following manner:

PRN.TXT   Use the printer for input or output

PRN is a reserved device name that represents the printer. If you use this file name, one of three things may happen. First, DOS may go to get information from the "file" (try to input from the printer), then quickly return without getting anything. What happens next depends on the program used. In most cases, the result will not be what you want.

Second, if you are putting information into this file and the printer is turned off or not selected, DOS will wait for 20 to 30 seconds, then give an error message telling you that PRN (the printer) is not ready.

Third, if the printer is on and selected, DOS will write the information to the printer and not save the information in a disk file.

This example applies any time you use a device name as a root name. DOS will use the device rather than make a disk file. If you use names such as AUX.TXT, LPT2.MAC, or NUL.COM, the results will not be what you want. (Remember this when device names are discussed in Chapter 6.)

A word about uniqueness. Two files in the same directory cannot have the same name. You might call this the "identity property" for disk files. Each file name must be made different, by adding, subtracting, or changing characters in either the root name or the extension. If the names are not different, DOS will be confused and not know which file you are designating.

If you try to change a file name to match a name already in the directory, DOS will give you a `Duplicate file name` or `File not found` error message, and will not rename the file. DOS is protecting you and it from having two files with the same name in the same directory.

COPYing can be dangerous if you are not careful about file names. For example, suppose that the diskette in drive A has a file called MYFILE.DAT. This file holds the names and addresses of your clients. The diskette in drive B also has a file called MYFILE.DAT, but this file holds the names and addresses of your personal friends. If you copy MYFILE.DAT from drive A to drive B, DOS will first delete the file with your friends' names on drive B, then copy the file holding your clients' names to the diskette in drive B. You will have just lost the file that holds the information on your friends.

DOS deleted the MYFILE.DAT on drive B as a self-defense move. No two files in the same directory can have the same name. When you tell DOS to copy files, it will check the names. If a file in the directory you are copying to has an identical name, DOS will delete that file first. The contents of that file are lost. Then DOS copies the file. No warning is given. Therefore, it is wise to check both directories for duplicate file names when you copy files so that you do not inadvertently lose a good file.

The preceding lists of examples held valid and invalid file names. A valid file name is correctly phrased; an invalid name has an illegal character. There are also good and bad file names. A valid file name can be good or bad.

A *good* file name is one that means something to you and the other people who use your files. You can use the name %$!12.XYZ, but how can you tell what is in the file? Will you remember what is in the file when you come back to use it several days or weeks later?

Give each file a name that refers to how the file is used or what it contains. For example, it is easy to remember that the file FRIENDS.DAT is a data file holding your friends' names and addresses, that CHAPT4.TXT is a text file that holds the fourth chapter of a book, and that SMITH3.LET holds the third letter you wrote to Mr. Smith.

Grouping and using good file names will help you quickly locate files on your disk.

Some special characters may be used in file names. The question mark (?) and asterisk (*) have a special meaning to DOS. These characters are known as *wild card* or *global* characters. When you use them in a file name, your file name becomes *ambiguous*. This means that the file name you are using can match more than one file on the disk. Some programs and DOS commands allow wild cards, and others do not.

When used, DOS interprets these characters as

> ?   Match any *one* character in the file name.

> *   Match any number of characters in the file name.

Both ? and * will match places where there are not characters in the file name. In other words, the file name WORDS? will match the files WORDS1, WORDSA, WORDST, and WORDS. In the case of WORDS, the ? matches the nonexistent character after the "S" in the file's root name.

These wild-card characters are very useful with the DIR (directory), ERASE (delete files), CHKDSK (check disk), and RENAME (change file name) commands, as well as with other programs.

The most commonly used ambiguous file name is *.*. It says, "Match any number of characters in both the root name and the extension." The longhand form would be "????????.???" In other words, *.* matches every file in the directory. This can be the most dangerous ambiguous name when used with ERASE. The command

ERASE *.*

will delete every file in the current directory of the disk. (DOS V2 will ask you to confirm your intent if you type this.)

Combinations of ? and * can be used to designate groups of files. **DIR *.BAS** will show all the BASIC files in the directory. **DIR ??FILE.DAT** will display all files that start with any two characters and the word FILE as the root name, and DAT for the extension.

As an exercise, try the wild-card characters with the directory (DIR) command. This will not harm your files. Experiment with these characters. It will help you become comfortable with wild-card characters. Try using the disk or directory that you created in Chapter 2 for this exercise. The more files on the disk, the better.

Wild-card characters also save you from having to reissue a command several times. When you copied the BASIC files from the DOS diskette, the command with the file name ***.BAS** copied every BASIC file. This illustrates why using common extensions is helpful; one command can cover many files.

But remember the caution about COPY. When you use wild-card characters, you can overwrite a good file with a completely different one if the files have the same file name. If in doubt, use the DIR command to check the file names.

6
Devices and Device Names

Device is another name for peripheral. The keyboard, video screen, terminal (if you use one), printer, modem, game adapter, and any other items you connect to the computer are all devices.

Each device uses some connection to talk to the computer. The technical name for this connection is *interface.* An interface represents the physical connection (the cable, plugs, and wires) and the electronics that handle the communications between the computer and the device.

Some interfaces are built into the computer, such as the keyboard interface for using the Keyboard Unit. Other devices may need a special card or adapter that you place in the computer.

The computer and its devices usually communicate one byte at a time. A byte can be transmitted and received in one of two ways. *Parallel* connections, interfaces, adapters, and devices transmit the entire byte at one time. A parallel connection uses eight separate wires or lines for the eight bits in a byte, and other electrical lines to coordinate the movement of the character. IBM printers use the parallel method. The other method is *serial,* by which the eight bits are sent one at a time.

Some additional bits are also sent to coordinate the moving of information between the devices. Most modems, terminals, and the Keyboard Unit use the serial method of communication.

The video screen is an exception. Video adapters use *memory-mapped video*. The adapters project a video image based on the memory inside the adapter. That is why the video screen is so fast. It is quicker to move characters in memory than to move them to another device. For video displays, the terms parallel and serial have no real meaning.

Disk drives are serial, character-oriented devices. Bytes are stored on the diskette, or platter, one bit at a time. The electronics of the adapters collect and combine the bits into characters, and the characters into blocks. This action is so fast that you don't notice the extra work the adapters and hard disk drives perform. From the standpoint of the computer system, these peripherals are block-oriented devices.

The computer system sees all devices as falling into two sets of classes: character-oriented devices and block devices, and parallel interfaces and serial interfaces.

Character-oriented devices are peripherals that communicate to the computer one character at a time. Almost all devices attached to the computer system are character oriented, including printers, modems, the keyboard, and the display (or terminal).

Block-oriented devices are peripherals that move information in a group of characters. By this definition, disk drives fit in this category and are the main block devices.

The software used to control these devices is in the BIOS of the computer system. The higher-level routines are in the disk and nondisk filing system of DOS.

Every device has a name. MS-/ PC DOS "knows" several device names. In most cases, the name is based not on the device itself, but on the type of adapter.

The names are three to four characters long. All device names, except PRN, end with a colon, although this is optional with most commands. (The MODE command is an exception.) When a device name is used, DOS will attempt to use the specified adapter or device.

Because of the way DOS is constructed, you can use a device name anywhere that a file name can be used. This means that you can direct DOS to get information from a device (such as a modem) or send information to a device (such as the printer).

Each device name is *reserved.* You cannot use the device name as the root name of a disk file.

The character-oriented device names that DOS recognizes are listed below. Also included are two additional device names that Microsoft BASIC-86 (Disk BASIC) and GW (Advanced) BASIC use, but are not recognized by DOS. The colon is included after the device name, although the colon is usually optional.

Character-Oriented Device Names

PC DOS

Name	Device
CON:	The video display and keyboard. As for MS-DOS, input from CON: comes from the keyboard; output to CON: goes to the video display.
AUX: or COM1:	The first asynchronous communications port. If a second asynchronous port is available, it is called COM2:.
LPT1: or PRN	The first line or parallel printer. Like LST:, this device is used only for output.
LPT2: LPT3:	The second and third parallel printers
NUL:	The same as for MS-DOS
CAS1:	The cassette recorder

Microsoft BASIC-86 and GW BASIC

Name	Device
KYBD:	The keyboard of the system, an input-only device
SCRN:	The video display, an output-only device

Rules for Using Character-Oriented Device Names

1. Valid names for character-oriented devices are CON:, AUX:, COMx:, LPTx:, PRN, NUL:, and CAS1:.

2. The colon following these names is usually optional.

3. A character-oriented device name can be used anywhere a file name can be used.

4. If an extension is given with a device name, the extension is ignored. For example, CON.TXT is treated as CON:.

5. You may use the UNIX/XENIX-compatible path name for a device, \dev*devicename*. For example, **\DEV\PRN** may be used instead of **PRN** (DOS V2 only).

6. Do not use a device name when the device does not exist, such as LPT2: when your computer has only one printer. NUL: is the exception to this rule.

These rules summarize how device names should be used. If the root name of a file is identical to one of these device names, DOS will use the device, not a disk file.

Rule 6 is especially important. Don't try to use a device you don't have. At best, DOS will give you an error message. At worst, DOS may act erratically.

To complete this discussion, try the following exercise. Put a formatted practice diskette into a disk drive and type:

```
A>COPY CON SHOWFILE.TXT
```

When you type this line, the system prompt will not appear. Next, type the following line:

This demonstrates copying between a disk and a device.

After hitting Enter, tap the F6 special-function key and one more Enter. A ^Z should appear on your screen when you tap the F6 key. You will see the COPY message that one file was copied.

Now type:

TYPE SHOWFILE.TXT

The line you typed should appear on your screen. You have just copied a "file" from the keyboard to a disk file. The **CON** is the console (the keyboard and the video screen). You told COPY to take what was typed on the keyboard and put the characters in the disk file called SHOWFILE.TXT.

Can this work the other way? Type:

COPY SHOWFILE.TXT CON

Yes, it does. This procedure is identical to TYPEing the file. You can copy files between the serial adapters, printer, console, and other devices as if you were copying disk files. This does not mean that you can use COPY as a general-purpose communications program, but it does show the versatility of DOS and COPY.

The next chapter extends what you have just learned about devices and files. It also introduces the concepts of I/O redirection and piping.

7

Redirection and Piping

Redirection

If your system has a printer, turn it on and make sure it is ready to print. Now type the Ctrl-PrtSc characters (hold down the Ctrl key and tap the PrtSc key). Then type **DIR**. The directory of the disk should print on both your screen and the printer.

Type one more Ctrl-PrtSc. The Ctrl-PrtSc sequence toggles the printer on and off. The first Ctrl-PrtSc turns on the printer. DOS will then print to both the video screen and the printer. The second Ctrl-PrtSC turns off this feature.

Now type **DIR >PRN**. What happened? DOS printed a directory of the disk on the printer, but the directory did not appear on the screen. You have just used a new DOS V2.0 feature: I/O redirection.

What is I/O redirection? We know that I/O stands for input and output. In *redirection,* you tell DOS to change the source or destination it normally uses for input and output.

To explain this, let's look at three new terms. *Standard input* is the keyboard, where your programs and DOS normally expect characters to be typed. *Standard output* is the video screen, where programs and DOS usually display information. *Standard error* is also the video screen, where your programs and DOS report any errors that occur. These are the standards DOS uses.

When you redirect I/O, you tell DOS to get characters from somewhere else or put characters to some device other than the video screen. Instead of getting characters from the keyboard, you can tell DOS to get characters from a disk file or any other device. You can also tell DOS to display characters into a disk file, printer, or other device. That's what happened when you typed **DIR >PRN**. When you run a program, DOS tricks the program into thinking that it is getting or putting information on the standard devices, standard input (the keyboard), and standard output (the screen).

Three new characters are involved in this process:

<	Redirects the input of a program
>	Redirects the output of a program
>>	Also redirects the output of a program, but adds to an established file

You can use these symbols only at the DOS system prompt level. You add these symbols and the file or device name to the command you type. The syntax is

   symbol devicename

or

   symbol *d:* **filename.***ext*

(Note: Although this point has not been covered yet, you can place a path name behind the disk drive name and in front of the file name.)

For example,

(1) **DIR >DISKDIR**

   Redirects the output of the directory command to a disk file called DISKDIR

(2) **CHKDSK >COM1**

Redirects the output of the CHKDSK program to the serial port

(3) **MYPROG <ANSWERS**

Redirects to MYPROG input from the disk file ANSWERS

In the last example, MYPROG is not expecting you to type anything from the keyboard. Instead, MYPROG will get its input from the disk file ANSWERS.

When you use the > to redirect output and the output is a disk file, DOS will erase any disk file in the directory by this name, then create a new file to hold the output. In example (1), if a file in the current directory has the name DISKDIR, it is erased first. Don't give a file name that you don't want erased with the > output redirection command.

If you want to add the redirected output to an established file, use >>. This appends the output to the file (adds to the end of the existing file), but does not erase its original contents. To change the first example and add this additional copy of the directory to DISKDIR, you would type:

DIR >>DISKDIR

If you look at the way the symbol points, you will remember how it works. The < sign points *away* from the device or file and says, "Get the input from here." The > and >> point *towards* the device or file and say, "Take the output and put it here."

The SORT.EXE program on your DOS disk sorts the lines in a file. I created a file called WORDS that has one word on each line. To sort this file and put the sorted words in a file called SWORDS (sorted words), I type:

SORT <WORDS >SWORDS

This command tells DOS to run the SORT program, get the lines for SORT from the file called WORDS, and put the output of SORT into a file called SWORDS.

For programmers, DOS grabs the redirection command, which never appears on the command line passed to the program.

The example above illustrates how you can redirect both the input and the output of a program.

The most common use for redirection is to print what is normally displayed on the video screen. Redirection is also frequently used to put what would be displayed on the video screen into a disk file and to debug programs. Programmers debug programs by establishing a file of "answers" for the program, then running the program and redirecting the input to the disk file. This use of redirection reduces debugging time.

If you think about what can happen to error messages when you redirect the output, such as to a printer or disk file, you are one step ahead. The answer to this question depends on the program. If your program uses the new concept of *standard error,* the message will appear on your video screen, not at the redirected file or device. If the program does not use standard error, then the error messages will be redirected. This means that you may not see the error messages the program displays because they are sent to a file, not to the video display. Fortunately, all DOS V2 commands and programs use standard error. (Microsoft BASIC V2, Disk BASIC, and Advanced BASIC, have provisions for standard input, output, and error.)

As an exercise, experiment first with the redirection of output. Use the > and >> symbols to redirect the output of the DIR and CHKDSK commands. Put the output to the printer and into a disk file.

Once you are comfortable with the redirection of output, make a text file that answers a program's questions. See what "responses" can come from a disk file.

Be careful. There is a bug in DOS V2.00. If you don't place enough answers in the text file to answer all of the program's questions, DOS will wait forever for the rest of the answers. The computer will actually "lock up," and the only way to free it will be to reset your computer. This bug exists only in V2.00. If you have a later version of DOS, you don't have to worry about this problem.

Piping

The concept of piping goes with I/O redirection. A *pipe* is a computer-made line that connects two programs. The output of the first program becomes the input for the second.

A simple example is the program MORE. It displays one screen of information that it gets from the standard input, then displays the message -- More -- . When you tap a key, MORE will display the next screenful of information and repeat this process until the entire input is displayed.

MORE is a *filter,* a program that performs some manipulation on the stream of characters that come from the standard input, one character after another, and go to the standard output. A filter gets data from the standard input, modifies the data, then writes it to the standard output (screen). This modification is called "filtering" the data. In this case, the manipulation MORE performs is waiting for you to press a key after a screenful of information is displayed.

If you are confused, try the example below. If you are wondering what good a filter like MORE is, the example will show you.

Use the diskette that contains all your DOS and sample BASIC programs. Put it in drive A:, then type:

```
A>DIR | MORE
```

and hit the space bar when you see -- More -- at the bottom of your screen. The character between the words DIR and MORE is a vertical bar. This is the pipe character.

Here's what happens when you issue the previous command:

1. DOS executes the DIR command.

2. Instead of printing the information on the video screen, DOS places the information in a file called %PIPE1.$$$

3. DOS executes the MORE filter.

4. DOS tricks MORE into using the file %PIPE1.$$$ for input.

5. MORE performs its work and displays its information on the screen.

6. DOS deletes the file %PIPE1.$$$

You could do the same thing by issuing these three commands:

A>DIR > %PIPE1.$$$
A>MORE < %PIPE1.$$$
A>ERASE %PIPE1.$$$

Technically, *piping* is the chaining together of two or more programs with automatic redirection. Temporary files are created in the root directory of the disk for this redirection. (Don't worry now about root directories. They are the subject of the next chapter.) The names of the files are **%PIPEx.$$$**, where DOS assigns a number to **x**.

Redirection of I/O and piping are UNIX features. Although DOS acts like UNIX in this respect, DOS does not perform these functions the same way. DOS uses temporary disk files. UNIX does not. When you use piping, make sure that your disk has enough room to hold the temporary file or files; otherwise, the piping will not work.

You are not restricted to using just one pipe at a time. However, only one program name may be on each side of the pipe. You can redirect the input of the first program and the output of the final program in the pipe.

Piping, like redirection, works only at the DOS command level. You cannot use piping after you have run a program. You must pipe things when you type the line to run the program.

Earlier, we saw that MORE is a filter. Three standard filters are provided with DOS V2:

FIND   Finds a string
MORE   Displays a screenful, then waits for a keystroke
SORT   Is a sorting utility

You may want to skip to the Command Summary at the back of the book to find out how each filter is used. I would suggest, however, that you read about these filters after you have finished reading this chapter.

The following example uses two filters: SORT and MORE. As before, I have a text file called WORDS that has several words in it. Each word is on a separate line. This example sorts the WORDS file and uses MORE to display one screenful of words.

SORT < WORDS | MORE

This command tells DOS to take the words from the file called WORDS, sort the lines (remember that I put one word to a line), and run the results through MORE to display one screenful of lines at a time. It also shows that the first program can have its input redirected.

The example below shows the redirection of the final program and how piping can be used with several filters.

DIR | FIND "1-01-80" | SORT > DIRS

This command tells DOS to find any line from the DIR command that has the characters "1-01-80." The result is passed to SORT, which sorts the lines and places the output into the file called DIRS. This example shows you the files created on "1-01-80," the default starting date for DOS. Try this with your diskettes or hard disk. If you have always answered the date and time questions when DOS started up, you should not have any files like this.

The best way to learn about redirection, piping, and filters is to try them. Read about FIND, SORT, and MORE. Experiment with these filters and piping. Don't forget the caution about redirection. If you redirect a program's output to a disk file with the > symbol, anything in that disk file will be erased before DOS uses it. Be careful about the file names you use.

This chapter introduced two UNIX features—redirection and piping—used by PC DOS. The next chapter introduces a third, the hierarchical directory system.

8

Hierarchical Directories

If you have used DOS V1.1 or other operating systems, you know that each diskette has its own directory. Every diskette has one, and only one, directory. This system works well. If, by chance, you store 112 files on a diskette (the maximum for a double-sided PC DOS diskette), you can still "wade" through the directory to find a file.

When you have a large number of files in a directory, however, the DIR command is clumsy to use. You must often pause the listing of the files so that the file you are looking for does not scroll off the top of the screen.

DOS V1.1 added a new option to the directory command to aid in searching for a file. The **/W** switch gives a short, wide listing of just the file names. DOS V2 adds the **/P** switch that pauses the display after a screenful of files. When you tap a key, the next screenful of files is listed. These switches allow both versions of DOS to address the problems associated with long directories.

The **/W** and **/P** options to the DIR command address only the displaying of the directory. They do not address the limitations in how DOS handles the disk's directory.

The hard disk is a device capable of storing hundreds or thousands of files. Somehow, the directory of the hard disk needs to be expanded to accommodate these files. If you make the single directory of the diskette bigger, it will slow DOS down. When you look for a file, DOS must wade internally through the directory to find the file you want. From the standpoint of performance, this simple solution does not work.

To solve this problem, Microsoft, the author of DOS, borrowed a concept from the UNIX operating system: hierarchical directories.

Why Hierarchical Directories?

With hierarchical directories, files can be grouped and organized on the hard disk in a manner similar to the way most people organize floppy diskettes. Floppy diskettes are usually organized by purpose. Each diskette contains the programs and data files needed for a certain task. I have one floppy diskette for my word-processing program; another for infrequently used DOS utilities; and some diskettes for programming in BASIC, C, and machine language. I have other diskettes for my spreadsheets, and still other diskettes for creating models.

This arrangement logically groups programs and data files across many diskettes. It, therefore, works well for floppy diskettes.

How about the hard disk? Can files be organized the same way on the hard disk? They can if you place almost every diskette into a subdirectory on the hard disk. What is a subdirectory? Let's look at the directory system as a whole.

Every disk or diskette starts with one directory. It is stored on the disk and holds the names of your files as well as other information. The directory itself is really a file. Although you cannot store programs or data in the directory, DOS stores its own data in the directory file. You might not have thought of this before, but if you can visualize the directory as a file, the rest is easy.

The starting directory of every disk is the *root* or *system* directory. It holds program or data files but now can also hold the names of other directories. These additional directories are called *subdirectories*.

Subdirectories are also files. A subdirectory is set up just like the main or root directory and can hold the names of your files and other information. Like the root directory, subdirectories can hold the names of other subdirectories.

The only restriction on subdirectories is the amount of free space on the disk. Otherwise, subdirectories can hold an unlimited number of files. As you add more files, DOS will automatically make the subdirectory bigger. This is the major difference between subdirectories and the root directory of a disk. The root directory is fixed both in size and in the number of files it can hold. The subdirectory can be extended as needed, subject only to free disk space.

To understand how directories work, imagine a family tree with the founding parents as the base of the tree. Their children are branches on the tree. When the children themselves grow up, marry, and have children, the tree grows more branches. The process continues for each generation as children marry and have children.

The root directory is like the founding parents. Just as the founding parents have children, the root directory can have subdirectories. Each subdirectory (child) of the root (parent) directory can in turn become a parent to another generation of subdirectories. As you create each new subdirectory, you create a new branch on the tree.

The terms *parent* and *child* are often used in discussing the directory system. The parent directory "owns" its child subdirectories. In turn, each child can trace itself back to its parent. A subtle fact to remember is that although a parent directory can have many child subdirectories, a child subdirectory is owned by only one parent directory. You can, therefore, trace any subdirectory back to the root directory of the disk.

Look at Appendix B. You will see a sample directory setup that illustrates how hierarchical directories work. This illustration will be used only to demonstrate how the directory system works and is not intended to show the best way to organize your files.

The root directory is at the top. It contains several normal (non-directory) files: IBMBIO.COM, IBMDOS.COM, AUTOEXEC.BAT, CONFIG.SYS, and VDISK.SYS. You may recognize some of these file names. The root directory also has two subdirectories: DOS and WORDS. The DOS side contains DOS programs and programming files. The WORDS side has word-processing files. In this case, the parent directory owns two children: the DOS and WORDS subdirectories.

Note that there is no directory by the name "root." The topmost root directory uses a special symbol for its name: the backslash (\). If you see only a backslash as the directory name, that backslash signifies the root directory. Call for a directory of any DOS diskette in drive A. You will see the line

```
    Directory of A:\
```

The single backslash tells you that you are getting a directory listing of the root directory of the diskette.

Let's descend one level on the word-processing side. You have moved down to the WORDS subdirectory. If you are familiar with WordStar, you will recognize the names of three files. These are the WordStar program files. In addition to the WordStar program files, WORDS also owns two children: the subdirectories LETTERS and CONTRACTS. The LETTERS subdirectory holds letters that I wrote. In this case, it holds letters to IBM, JACK, and DOUG. LETTERS also holds the previous revisions of the letters to IBM and JACK (the files that end in .BAK). The CONTRACTS subdirectory holds the drafts of my contracts with MEYER and ANDRESON.

In this case, the hierarchical directories were used to organize word-processing files by purpose—letters and contracts.

(This example is not completely accurate. When this book was written, WordStar would not allow the use of files that were not in the same directory as the WordStar program. This is discussed later.)

Let's go back to the root directory, moving back up through WORDS. Now we will move down one level to the DOS directory. The DOS directory holds a copy of the Microsoft Macro Assembler (MASM1.EXE) and an assembly language file called VDISK.ASM. (This is the RAM disk program that is in the IBM DOS V2.0 manual on pages 14-27 through 14-34. If you have a copy of the Macro Assembler, you may want to try your hand at that program later.)

DOS owns three children: BASIC, UTIL, and HARDDISK. Two versions of the BASIC language are in one directory, some DOS utilities programs in the UTIL directory, and programs for the hard disk are in the HARDDISK directory.

Did you notice that I used the term directories for subdirectories? The two terms are interchangeable if you are referring to any directory other than the root directory of a disk. The root directory cannot be a subdirectory, but any subdirectory is a directory in its own right. From this point on, the term subdirectory is used only when needed for clarity.

Let's step down one more level into the BASIC directory. BASIC owns two directories: a SAMPLES directory, which contains the sample programs provided with IBM DOS V2.0; and a TEST directory with some BASIC programs I created to test the disk speed (DSKSPED.BAS) and the screen (SCRNTST.BAS).

Before we start using the new directory system, let's look at one new term, path. A *path* is a chain of directory names. It tells DOS how to maneuver through the directories to find the directory or file you want. Each directory name is separated by the path character, the backslash (\).

Don't let this dual use of the backslash confuse you. Remember that if the backslash is the first character of the path, it means start at the root directory of the disk. Otherwise, the backslash just separates directory names. Also remember that if you need to use a file name with a path, one more path character is required before the file name.

In the chapter about file names, you learned that no two files can have the same file name in the same directory. You cannot substitute disk for directory in this rule. However, because a diskette or hard disk can have several directories, the same file name can exist in several directories on the same disk or diskette. This does not confuse DOS at all.

A word of warning: Never put a program or batch file with the same root name as a subdirectory in the subdirectory's parent directory. When executing a program or batch file, you only use the root name of the file. If a subdirectory's full name is identical to the root name of a program or batch in the parent directory (where the subdirectory name is held), DOS may not be sure whether you are talking about the program or the directory when you execute a file or attempt to give a path name.

Look at the following rules about directories and path names. You may notice some similarities between directory names and file names. They are closely related.

Rules for Directory Names

1. A directory name has

   A. A root name one to eight characters long

   B. An optional extension one to three characters long

   C. A period separating the root name from the extension

2. Valid characters for a directory name are

   A. The letters A to Z (Lower-case a to z are transformed to upper-case A to Z.)

   B. The numbers 0 to 9

   C. The special characters and punctuation symbols

   $ # & @ ! & ( ) - { } ' _ ` ~

3. The following characters cannot be used in a directory name:

   A. Any control character, including escape (27d or 1Bh) and delete (127d or 7Fh)

   B. A space

   C. The characters

   ^ + = / [ ] " : ; , ? * \ < > | .

4. You cannot create a directory called . (single period) or .. (double period). The single period is the shorthand way of designating the current directory, and the double period (..) is the shorthand for the parent directory.

5. A device name may be part of a directory name, but not the entire directory name. For example, CONT is okay, but CON is not.

Rules for Path Names

1. A path can be from 1 to 63 characters long.

2. The path is composed of directory names separated by the backslash (\).

3. A drive name may precede a path.

4. Generally, a file name may follow a path. When it does, separate the path name from the file name by a backslash.

5. Each drive has its own path, which DOS keeps in memory.

6. The symbols . (current directory) and .. (parent directory) are valid in a path name.

7. To start with the root (uppermost) directory, precede the path name with a backslash. (A drive name before the path does not contradict this rule.)

8. If you don't start with the root directory, DOS will start with the current directory of the disk.

You will recall the notation used for a disk drive and file name earlier in this book. The new (and correct) notation is

d:path**filename**.*ext*

This is a full-file specification. It starts with the optional disk drive name, followed by an optional path name, the mandatory root file name, and finally the optional extension. This file specification is called *filespec* in the DOS manual.

In Chapter 6, device names in the format *dev**dev were discussed. An invisible subdirectory called* **dev** is in the root directory of every disk. You don't see **dev** on any diskette or disk because DOS keeps this subdirectory internally. The designation **dev** refers to the device directory and is used to specify devices. For example, **dev****lpt1** or

\dev\prn refer to the printer, and **\dev\con** specifies the system console. Both UNIX and XENIX use device directories to handle their devices. Now DOS V2.0 also has this capability. To use this feature, type **\dev** and the device name in upper- or lower-case letters. Because the standard for UNIX is lower-case letters, they are used in this discussion.

Moving through Directories

For these examples, look at the sample disk directory in Appendix B. Use your sample disk.

We'll start at the root directory. The objective is to get to the LETTERS directory to see what I wrote to Doug (DOUG.LET), then run CHKDSK to see how much space is left on the disk.

There are two ways to accomplish this task: the hard way and the easy way. The hard way is to move down to the WORDS directory, then to the LETTERS directory. At this point you can ask DOS to show you what is in the DOUG.LET file, using the TYPE command. TYPE displays the contents of a disk file on the video screen.

To move down to the WORDS directory, use the DOS V2 command CHDIR (change directories). Type:

```
A>CHDIR WORDS
```

DOS checks the root directory to find a subdirectory called WORDS. If DOS finds the subdirectory, DOS will go there. Now you can move another level down to the LETTERS directory by typing:

```
A>CHDIR LETTERS
```

Once you are in the correct directory, typing:

```
A>TYPE DOUG.LET
```

will display the characters in this file. (Because WordStar does some funny things to a file, the display will have some strange characters in it. If you type a WordStar document file, you will see what I mean.)

Now we must return to the root directory. To do this, type:

```
A>CHDIR \
```

The path given to DOS was just the backslash character. DOS sees the backslash character and moves back to the root directory. Remember that when the path starts with a backslash, it tells DOS to start with the root directory. In the case of **CHDIR LETTERS**, DOS assumed that I meant to start with the directory I was in, because I did not start the path with a \ character.

The easy way to type this file would be to enter:

TYPE WORDS\LETTERS\DOUG.LET

The TYPE command will take a path name before the file name. DOS interprets this command to mean: look in the current directory for the subdirectory called WORDS; move into this directory and find the subdirectory called LETTERS; move into this directory and find the file called DOUG.LET; display on the video screen the characters in this file; and, finally, move back to the directory where you began.

Notice that the path character was used between each directory name. The path character was also used between the last directory name and the name of the file to be typed. You must phrase your command to DOS this way when you use a path name and a file name.

Notice the last thing DOS did when executing the TYPE command. DOS returned to the directory where the TYPE command was issued. DOS remembers the current directory for every disk you use. If you give DOS a command to go into a different directory to get a file, DOS will bounce back to the starting directory after getting the file. The only way you can change the current directory on a disk is to use the CHDIR command.

The second objective in this example is to run the CHKDSK (check disk) program on this diskette. To do this, you would first move to the UTIL directory from the root directory by typing:

```
A>CD DOS\UTIL
```

CD is the abbreviation for the CHDIR command. Both CD and CHDIR are recognized as the same command. In this example, DOS is told to move down from the root directory through the DOS subdirectory to the UTIL subdirectory. Once the UTIL directory is the current directory, type:

```
A>CHKDSK
```

DOS will then load and execute the check disk program.

(Why we moved into the UTIL directory, then executed the CHKDSK program is explained in the next section.)

Some Hands-on Experience

In this session, we will use the hierarchical directory commands CHDIR (change directory), MKDIR (make a new directory), and RMDIR (remove a directory). The abbreviations for these commands are CD for CHDIR, MD for MKDIR, and RD for RMDIR. Because DOS recognizes both forms, the abbreviations are used here. For this session, you will need:

1. Your computer with two disk drives. One drive must be a floppy disk drive; the other can be either a floppy disk drive or a hard disk. The floppy disk drives should be double-sided.

2. A copy of your DOS diskette with the sample BASIC programs.

3. If you are using two floppy disk drives, you will also need one formatted diskette with the DOS operating system on it. Label this diskette "Practice Directory Diskette," or something similar.

If you have an XT or similar computer, make one important change in the directions. Whenever drive B is mentioned, change it to the letter for your hard disk drive. For example, in the command:

A>**COPY A:*.BAS B:**

IBM XT owners should change the B: to C: (the letter for the hard disk). This alteration would change the directions to:

A>**COPY A:*.BAS C:**

Keep this requirement in mind as you read the directions. If you make a mistake and hit Enter, type the panic button (Ctrl-Break) and try the command again. Otherwise, use your backspace or Esc key and retype the command.

Step 1

Put your copy of the DOS diskette into drive A.

Step 2 (For those with two floppy disk drives)

Put the practice diskette into drive B.

Step 2 (For hard disk owners)

Make sure that you are at the root directory of the hard disk by typing **CD C:**. If your hard disk is not drive C:, substitute the appropriate letter of the hard disk drive for the letter C.

Step 3

Type **MD B:COMS**

If you have a hard disk, don't forget to change the B: to C:, or whatever is appropriate for your system.

This command makes a new subdirectory called COMS on the disk.

Step 4

Type **MD B:COMS\SAMPLES**

This command makes a new subdirectory called SAMPLES in the subdirectory COMS. At this point, the root directory owns a directory called COMS, which, in turn, owns a directory called SAMPLES. Notice that you have used a path name in this command. DOS moves down through the path name and knows that when it reaches the last name in the path (SAMPLES), it should create a new directory called SAMPLES rather than try to move again.

This path sequence can be a source of confusion for beginners. To keep the order of implementation clear in your mind, think of the path as instructions that tell DOS where to do things, and regard the last name in the path (**SAMPLES**) as the object of your action.

Step 5

Type **DIR B:**

What you see is the listing of root directory files on the disk. You may see several files if you are using the hard disk. Look for a listing in the directory that starts like this:

```
COMS      <DIR>
```

The <DIR> in the directory tells you that this "file" is a directory, not a normal file. The date and time when you created the directory should also appear on this line. Make a note of the time you see on the screen. Look at the rest of the screen. Notice the line that tells you what disk drive you are using and the directory you are viewing. Study the screen for a few seconds, then move to the next step.

Step 6

Type **DIR B:COMS**

Now you will see a directory of the COMS directory. You should see just three files listed as

```
      .          <DIR>
      ..         <DIR>
    SAMPLES      <DIR>
```

The SAMPLES directory should be no surprise, but what are the period and double-period directories?

The period represents the subdirectory you are viewing. You can think of it as the subdirectory's "I exist to myself" symbol. The double period represents the parent directory of the COMS subdirectory.

Notice that the root directory does not contain these directory symbols. Only subdirectories have the period (.) and double-period (..) symbols.

If you want to tell DOS specifically to start with the directory you are using, use the period as the first character in the path. To tell DOS to move up one level of subdirectories, use the double period.

Take a look at the dates and times on the lines with the period and double-period symbols. These dates and times should be the same as those for the entries for COMS <DIR> in the root directory. When DOS creates subdirectories, it not only makes an entry in the parent directory, but also establishes the . and .. files, giving all three items the same date and time.

Step 7

Type **COPY A:*.COM B:\COMS /V**

This command copies from drive A to the subdirectory COMS on drive B (**B:\COMS**) all the files that end with .COM (**A:*.COM**). As before, the **/V** tells DOS to verify that the copies are correct.

Notice that when a disk drive name must be specified, it appears first. The path comes next, then the file name. With **A:*.COM**, a path was not needed because we were using the directory containing all of the DOS programs we wanted. For **B:\COMS**, a disk drive (drive B) and a path (**\COMS**) were specified. Because we did not want to give the files a new name when they were copied, we did not need to use a file name.

A drive name, followed by a path, and finally a file name is the usual order. If you don't need one part, such as the path or drive name, leave it out.

Step 8

Type **CD B:\COMS**

This command makes COMS the current directory on drive B.

Step 9

In this step, you will copy two files to the COMS directory. Type:

    COPY A:SORT.EXE B: /V

After SORT.EXE is copied, type:

    COPY A:FIND.EXE B: /V

Because COMS is the current directory for drive B, which is where we want to move the new programs, we do not need to specify a path name.

Step 10

Display a list of the files for the root, COMS, and SAMPLES directories on drive B. Briefly look at each directory before doing the next one. The required commands are

    DIR B: ..
    DIR B:
    DIR B:SAMPLES

The first command tells DOS to step up one level of directories and show the list of files. The second tells DOS to list the files in the current directory, and the final command tells DOS to list the files in the SAMPLES subdirectory.

Step 11

At this point, you will copy the BASIC programs from the DOS diskette. To copy the BASIC program files from drive A to the SAMPLES directory, type:

COPY A:*.BAS B:SAMPLES /V

Step 12

To move to the SAMPLES directory, type:

CD B:SAMPLES

Step 13

If your system has two floppy disk drives, exchange the diskettes in drives A and B. Then call for a directory of drive A and a directory of drive B. What happened?

In both cases, you got a listing of the files in the root directory. If you change diskettes, DOS will reset the current directory back to the root directory. This way DOS does not get confused when you change diskettes.

If you have a two-floppy disk system, move back to the SAMPLES directory by typing **CD COMS\SAMPLES**.

If you are using a hard disk, make it the current disk drive. Type the letter of the disk drive, a colon, and hit Enter. For the XT, type **C:** ⟵.

Step 14

Create a new directory called TEST in SAMPLES. The command is

MD TEST

Now call for a directory of TEST. (Use the command **DIR TEST**.) You should see only the . and .. entries.

Step 15

Copy BASIC into the TEST directory by typing:

COPY ..\BASIC.COM TEST /V

This command tells DOS to step up one directory to COMS to get BASIC.COM (Disk BASIC) and copy it into the TEST subdirectory.

Step 16

Type **RD TEST**

You should see an error message. RD, or RMDIR, is the remove directory command. You just told DOS to erase the TEST directory. The message you see on your screen tells you that you cannot remove a directory which is not empty. You can remove a subdirectory if the only files in the subdirectory are the . or .. directory symbols. No other files or subdirectories are allowed. This is for their safety. DOS assumes that if you want to remove a subdirectory, you will empty it first.

You cannot use RD on the current directory, nor can you remove the root directory of the diskette. If you try to do either, you will get a different error message.

Move to the TEST directory and try to remove it. Move back to the SAMPLES directory before going on to step 17.

Step 17

To remove the TEST directory successfully, type the following command. Make certain that you type it correctly before you hit Enter.

ERASE TEST*.*

DOS will now ask, Are you sure (Y/N)? This is another safety precaution. You have just told DOS to erase all files in the TEST subdirectory. Whenever you tell DOS to erase all files, DOS will ask you to confirm your request.

Because we do want to erase all of the files, answer **Y**. Otherwise, you would answer **N**, and the system prompt would return.

Next, call for a directory of TEST (**DIR TEST**). You will see that BASIC.COM was erased, but the . and .. entries remain. You cannot erase a subdirectory with the ERASE command. The only way to remove a directory is to use the RMDIR (or RD) command.

You can remove the directory by typing:

RD TEST

Now call for a DIR. You will see that the TEST directory has been removed.

Step 18

In this step, you will try to run the BASIC sample programs. To do this, load the BASIC language, then run the sample programs.

First, we'll try to invoke Advanced BASIC, which is in the UTIL directory. Type:

..\BASICA SAMPLES

Nothing happened. Why? Let's try telling DOS to start at the top, move down to UTIL, and get BASIC. Type:

\UTIL\BASICA SAMPLES

The same thing happened. The system prompt reappeared. Why?

You did not do anything wrong. You have just seen a limitation of DOS. It will not let you execute a program that is not in your current directory. Unlike UNIX and XENIX, which allow a path name in front of a command or program name, DOS currently does not.

You are now faced with two choices. You can copy BASICA.COM into the SAMPLES directory. This will work well, but it means that you will have to keep a copy of BASICA.COM or Disk BASIC (BASIC.COM) in each subdirectory. This is not a very efficient way of conserving disk space.

The PATH command is the other choice. It allows you to tell DOS to search in other subdirectories for the programs you want to run. If DOS does not find the program in the current directory, DOS will search the directories you named in the PATH command.

Try typing:

PATH \COMS

This command tells DOS to look in the COMS subdirectory if DOS cannot find in the current directory the program you want to run. As with many other DOS commands, the last directory named in the path (COMS) is searched and no other (in this case, the root directory of the disk). If you want DOS to search both, you must use the PATH command and type in the directories to be searched, separating them with semicolons. If you want DOS to search both the root directory and the COMS directory, you would type **PATH \;\COMS**.

Now that the PATH command has been properly set, type:

BASICA SAMPLES

This should load and run Advanced BASIC from the COMS directory. BASIC will then load and execute the BASIC samples menu.

Three Notes about the PATH Command

The PATH command can accept a disk drive name in front of the path name. Give the PATH command the name for your hard disk (such as C:, then the path) if you have one. DOS will automatically return to the hard disk drive to find a program in the specified path.

When you use the PATH command, always start paths with the root directory. This way you can be in any subdirectory on the disk, and DOS will always start at the root directory. If you don't specify the root directory as the beginning of these paths, DOS will try to move down your specified path, starting with the current directory. This means that you must give a new PATH command every time you change subdirectories. The easy way is to start your paths for the PATH command with a disk drive name and a backslash.

Unfortunately, the PATH command works only when you are running programs or batch files from the DOS system prompt. (Batch files are discussed in the next chapter.) Your programs must know where to get any additional program or data files. You cannot change this with the PATH command.

Some Final Thoughts

Hierarchical directories are a powerful tool for organizing your files. This system allows you to group your files by purpose, which is a major benefit to hard disk owners.

Unfortunately, at the time of this writing, most programs do not take advantage of the hierarchical directories. This means that you may have to keep your programs and data files together in a directory instead of having programs in one directory and data files in separate sub-directories. Program publishers should catch on to this feature and allow you to tell the program which subdirectory holds program or data files.

The biggest problem is programs with additional program files that are constantly used while the program is running. WordStar is one example. The WordStar program uses the two overlay files, **WSOVLY1.OVR** and **WSMSGS.OVR**, while it is running. Although you can put the main WordStar program file in the subdirectory used by the PATH command, you must keep a copy of the two overlay files in each subdirectory you use with WordStar.

I keep all my common programs (the DOS utilities, other disk utilities, text editors, etc.) on my hard disk in a subdirectory called BIN. The PATH command I use is **C:\BIN**. I can be anywhere and run programs or batch files that are in the BIN subdirectory. This includes the times when the floppy disk drive is the current drive.

After you use the new directory system for a while, you will probably have many subdirectories. Two commands will help you find all the subdirectories on a disk: CHKDSK with the **/V** (verbose) switch and TREE. Each of these commands can be used to find all the sub-directories on a disk. Occasionally, use I/O redirection to print a copy and keep it on hand. A newcomer using your computer will appreciate this directory road map.

If you'd like to try the **\dev** subdirectory, type **DIR>\DEV\PRN** while your printer is on and selected. Typing **PRN** is easier than **\dev\prn**, but the latter will help you use UNIX later.

Experiment with the new directory system. Make some directories, copy files, erase files, and subdirectories while you are in a different directory. Practice with the hierarchical directories. This is the best way to learn the new system.

9

Batch Commands

Up to this point, you've learned most of the facts about using DOS, but how do you make DOS use itself? Batch files are the convenient and time-saving feature of DOS that allows you to make DOS do work for you.

What Is a Batch File?

A *batch file* is a series of DOS commands that is placed into a disk file. When instructed, DOS executes the commands in the file, one line at a time. DOS treats these commands as if they were individually typed from the keyboard.

Batch files have several advantages. Once the correctly phrased commands have been placed in the file, you can direct DOS to execute them by typing the batch file's root name. This is very convenient. You don't have to worry about misspelling the commands in the file once they have worked correctly because you don't have to re-enter commands in a batch file each time you want to execute them. You can direct DOS to perform one or hundreds of commands just by typing the batch file's root name.

Once a batch file has been invoked, DOS does not need your attention until it has finished running the batch file. Some programs may take a long time to run. In the past, if you needed to run several long programs back-to-back, you started each program and waited until it was finished before starting the next one. Waiting can be tedious. Why should you have to wait for the computer if you don't have to?

A batch file will execute each command without your intervention, freeing you to do other tasks or just relax while the computer does the hard work. However, if a program needs your input to answer a question or change diskettes, the batch file cannot do these tasks for you. Your attention is still required. You can, though, use a batch file to execute programs or commands without having to type the program or command name each time. By redirecting the input of the program to a file, you can avoid having to answer manually a program's questions. (Batch files and redirection are discussed later.)

Batch files are for your convenience. You may never need to use a batch file, but you may find this DOS facility very handy.

Batch File Rules

Rules for Creating Batch Files

1. A batch file contains ASCII text. You may use the DOS command COPY; EDLIN, the DOS line editor; or another text editor to create a batch file. If you use a word processor, make sure that it is in the programming, or nondocument, mode.

2. The root name of a batch file can be one to eight characters long and must conform to the rules for file names.

3. The file-name extension must be .BAT.

4. The root name of the batch file should not be the same root name as a program file (a file ending with .COM or .EXE) in the current directory. Nor should the root name be the same as an internal DOS command, such as COPY or DATE. If you use one of these root names, DOS will not know whether you want to execute the batch file, the program, or the command.

5. You may enter any valid DOS commands that you might type at the keyboard. You may also use the parameter markers (%0 to %9) and the batch subcommands.

6. To use the percent sign (%) in a command, such as for a file name, enter the percent symbol twice. For example, to use a file called A100%.TXT, you would enter **A100%%.TXT**. This rule does not apply to the parameter markers (%0 to %9).

To run batch files, the syntax is

d: **filename** *parameters*

where *d:* is the optional name of the disk drive holding the batch file, **filename** is the root name of the batch file, and *parameters* is the additional information to be used by the batch file.

Rules for Running Batch Files

1. If you do not give a disk drive name, the current disk drive will be used.

2. To invoke a batch file, simply type its root name. For example, to invoke a batch file called OFTEN.BAT, just type **OFTEN**.

3. If the batch file is not in the current directory of the disk drive, DOS will search the directory(ies) specified by the PATH command to find the batch file.

4. DOS will execute each command, one line at a time. The specified parameters will be substituted for the markers when the command is used.

5. DOS recognizes a maximum of ten parameters. You may use the SHIFT subcommand to get around this limitation.

6. If DOS encounters an incorrectly phrased batch subcommand when running a batch file, a Syntax error message will be displayed. DOS will ignore the rest of the commands in the batch file, and the system prompt will reappear.

7. You can stop a running batch file by typing Ctrl-Break. DOS will display the message:

```
Terminate batch job (Y/N)?
```

If you answer **Y** for yes, the rest of the commands will be ignored, and the system prompt will appear.

If you answer **N** for no, DOS will skip the current command but continue processing the other commands in the file.

8. DOS remembers which disk holds the batch file. If you remove the diskette that holds the batch file, DOS will prompt you to place that diskette into the original drive to get the next command.

9. DOS remembers which directory holds the batch file. Your batch file may change directories at any time.

10. You can make DOS execute a second batch file, immediately after finishing the first one, by entering the name of the second batch file as the last command in the first file.

AUTOEXEC.BAT

Rules for AUTOEXEC.BAT

1. The file must be called AUTOEXEC.BAT and reside in the root directory of the boot disk.

2. The contents of the AUTOEXEC.BAT file conform to the rules for creating batch files.

3. When DOS is booted, it automatically executes the AUTOEXEC.BAT file.

4. When AUTOEXEC.BAT is executed after DOS is booted, the date and time are not requested automatically. To get the current date and time, you must put the DATE and TIME commands into the AUTOEXEC.BAT file.

To understand batch files, let's look at an example. We'll use the AUTOEXEC.BAT file on the IBM VisiCalc® diskette. When you TYPE this file, you will see:

```
VC80
```

When you boot the computer, DOS loads itself into the computer's memory. Next DOS scans the root directory of the diskette for the AUTOEXEC.BAT file. After finding the file, DOS starts executing the commands in the file. In this case, the only command is VC80, which loads and executes the 80-column version of VisiCalc, VC80.COM.

AUTOEXEC.BAT is a useful feature. It allows the computer operator to insert a diskette into drive A, turn on the computer, and have the computer automatically load VisiCalc. This process is called *turnkey capability.*

Another advantage to this approach is that the contents of the AUTOEXEC.BAT file can easily be modified to perform different or additional functions. If you use a 40-column video screen, say a television set, you would want to run the 40-column version of VisiCalc, VC40. To do this, you would simply edit the AUTOEXEC.BAT file on the VisiCalc diskette, changing the VC80 to **VC40**. DOS would then execute the 40-column version instead of the 80-column.

This batch file has one slight disadvantage. No provision is made to get the current date and time. DOS date-stamps each VisiCalc data file with "1-1-80," the default DOS date. When you do a directory of the disk, it is difficult to tell when a VisiCalc data file was created or changed.

Lotus Development Corporation, author of 1-2-3™, uses a slightly different AUTOEXEC.BAT file. When you type the file, you see:

```
DATE
TIME
LOTUS
```

When DOS is booted from this diskette, DOS executes the DATE command to get the current date and the TIME command to get the current time, then loads and executes the 1-2-3 menu program, LOTUS.EXE.

You can make you own AUTOEXEC.BAT files by creating a file containing all the commands needed to start your program. To make a batch file that would automatically run the IBM BASIC sample programs, you would put the following command in the AUTO-EXEC.BAT file on a copy of the DOS diskette:

BASICA SAMPLES

This command loads Advanced BASIC, which then loads and executes the SAMPLES.BAS program. If you would like to try this, format a diskette and place the operating system on it (**FORMAT /S**). Copy BASICA.COM from your DOS master diskette to the new diskette. Then copy all the .BAS (BASIC) programs from the DOS Supplemental diskette. Make your AUTOEXEC.BAT file and reboot the computer with the new diskette in drive A.

The concept of a batch file is simple. The computer executes the commands from the file as if you typed them at the keyboard. The AUTOEXEC.BAT file is slightly different. DOS automatically executes this file when you start the computer. You can also execute this batch file at any time by typing **AUTOEXEC** while the diskette is in the current disk drive. The only "magic" to this file occurs when DOS starts up. After DOS is up and running, AUTOEXEC.BAT is just another batch file.

Another convenient feature of a batch file is that it allows you to execute a long series of commands without having to type them in. Let's look at 1-2-3's installation batch file, INSTALL.BAT. The instructions in this file are to place a DOS system diskette in drive A, place the 1-2-3 Utility disk in drive B, then type **B:INSTALL**. The contents of the IN-STALL.BAT file are listed on the next page.

The first four lines of the file are the message that is displayed when the batch file is run. *REM* is short for remark, a batch command that displays whatever follows it on the video screen. The message tells you to make sure that you have the correct diskettes in the right drive and hit any key to continue, or a Ctrl-C to stop the batch file.

```
REM Please check that you have placed a DOS disk in Drive A.
REM Also check that the LOTUS Utility disk is in drive B.
REM If this is not the case, press [Ctrl] and ''C'' and start over.
REM If the disks are correct, press any other key.
PAUSE
A:SYS B:
COPY A:COMMAND.COM B:
COPY A:DISKCOPY.COM B:
COPY A:DISKCOMP.COM B:
COPY A:FORMAT.COM B:
COPY A:CHKDSK.COM B:
```

Next PAUSE, another special batch file subcommand, puts a message on the screen, Press any key to continue, and waits. When you press a key, the batch file will continue. The PAUSE subcommand is used when you want the operator to read a lengthy message or change diskettes. After the appropriate action has been taken, pressing any key on the keyboard will allow DOS to continue with the batch file.

The next command, A:SYS B:, tells DOS to place a copy of the operating system on the diskette in drive B, the 1-2-3 Utilities diskette. This will make the Utilities diskette *bootable* (able to be used to start DOS).

The command in line 7 copies the DOS command processor, COM-MAND.COM, to the 1-2-3 diskette. The rest of the commands copy some DOS utility programs to the 1-2-3 Utilities diskette.

You can execute each command separately by typing it at the keyboard. However, it is much simpler just to type **B:INSTALL** than to type the last six lines in the batch file.

Parameters

What is a batch file parameter? In DOS, many commands accept information that you type in when you run the program. COPY is one example. The name of the file you want to copy, the destination to copy the file to, and the additional switches you enter are all parameters. *Parameters* are the additional information that is typed on the command line after the program name. Programs, in turn, can use whatever information is in the parameters.

For example, in the line

COPY FORMAT.COM B: /V

FORMAT.COM, B:, and **/V** are parameters. Each parameter tells COPY what to do. In this case, the parameters tell COPY to copy the program FORMAT.COM from the default disk to the diskette in drive B and verify that the copy was made correctly.

Batch files also use parameters but in a different way. When you type the name of the batch file, you can type additional information on the same line before you press ←. Your batch file, in turn, can use these parameters.

Markers tell DOS where to use the parameters you typed when you invoked the batch file. A marker starts with a percent sign (%), followed by a number from 0 to 9. These ten markers tell DOS to substitute whatever is typed on the command line for the markers.

If you look at the command line, every word (including the name of the program or batch file you are going to run) that is separated by a space, comma, semicolon, or other valid delimiter is a parameter.

The first parameter on the command line is the program or batch file name. This is the 0 parameter. Computers usually start numbering with 0. For them, 0 is a true number, not a placeholder as you were taught in arithmetic.

The second word on the command line is parameter 1. The third word is parameter 2, and so forth. This system works well because the name of the program or batch file is often ignored when parameters are counted. The first item placed on the command line after the program or batch file name is usually considered the first parameter.

With a text editor or COPY, place the following line into a file called TEST.BAT.

echo Hello, %1

Now type **TEST**, a space, then your first name, and press ◄─┘. In my case, I saw:

```
A>TEST CHRIS
A>echo Hello, CHRIS
Hello, CHRIS
A>_
```

The ECHO subcommand is a new batch command. It shows the text on the line following the word "ECHO" on the video display. The "%1," however, is the real object of this discussion. Why didn't DOS print "Hello, %1"?

DOS substituted your name in the spot where the "%1" was in the line. Your name, the second word on the line, became the first parameter.

Now create another batch file called TEST1.BAT. This is also a one-line file.

   ECHO %0 %1 %2 %3 %4

After you have created this file, type **TEST1**, a space, your name, another space, and your address. Here's how my file looked.

```
A>TEST1 CHRIS 1234 THUNDERBIRD AVENUE
A>ECHO TEST1 CHRIS 1234 THUNDERBIRD AVENUE
TEST1 CHRIS 1234 THUNDERBIRD AVENUE
A>_
```

Looking at the batch file line, we have requested that DOS show parameters 0 through 4 on the video display. This worked out to be

WORD:	TEST1	CHRIS	1234	THUNDERBIRD	AVENUE
PARAMETER:	%0	%1	%2	%3	%4

What happens if you don't give enough information on the command line to fill each parameter? Run TEST1 again but this time give only your first name. I saw the following:

```
A>TEST1 CHRIS
A>ECHO TEST1 CHRIS
TEST1 CHRIS
A>_
```

DOS displayed the batch file name and my name. No other information was "echoed" on the video display. If you do not give enough parameters on the command line, DOS will replace the unfilled markers with nothing. It ignores the unfilled markers. In this case, only parameters 0 and 1 were printed. Parameters 2, 3, and 4 were ignored.

One last comment about the 0 parameter. If you give a drive name with the name of the batch command, the drive name will appear with the batch file name. If I had typed **A:TEST1 CHRIS**, I would have seen:

```
A>ECHO A:TEST1 CHRIS
A:TEST1 CHRIS
A>_
```

Let's construct a batch file that takes advantage of blank parameters. Because I use a hard disk system, I use floppy diskettes for moving information between computers or for backing up information on the hard disk. Sometimes, I edit a file on another computer, then move the information back to the XT. I don't need the copy of the file on the floppy disk after the file has been copied to the hard disk. Many times, I remove the file from the floppy diskette. To do this, you must:

1. Copy the file from the floppy diskette to the hard disk

2. Erase the file from the floppy diskette

You can do this with a batch file by typing just the batch file name. Suppose that you constructed a batch file called C&E.BAT (copy and erase).

COPY A:%1 C:%2
ERASE A:%1

To use this file, you would type:

C&E oldfilename newfilename

where the **oldfilename** is the name of the file you want to copy to the hard disk, and **newfilename** is the new name for the file you copied (if you want to change the file name as it is being copied). Now suppose that you put a diskette containing the file NOTES.TXT into drive A and want to copy it to the hard disk. To do this, type:

```
A>C&E NOTES.TXT
A>COPY A:NOTES.TXT C:
1 file(s) copied
A>ERASE A:NOTES.TXT
A>
```

In this example, ignoring empty markers worked well. Because we did not want to change the file name, we did not give a second parameter. DOS copied NOTES.TXT from drive A to drive C, then deleted the file. The "%2" parameter was "dropped" in the batch file so that the file did not get a new name when it was copied.

One of the benefits of constructing a batch file this way is that you can also use a path name as the second parameter and copy the file from the floppy disk into a different directory on the hard disk. For example, to copy NOTES.TXT to the a second-level directory called WORDS, type:

C&E NOTES.TXT \WORDS

Line 2 from the batch file becomes:

COPY A:NOTES.TXT C:\WORDS

Because WORDS is a directory name, DOS knows that it should copy the file NOTES.TXT into the directory WORDS instead of copying the file into the current directory and giving it the new file name WORDS.

Batch Subcommands

Batch Subcommands for DOS V2	
ECHO	Turns on or off the display of batch commands and can display a message on the screen
FOR..IN..DO	Allows the use of the same batch command for several files
GOTO	Jumps to the line after a label in the batch file
IF	Allows conditional execution of a command
SHIFT	Shifts the command line parameters one parameter to the left
PAUSE	Halts processing until a key is struck and can optionally display a message
REM	Displays a message on the screen

ECHO

The ECHO command does two things. It turns on or off the display of commands from the batch file. Turning ECHO OFF is useful when you don't want to display the commands or remarks from the batch file. The screen stays uncluttered and does not confuse the operator. ECHO OFF also stops the display of remarks from the batch file.

The second part of the ECHO command displays a message on the screen. REM (remark) also displays a message on the screen. In this sense, the two commands do the same thing. However, if ECHO is OFF, no REM statement will appear on the video screen. When you ECHO a message, it always appears on the video display, regardless of whether ECHO is ON or OFF. If you always want to display a message in your batch file, use ECHO rather than REMARK.

PAUSE

The PAUSE command stops the processing of the batch file, shows any message on the rest of the line (just like the REM subcommand), displays the message Strike a key when ready . . . , and waits for you to press a key. After you press a key, DOS continues processing the batch file. The PAUSE command allows you to change diskettes while in the middle of a batch file. The other use for PAUSE is discussed in the GOTO section.

As mentioned above, PAUSE, like REM, can also display a message. Like REM, if ECHO is OFF the message is not displayed. The message Strike a key when ready is always displayed, whether ECHO is ON or OFF.

GOTO

GOTO is a new DOS V2.0 command. It allows you to jump to a part of your batch file, like the GOTO command of the BASIC language. The major difference is that you don't use a line number with DOS' GOTO, but a label. A *label* is a line in your batch file that starts with a colon (:), which is followed by a one- to eight-character name. The name can be longer, but only the first eight characters are significant to DOS. Anything after them is ignored.

When you enter **GOTO label**, DOS jumps to the line in your batch file after the one holding the label. The batch file TEST2.BAT is shown below. It is very similar to TEST.BAT but also contains the GOTO and PAUSE subcommands.

```
:START
ECHO Hello, %1
PAUSE
GOTO START
```

When I type **TEST2 CHRIS**, the following is displayed.

```
A>TEST2 CHRIS
A>ECHO Hello, CHRIS
A>PAUSE
Strike a key when ready . . .<space bar>
A>GOTO START
A>ECHO Hello, CHRIS
A>PAUSE
Strike a key when ready . . .Ctrl-C

Terminate batch job (Y/N)? Y
A>
```

The batch file starts by echoing the message with my name in it. The file then pauses for me to hit a key before continuing. After I hit a key, DOS executes the GOTO START command. DOS then jumps to the line after **:START** and continues processing. When DOS pauses a second time, I type a **Ctrl-C** to stop the batch file. DOS then asks if I want to stop the batch file. I answer **Y** for yes, and DOS quits processing the batch file. With this type of batch file, the only way to stop DOS from looping continuously is to type the Ctrl-Break sequence.

This "endless looping" type of batch file can be used to repeat the contents of a batch file several times, but also a variable number of times every time you invoke it. For instance, suppose that I want to put CHKDSK.COM, FORMAT.COM, DISKCOMP.COM, and DISK-COPY.COM on several diskettes. This time, I want to put these programs on four diskettes. But the next time I run this batch file, I may want to copy these programs onto one, two, or as many as ten diskettes. I can write a batch file to make DOS do the hard work. For this example, we'll assume that the computer has two disk drives. The disk with CHKDSK.COM, FORMAT.COM, DISKCOMP.COM, DISK-COPY.COM, and my new batch file will be on drive A. The diskette to receive the programs will go into drive B.

First, I'll create a file called FLOPPY.BAT.

```
 1    ECHO OFF
 2    :START
 3    ECHO Place the diskette to receive CHKDSK.COM, FORMAT.COM,
 4    ECHO DISKCOMP.COM, and DISKCOPY.COM in drive B or ...
 5    ECHO
 6    ECHO To quit, type Ctrl-C Y instead
 7    PAUSE
 8    COPY A:CHKDSK.COM B: /V
 9    COPY A:FORMAT.COM B: /V
10    COPY A:DISKCOMP.COM B: /V
11    COPY A:DISKCOPY.COM B: /V
12    ECHO Files are copied.
13    GOTO START
```

The GOTO subcommand in this file causes an endless loop. It can be used to copy these four programs to one diskette or to one hundred or more diskettes. This file also illustrates several batch commands.

Line 1 turns off ECHO to avoid confusing the operator. When ECHO is turned off, the commands are not displayed.

Lines 2 through 6 tell the operator either to put a diskette into drive B or to type Ctrl-C to quit.

Line 7 is the PAUSE command that displays the message telling you to strike a key to continue. At this point, if the operator has finished copying these files, typing **Ctrl-C** and a **Y** (to answer the question about terminating the batch job) will mean quitting the batch file. I could not place a message on the line with the PAUSE command because ECHO had been turned off, and any message on the same line with the PAUSE subcommand would not be displayed.

Lines 8 through 11 transfer the four programs to the diskette in drive B.

Line 12 is the reassurance line. It tells the operator that the files have been transferred. This line is unnecessary. It performs no work whatsoever. However, it is a good idea to put lines like this in a batch file because they assure the operator that all has gone well. They also make the computer less intimidating.

Line 13 is the GOTO line that starts the process over again.

The only batch commands we have not covered are IF, FOR..IN..DO, and SHIFT. All three are simple, once you understand how they work.

IF

The IF command is a "test and do" command: perform the test; if the test is true, do what's on the rest of the line; if the test is false, ignore the line. The command can be used to test three conditions:

1. The ERRORLEVEL of a program
2. If a string is equal to another string
3. If a file exists

You can also test for the opposite of these conditions (test if a condition is false) by adding the word "NOT" after "IF." Let's look at each condition and how the command can be used.

The first condition is ERRORLEVEL. A better name for this would have been "exit level." ERRORLEVEL is a number your program leaves for DOS when it is finished executing. You will notice in the commands that only two current DOS commands, BACKUP and RESTORE, have an exit code. A 0 exit code means everything was okay. Anything above 0 indicates that something was wrong, such as no files were found to back up or restore, the operator aborted the program, or the program encountered an error. ERRORLEVEL lets you test to see if the program worked properly.

ERRORLEVEL is true if the exit code of your program is equal to or greater than the number you specify in the batch file. You can think of this condition as a BASIC-like statement:

    IF ERRORLEVEL >= number THEN do this

For example, if your batch file invoked PROGRAM.COM, you could test to see if the PROGRAM worked successfully by inserting the lines:

PROGRAM
IF ERRORLEVEL 1 ECHO PROGRAM DID NOT WORK!!

These lines would test the exit code of PROGRAM. If the exit code was 1 or greater, PROGRAM DID NOT WORK! would be displayed on the screen. Otherwise, nothing would be displayed. If the condition (ERRORLEVEL 1) is false (the exit code was 0 or less), the line is skipped. This example supposes that PROGRAM.COM actually gave DOS an error code, something that is not true for most programs (including most current DOS utilities).

The best way to test the ERRORLEVEL with a batch file is to use the IF statement to move around the rest of the batch file like this:

PROGRAM
IF ERRORLEVEL 1 GOTO OPPS

    .
    .
    .

GOTO END
:OPPS
ECHO PROGRAM DID NOT WORK!
:END

This batch file invokes PROGRAM. If the exit code is 1 or greater, the batch file jumps to the line after the OPPS label. If the exit code is 0 or less, the rest of the batch file is processed. Notice that the GOTO END statement was placed before the OPPS. You don't want the batch file to say PROGRAM DID NOT WORK when the program did work. If the batch file does the rest of the work correctly, DOS jumps to the end of the batch file, the END label. When DOS reaches this label, it has no more lines to execute and will stop processing the batch file.

The *IF string1 == string2* is normally used with command line parameters and markers. One simple example is the batch file ISIBM.BAT, shown below.

IF %1 == IBM ECHO I'm an IBM computer

If you type:

ISIBM IBM

you will see:

```
    I'm an IBM computer
```

If you type anything other than **IBM** as the first parameter, you won't see anything on the screen. A better example is the batch file I have for the Computer Innovations C86 C compiler.

The C86 compiler takes four steps to compile a C program. First, you must run CC1.EXE, CC2.EXE, and CC3.EXE. Each time you run one of these programs, you must give the root name of your C program. In the final step, you "link" (bring together) your C program with the compiler's library of subroutines. A separate library of subroutines for using the 8087 numeric coprocessor is also provided.

To compile and produce a program called TEST.C, I would normally type:

```
A>CC1 TEST
A>CC2 TEST
A>CC3 TEST
A>CL TEST CLIB
```

The last line runs the C86 linker and joins my program with the library of subroutines (CLIB). To eliminate having to type all of these commands each time, I created a batch file called CC.BAT, shown below.

```
CC1 %1
CC2 %1
CC3 %1
CL %1 CLIB
```

When I type **CC TEST**, the batch file does all the work of the previous example. Like most computer-oriented things, there are two hitches. First, to use the subroutines for the 8087 coprocessor, I must tell the CL program to link the subroutines for the 8087—a file called 8087. The last line must be changed to:

```
CL %1 8087 CLIB
```

The second hitch is that sometimes I don't want to run the CL program. In this case, the last line, with the CL command on it, must be removed. The IF command allows me to do all of these things with one batch file. This batch file, CCS.BAT, is shown below.

```
1   CC1 %1
2   CC2 %1
3   CC3 %1
4   IF %2 == 8087 GOTO 8087
5   GOTO END
6   :8087
7   CL %1 8087 CLIB
8   :END
```

This file is two batch files in one. As before, lines 1 through 3 compile the C program. Line 4 tests whether the second parameter given on the command line is "8087." If it is, DOS jumps to the line after the 8087 label. Line 7 runs the CL program with the correct subroutine libraries. For any other second parameter, DOS jumps to the end of the batch file.

To compile the TEST program, I type **CC TEST**. To compile the program *and* use the 8087 coprocessor routines, I type **CCS TEST 8087**. If I want to compile my C program but not run the CL program, I type **CCS TEST NOLINK**. I could actually type anything but 8087 for the second parameter, and the same result would occur.

Two important facts should be noted about this part of the IF command. DOS will give you a Syntax error and abort the batch file if you don't give enough parameters for use with the IF subcommand. For example, if I type **CCS TEST**, the "%2" in the fourth line will be changed to nothing. It becomes a null parameter. DOS does not like to compare null parameters and returns a syntax error if you try it. That's why a second parameter must be given when you use CCS.BAT; otherwise, DOS will abort the batch file when it encounters line 4.

DOS compares the strings literally. This means that upper-case characters are different from lower-case. If I invoke the earlier batch file, ISIBM.BAT, with the line:

ISIBM ibm

DOS will compare the lower-case "ibm" with the upper-case "IBM" and decide that the two strings are not the same. The IF test would fail, and the ECHO I'm an IBM computer would not be performed.

The last part of the IF subcommand is *IF EXIST filename*. This IF tests whether the file *filename* is on the disk. If you are testing for a file on a disk other than the current drive, put the disk drive name in front of the file name (for example, B:CHKDSK.COM). IF NOT EXIST filename can also be used to check whether a file is not on the disk. As with the other IF commands, the file name to check is placed after IF NOT EXIST.

FOR..IN..DO

FOR..IN..DO is an unusual and extremely powerful batch command. Its syntax is

FOR %%*variable* **IN (***file set* **) DO** *command*

The *variable* is a one-letter name. The **%%** in front of the *variable* is important. If you use a single **%**, DOS may confuse the symbol with the parameter markers. The *command* is the command you want performed.

The *file set* is the name (or names) of the disk file(s) you want to use. Wild cards in the file names are okay here. However, path names are not allowed with the file name (an exception to most DOS commands). If you have more than one file name in the *file set*, use a space between each name.

An interesting example is a simple batch file that compares file names on a copy of the DOS master diskette with those on any other diskette. Find a working DOS diskette and put the batch file CHECKIT.BAT on it.

```
ECHO OFF
FOR %%a IN (*.*) DO IF EXIST B:%%a ECHO %%a is on this disk also.
```

Now put the diskette with the CHECKIT.BAT file in drive A and a copy of your DOS master diskette in drive B. Type CHECKIT and watch the results.

In this illustration the first part of the FOR..IN..DO command means: For every file that is specified, do the command. Here, every specified file corresponds to all the files on drive A because we gave the wild-card file name *.*, which matches every file on the disk. The rest of the command says: If the file exists on drive B, then display the message that the file is on the DOS disk.

I wrote a simple program in C, called PR.EXE, that produces a line-numbered printout of a text file. To print all of my C text files and my macro assembler files, I wrote a very simple batch file. All C text files end with a .C extension, and all macro assembler files end with an .ASM extension. The batch file created to print all of these files contained only one line:

```
FOR %%a IN (*.C *.ASM) DO PR %%a
```

The FOR..IN..DO command finds every C and assembler text file and invokes the PR command for every matching file name. I was able to get a numbered listing of 35 C and assembler programs with one batch file command.

This last example of FOR..IN..DO developed out of necessity. I was faced with updating more than 40 DOS V1.1 diskettes to DOS V2.0. In the process of updating each diskette, I had to:

1. Place the DOS V2.0 operating system on the diskette if it had a copy of DOS V1.1 on it

2. Remove any old versions of the DOS utility program

3. Put the V2.0 versions of the DOS utility programs on the diskettes

I made one assumption about the diskettes. If a diskette did not have the COMMAND.COM file on it, it didn't have a copy of DOS on it either. When you do a **FORMAT /S** command, DOS places not only the operating system on the diskette, but also a copy of COMMAND.COM. I assumed that if the diskette didn't have COMMAND.COM, the diskette was not set up to hold the DOS operating system.

(This may or may not be true for your diskettes. To find out if DOS is on an old diskette, do a CHKDSK of the diskette. If CHKDSK reports two or more hidden files on the diskette, then it probably has DOS on it. Make sure that you use Version 2 of DOS with CHKDSK!)

To complicate the matter, some diskettes did not have all of the DOS utility programs. Some had FORMAT.COM, and others did not. Some diskettes had CHKDSK.COM, and others did not. This was true for all of the DOS utilities on all of the old diskettes. Because some of the diskettes were almost full, I did not want to copy all of the DOS utilities, just replace the utilities that were already there.

One way to accomplish this task would be to do a directory of each old diskette, decide if I should put DOS on the diskette, then replace the old version of the DOS utility programs with the new version. However, there is a better way.

I created a copy of my DOS V2.0 master diskette that held all of the utility programs (all .COM and .EXE files) and DOS itself. Then I created the following batch file, called UPDATE2.BAT.

```
 1   ECHO OFF
 2   :START
 3   ECHO Place the diskette to be updated in drive B and press a key
 4   ECHO or type Ctrl-C to quit updating diskettes
 5   PAUSE
 6   IF EXIST B:COMMAND.COM SYS B:
 7   B:
 8   FOR %%a IN (*.*) DO IF EXIST A:%%a COPY A:%%a B:
 9   A:
10   ECHO Done!
11   GOTO START
```

This batch file is powerful, yet simple. Line 1 turns off the display of batch file commands. Line 2 is the label for the endless loop. Because I had to update many diskettes, I decided to use the GOTO command and type a Ctrl-C when I was finished. Lines 3 and 4 tell the operator to put the diskette to be updated in drive B, or type a Ctrl-C to exit. Line 5 pauses the batch file while the operator changes diskettes or exits the batch file.

Line 6 involves the IF EXIST filename construction. DOS checks to see whether the file COMMAND.COM is on the diskette in drive B. If it is, DOS performs the SYS command that places a copy of DOS V2.0 on the diskette. (This is the assumption that I made. If COMMAND.COM is on a diskette, the DOS V1.1 operating system should also be on the diskette and must be replaced by DOS V2.0.)

Line 7 makes B: the current disk drive. Because DOS will remember where the batch file is, I can change the current disk drive (and current directory) without confusing DOS.

Line 8 does the major work and means: For every file on the current disk (drive B), check to see whether the file also exists on drive A; if the file exists on drive A, copy the file to drive B.

Only the DOS V2.0 programs and this batch file can be on the diskette in drive A. DOS checks every file on the diskette in drive B. Then it checks to see whether a file by the same name exists on drive A, the copy of DOS V2.0. If it does, then DOS copies the new V2.0 version of the program to the diskette in drive B. If a file on drive B is not a DOS utility, then it doesn't exist on drive A and, in this case, no file is copied.

Line 9 switches the current disk drive back to A. Line 10 is my reassurance line. Line 11 goes back and repeats the process.

There is a good reason for switching the current drive from A: to B:. The first version I tried of this program used the line

FOR %%a IN (B:*.*) IF EXIST %%A COPY A:%%A B:

instead of line (8) in the batch file above. When I tried this program, it failed miserably. Remember that the variable **%%a** becomes each matching file name which appears in parentheses. This includes any disk drive names you have added to the file name. When I tried the program the first time, the disk file on drive B was COMMAND.COM. This is what DOS translated line (8) into:

```
IF EXIST B:COMMAND.COM COPY A:B:COMMAND.COM B:
```

DOS correctly added the B: in front of each file name. Because A: was specified as the drive for the copy, DOS found this syntax objectionable. Nor did the batch-file line accomplish what I wanted, which was to test whether the file was on drive A, not drive B. A little more testing produced the correct results.

This example works with any two-floppy or minifloppy diskette drive system. With some changes, you can make this file work on a computer like the Personal Computer XT, if DOS is already on the hard disk. First, create a new subdirectory on the hard disk. Copy all the DOS utility programs, including COMMAND.COM, to this subdirectory. Edit the UPDATE2 batch file by replacing all occurrences of A: with C: (lines 8 and 9), then replace all references to B: with A: (lines 3, 6, 7, and 8). Move into the new subdirectory and run the batch file, using drive A for the floppy diskettes.

SHIFT

SHIFT is the last batch command. It moves the command line parameters one parameter to the left. SHIFT is used to trick DOS into using more than 10 parameters. The diagram of SHIFT is

$$\%0 \leftarrow \%1 \leftarrow \%2 \leftarrow \%3 \leftarrow \%4 \leftarrow \%5 \dots$$

$$\downarrow$$

bit bucket

The 0 parameter is dropped. The old parameter 1 becomes parameter 0. Old parameter 2 becomes parameter 1, 3 becomes 2, 4 becomes 3, etc.

SHIFTIT.BAT is a simple example.

```
:START
ECHO %0 %1 %2 %3 %4 %5 %6 %7 %8 %9
SHIFT
PAUSE
GOTO START
```

When you type:

SHIFTIT A B C D E F G H I J K L M N O P Q R S T U V W X Y Z

the first time, ECHO shows:

```
SHIFTIT A B C D E F G H I
```

After you strike a key to continue, ECHO will show:

```
A B C D E F G H I J
```

Strike any key to keep moving down the line, or hit a Ctrl-C when you want to stop.

I have yet to find a good use for SHIFT. However, don't let that stop you from experimenting with the SHIFT command.

Summary

Batch files make your computer do the hard work for you. For example, they perform tedious typing. Additional commands, such as IF, FOR..IN..DO, and GOTO, can make your batch files powerful. Experiment with batch files. This helpful feature of DOS V2 can be very rewarding.

10

Configuring DOS with CONFIG.SYS

To configure means to set up for proper operation. Configuring your system is setting up your computer for operation. There are many levels of configuration.

You physically install your system. You plug your printer or modem into the computer, turn switches on and off, and construct and use various cables and adapters. This is the *physical configuration* of your system.

An *operating configuration* takes place when you set up your files in the various directories on diskettes.

Configuring the operating system usually means changing the Basic Input/Output System to meet your needs. In the past, the only way to do this was by writing assembly language routines that were added to the BIOS. It was not an easy task for newcomers.

DOS V2 has a major feature that assists in the configuration process: CONFIG.SYS. This special text file lies in the root directory of your boot disk and contains commands that can improve or alter the performance and flexibility of your computer. If you don't yet have this file on your disk, don't worry. By the end of this chapter, you will have made your own CONFIG.SYS file.

In earlier chapters, you learned how DOS starts up, or boots. After DOS starts, but before the AUTOEXEC.BAT file is searched, DOS looks for the CONFIG.SYS file. What can CONFIG.SYS do for you?

The CONFIG.SYS file name really tells the story. It is a *system configuration* file. In the file are commands that DOS uses to alter some of its functions and features. Some of the functions can be used immediately. Others are advanced features that you should not use until you are very experienced with DOS and are comfortable with your computer.

Configuration File Commands

The following commands can be in the configuration file: BREAK, BUFFERS, DEVICE, FILES, SHELL, and SWITCHAR. Interestingly, when the commands are assembled alphabetically, they are almost arranged in order from least to most complex.

If you are a beginner, the command you will be most interested in is BUFFERS. DEVICE would probably be next in importance, and BREAK would follow.

BREAK

CONFIG.SYS' BREAK command is identical to the normal DOS command. If BREAK is ON, DOS will check to see whether you have typed a Ctrl-Break every time a program requests some activity from DOS (performs a DOS function call). If BREAK is OFF, DOS will check for a Ctrl-Break only when DOS is doing work with the video display, the keyboard, the printer, or the asynchronous serial adapters.

For long, disk-bound programs that do a lot of disk access, but very little keyboard or screen work, you may want to set BREAK ON. This would allow you to break out of a long program if it goes awry.

The syntax for this command is

     BREAK ON   (to turn BREAK ON)

or

     BREAK OFF   (to turn BREAK OFF)

Because DOS starts with BREAK OFF, you do not have to give the command at all if you want to leave BREAK OFF.

BUFFERS

This command tells DOS how many disk buffers to use. Of all the commands, BUFFERS can have the greatest impact on disk performance. (I strongly recommend that you take advantage of this feature.)

The syntax is

BUFFERS = nn

where **nn** is the number of disk buffers you want. The number can be between 1 and 99. DOS will start with two buffers, unless you use this command.

What is a *disk buffer?* It is a reserved area of RAM memory that DOS sets up. The disk buffer is the same size as a disk sector, usually 512 bytes. When DOS is asked to get or put information on the disk that isn't the same size as a disk sector, DOS will put the information into the disk buffer. When the buffer is full, DOS writes the information to the disk. This is called *flushing* the buffer. When reading in information from the disk, DOS will go to the disk when the information inside the disk buffer is exhausted. The buffers are also flushed when you "close" a disk file in a program.

Whether a disk buffer becomes full or empty, DOS marks the buffer to indicate that it has been used recently. Then DOS goes through the list of disk buffers to find the buffer that hasn't been used for the longest time. The technical term for this is *least recently used.* This process is repeated for any disk activity.

In some ways, this process is similar to that of a RAM disk, except only parts of the disk (rather than the entire disk) are kept in RAM memory. When your program reads part of a data file, DOS brings this portion of the file into the RAM memory, the disk buffer. As your program writes information to the disk, the program goes into the disk buffer first. This method also applies to program overlays like those of WordStar. DOS will load an overlay into memory and give it to WordStar as needed. DOS handles all of this activity for you.

If you don't give a BUFFERS command in the CONFIG.SYS file, DOS will start with two disk buffers. This means that DOS will hold two sections of 512 bytes of memory each for transferring information to and from the disk drives. When your program wants a piece of information from the disk, DOS will check its disk buffers first. If that information is already in one of the two disk buffers, DOS will perform a high-speed, memory-to-memory transfer. If the information is not in memory, DOS goes to the disk and transfers the sector holding the information into the disk buffer. Then DOS hands the information to your program.

If your program does a lot of *random disk work,* (reading and writing information in different parts of a file), you will want more disk buffers. The more disk buffers you have, the better the chance that the information DOS wants is already hidden away in memory (the disk buffer). Using disk buffers will make your programs work faster when they are doing disk reading and writing. Data base programs, which do a lot of jumping around in a file, run much faster if you use more disk buffers.

Some programs do not benefit as much from using disk buffers. If your program does *sequential reading and writing* (reads and/or writes information from the start of the file straight through to the end), disk buffers won't help much. Because of the way you are moving through the file, one disk sector at a time, having many disk buffers doesn't give you any advantage. DOS still has to read each sector, then write it out. The same is true if your program reads and writes information in groups that are the same number of bytes as a disk sector. DOS will bypass the disk buffer and directly read and write each sector.

The real advantage of disk buffers comes when your program does much random reading or writing of information in amounts that are not exactly equal to a disk's sector. This applies especially to data base or accounting programs. Some word-processing programs can benefit from many disk buffers, but many other programs will not.

How many disk buffers should you have? The answer depends on what programs you run on your computer, whether you have a hard disk, and how much memory you have.

If your day-to-day use of the computer does not involve accounting or data base work, two disk buffers may be sufficient. Otherwise, increase the number to between 10 and 20.

If you use a hard disk, start with at least three disk buffers. In most cases, the more disk buffers your computer has, the better. Remember that DOS also holds a copy of the disk's or diskette's File Allocation Table (FAT) and directory in two or three disk buffers.

The memory issue is important. Each disk buffer takes 528 bytes of memory. This means that every two disk buffers you use will cost you just over 1K of RAM memory that could be used by your programs instead. If you are using a 64K system, you don't have much space to devote to disk buffers. If you have a 128K system, or larger, balance the number of disk buffers against the memory space your program needs. If you have over 192K, you can use as many disk buffers as you like. Otherwise, there is little sense in robbing Peter (your programs) to pay Paul (DOS' disk buffers).

Although DOS can have 99 disk buffers, avoid going over 20. There is a magic point at which DOS bogs down and becomes sluggish because it is spending so much time searching and handling the disk buffers rather than simply reading the information from the disk.

The best advice is to start with 10 disk buffers, then fine tune the number of buffers by increasing or decreasing them by one or two every day or several hours. Reboot DOS and examine its performance. Keep doing this until you think you have the best performance. You don't need to be exact, but just get the general "feel" of the computer's performance. When you have found the number of disk buffers that are best for your system, you are done. (I run 20 disk buffers on a 256K IBM Personal Computer XT and find that this number is "just right" for what I do.)

DEVICE

The DEVICE command is the "flexibility" command for DOS V2. With this command and the proper software, you can make better use of your current computer hardware and use other hardware that your computer could not easily use before.

The syntax for the DEVICE command is

DEVICE = *d:path***filename**.*ext*

where *d:* is the disk drive holding the device driver file, *path* is the directory path to the device driver file, and **filename**.*ext* is the name of the file holding the device driver.

What is a device driver? A device is any peripheral: a disk drive, keyboard, video display, terminal, printer, etc. A *device driver* is the software that links itself to the operating system so that the computer can use a particular device. DOS has the necessary software in it to control the peripherals provided with your computer.

However, what if you want to use a device that the operating system knows nothing about? The most common example is a letter-quality printer that uses a set of special characters (*software protocols*) to regulate information coming from and going to the computer. To use such a device, DOS needs to know what type of device it is, how to talk to the device, and how to listen to it. If there are two or more letter-quality printers, DOS simply will not know how to handle them.

A piece of software is needed to tell the operating system how to control the letter-quality printer. This software is the device driver. Earlier versions of DOS had few easy ways to tell DOS how to handle a new or different device. A simple method was needed for the user to install into DOS the necessary software for handling different devices.

The DEVICE command in CONFIG.SYS solves this problem. Device-driver software is written according to the specifications in the DOS manual. (This software may be written by the manufacturer of the device, by you, or by a third party.) Then the device driver is placed on the boot diskette. The CONFIG.SYS file can be edited (or created) with the line:

DEVICE = device driver filename

where you substitute the name of the file that holds the device driver software for **device driver filename**. When DOS boots, it loads and installs the appropriate device driver software. Now the computer system can use the device.

A device driver file called ANSI.SYS is provided with DOS. This software alters the way DOS handles the video screen and keyboard. The ANSI.SYS file allows you to control the video screen's color and graphics from any program, and to reprogram the entire keyboard if you desire.

To use the ANSI.SYS file, add the following line to your CONFIG.SYS file:

DEVICE = ANSI.SYS

Make sure that the ANSI.SYS file is in the root directory of your boot diskette. When DOS boots, it will automatically load and use the new device driver.

You can load as many device drivers as you like. To date, not many device drivers have been written. If you look in your IBM DOS manual, you will see an example of a device driver on pages 14-27 through 14-34. This is the device driver for a 180K RAM disk. You will need a text editor, Macro Assembler, and EXE2BIN.EXE to type in and use this driver. Otherwise, the DOS V2 market is just beginning to catch on to the concept of installing device drivers through the CONFIG.SYS file.

If you use floppy diskettes, you will probably want to put the device drivers in the root directory. Hard disk users should make a special subdirectory called SYS and put the device drivers in this directory out of the way of daily files. If you do this, be sure to add the directory path name in front of the device driver file name, as in **DEVICE=\SYS\ ANSI.SYS**.

FILES

The FILES command is new to DOS V2.0. The syntax is

FILES = nn

where **nn** is the number of XENIX-type files you want open at any time. The maximum number is 99, and the minimum is 5. If you give a FILES= command with a number less than 5, DOS will bump the number up to 5. DOS starts with 8 files. This number is usually sufficient. Each additional file over 8 increases the size of DOS by 39 bytes.

With the introduction of DOS V2.0, new operating system calls were added. These new calls closely resemble XENIX, Microsoft's version of UNIX. Most programs use the old CP/M-like system calls to handle files. The FILES command does not affect these older programs. FILES affects only newer programs that use the XENIX-like operating system calls for DOS V2. Because few programs use the new calls at this time, the default value of 8 is sufficient. As more programs begin to use the new features of DOS V2, you may have to increase this number.

The difference between the old and new ways of handling files comes from the use of *handles*. The old method involved the creation of a special area in memory called *FCB,* for file control block. When you told DOS to get information from a file or put it there, you used the FCB to tell DOS what file you were working with. The FCB contained much more information than just the file name. The new method uses a *handle*—a two-byte number. You give DOS the name of the file or device you want to use. It gives you back a two-byte handle. From this point on, you use the handle, rather than the FCB, to tell DOS what file you are going to use.

If you use BASIC or don't program at all, don't worry about handles. You may need to remember them only when a program gives you an error message about not having enough handles. Then you will want to add the FILES= command to the CONFIG.SYS file.

If you write assembly language programs, read the information about handles in the DOS manual. Handles and the new DOS system calls are powerful and very useful.

SHELL

The SHELL command is an advanced CONFIG.SYS command. Don't try to use the SHELL command until you are very comfortable with DOS.

The syntax for SHELL is

SHELL = **filename.ext** *d:path /P /C string*

where **filename.ext** is the name of the new command processor, *d:* is the drive containing the command processor, and *path* is the directory path to the command processor.

The switches are

/P	Stay *permanent*
/C	Give the new command processor this command *string*
string	The command you'd like the command processor to execute immediately

The normal command processor for DOS is COMMAND.COM. You can write your own command processor if you prefer. (I am not very good at assembly language programming and would not even attempt such a task.)

There is one possible everyday use for this command. SHELL allows you to move COMMAND.COM out of your root directory and into a subdirectory. This command may help some hard disk system owners. I put COMMAND.COM in the SYS subdirectory on my hard disk and used the following in CONFIG.SYS:

SHELL=COMMAND.COM C:\SYS /P /C AUTOEXEC

It worked. I also found that when I typed the SET command, I saw the line:

```
COMSPEC=C:\SYS\COMMAND.COM
```

telling me that DOS remembers where COMMAND.COM is located.

Don't try this with a floppy diskette system. Floppy diskettes can be changed, and the new floppy diskette might not have a subdirectory called SYS with the file COMMAND.COM.

SWITCHAR

The last CONFIG.SYS command is SWITCHAR. A word of warning about this command: SWITCHAR is an undocumented portion of DOS. Several DOS V2.0 commands do not use the SWITCHAR function and will not work properly if you reset SWITCHAR. The author of DOS, Microsoft, is not bound to support this function in any update or new major release of DOS. You use this function at your own risk.

To paraphrase, SWITCHAR is here now, but may not be here later. If you use it, several programs may not function properly. The one program I know that doesn't work properly with SWITCHAR is RESTORE, the IBM utility that restores files which have been backed up from the hard disk. I spent a very painful day learning this fact. If SWITCHAR does not exist in the next version of DOS, it will be your responsibility to "fix" any problems that have occurred through its use.

SWITCHAR is actually an innocuous character. It is the switch character for the DOS commands. DOS uses the slash (/) for the switch character. With SWITCHAR, you may use a different character.

The syntax for SWITCHAR is

SWITCHAR = newcharacter

where **newcharacter** is the new switch character. Because UNIX uses the minus sign (-) as its switch character, I tried the command:

SWITCHAR = -

with the CONFIG.SYS file. When you change the switch character from the slash to the minus sign, DOS changes the path separator from the backslash (\) to the slash (/). The slash is also the UNIX path separator. This change allowed me to type such lines as

COPY A:*.COM C:/BIN/BASIC -V

similar to the style used on UNIX/XENIX systems. All the DOS commands seemed to work correctly. The problem was not in resetting the ·switch character, but in resetting the path separator. Some programs were constructed to use only the normal path character, the backslash.

For example, one day I wanted to "clean up" my hard disk. First I backed up the entire hard disk with BACKUP. Then I reformatted the hard disk, erasing everything on it. When I tried to RESTORE all of the files from backup diskettes to the hard disk, I discovered that RESTORE would accept only the backslash as the path character.

I had more than six megabytes of files on backup floppy diskettes that I suddenly could not use. Every program was correctly backed up, but RESTORE would not recover the files.

If you are wondering how I got out of this predicament, I wrote a program in the C language that changed the slashes to backslashes on the backup diskettes. Then I ran RESTORE again. This time, it worked properly.

This is why I don't recommend that you use this undocumented function. If you take the risk, you may have to fix any problems that occur.

Making a CONFIG.SYS File

There are two major commands you may want to use with DOS V2.0: BUFFERS and DEVICE. You can use any text editor, including EDLIN, or the COPY command to make this file. Remember that the file must be called CONFIG.SYS.

BUFFERS = 10
DEVICE = ANSI.SYS

Put this file in the root directory of your DOS boot diskette. If you are using a hard disk system like the Personal Computer XT, put the file in the root directory of the hard disk. If you have included the second line, DEVICE=ANSI.SYS, copy the ANSI.SYS file to the disk you will use for booting.

After you have saved the file, reboot the system using your new disk. DOS will read the CONFIG.SYS file and alter itself to accommodate any commands in the file.

If you change the CONFIG.SYS file, the changes will be implemented the next time you boot the system from the disk. Remember that CONFIG.SYS is used only when DOS starts up.

11

Other DOS Commands

Now that you've learned and tried many of the commands, functions, and features of DOS V2, let's look at some of the more general commands.

DIR

You have already used the DIR command several times. This command allows you to get a listing of the files in the current or specified directory. If you give a file name, with or without a wild-card character, you can get a partial listing.

DIR has two switches. **/P** pauses the listing after 23 lines of files are displayed. When you hit a key, the next set of files is displayed. This feature is helpful when a directory is long and you don't want the listing to scroll off the screen. The disadvantage is that the top few lines containing the volume label, disk drive name, and path leave the screen before DIR pauses. You must use the pause-display sequence (Ctrl-Num Lock) to see these lines on long displays.

/W gives a *wide* display of the screen. Five file names are displayed per line. This switch is good for tight displays of long directories. The disadvantage is that the file size, <DIR> symbol for directories, and file date and time are not displayed.

The following examples illustrate how both switches can be used.

A>DIR C:\BIN\UTIL

```
Volume in drive C is QUE DISK
Directory of C:\BIN\UTIL

.                  <DIR>     8-06-83     5:03p
..                 <DIR>     8-06-83     5:03p
SYS       COM       1408     7-23-83     5:31p
DISKCOPY  COM       2444     7-23-83     5:31p
DISKCOMP  COM       2074     7-23-83     5:31p
EDLIN     COM       4608     7-23-83     5:31p
RECOVER   COM       2304     7-23-83     5:31p
COMP      COM       2523     7-23-83     5:31p
DEBUG     COM      11904     7-23-83     5:31p
EXE2BIN   EXE       1664     7-23-83     5:32p
LINK      EXE      39936     7-23-83     5:32p
BASIC     COM      16256     1-01-80    11:40p
BASICA    COM      25984     7-23-83     5:31p
BATHIDE   COM       7477     7-23-83     5:39p
BEEP      COM        151     7-23-83     5:39p
BLOAD     COM      17685     7-23-83     5:39p
SM        COM      19168     7-23-83     5:39p
DISKOPT   COM       6245     7-23-83     5:39p
DL        COM      32712     7-23-83     5:39p
FH        COM      14036     7-23-83     5:39p
FILEFIX   COM       7287     7-23-83     5:39p
FILESORT  COM       6924     7-23-83     5:39p
HL        COM      35607     7-23-83     5:39p
HM        COM      21590     7-23-83     5:40p
HU        COM      27490     7-23-83     5:40p
LABEL     COM       8063     7-23-83     5:40p
LPRINT    COM      24125     7-23-83     5:40p
REVERSE   COM       1298     7-23-83     5:40p
SCRATR    COM       3426     7-23-83     5:40p
SSAR      COM      23768     7-23-83     5:40p
```

```
TIMEMARK  COM      7045   7-23-83    5:40p
UE        COM     26026   7-23-83    5:40p
FDISK     COM      6177   7-23-83    5:31p
BACKUP    COM      3687   7-23-83    5:31p
RESTORE   COM      4003   7-23-83    5:31p
ASCOM     COM     20096   8-04-83    9:12a
DSORTE    BAT        46   8-08-83   12:50p
            37 File(s)     3809280 bytes free
```

```
A>DIR C:\BIN\UTIL /W

Volume in drive C is QUE DISK
Directory of C:\BIN\UTIL

.                    ..            SYS      COM  DISKCOPY COM  DISKCOMP COM
EDLIN    COM  RECOVER  COM  COMP      COM  DEBUG    COM  EXE2BIN  EXE
LINK     EXE  BASIC    COM  BASICA    COM  BATHIDE  COM  BEEP     COM
BLOAD    COM  SM       COM  DISKOPT   COM  DL       COM  FH       COM
FILEFIX  COM  FILESORT COM  HL        COM  HM       COM  HU       COM
LABEL    COM  LPRINT   COM  REVERSE   COM  SCRATR   COM  SSARCOM
TIMEMARK COM  UE       COM  FDISK     COM  BACKUP   COM  RESTORE  COM
ASCOM    COM  DSORTE   BAT
            37 File(s)     3809280 bytes free
```

A>**DIR C:\BIN\UTIL /P**

Volume in drive C is QUE DISK
Directory of C:\BIN\UTIL

```
.                <DIR>     8-06-83    5:03p
..               <DIR>     8-06-83    5:03p
SYS       COM     1408     7-23-83    5:31p
DISKCOPY  COM     2444     7-23-83    5:31p
DISKCOMP  COM     2074     7-23-83    5:31p
EDLIN     COM     4608     7-23-83    5:31p
RECOVER   COM     2304     7-23-83    5:31p
COMP      COM     2523     7-23-83    5:31p
DEBUG     COM    11904     7-23-83    5:31p
EXE2BIN   EXE     1664     7-23-83    5:32p
LINK      EXE    39936     7-23-83    5:32p
BASIC     COM    16256     1-01-80   11:40p
BASICA    COM    25984     7-23-83    5:31p
BATHIDE   COM     7477     7-23-83    5:39p
BEEP      COM      151     7-23-83    5:39p
BLOAD     COM    17685     7-23-83    5:39p
SM        COM    19168     7-23-83    5:39p
DISKOPT   COM     6245     7-23-83    5:39p
DL        COM    32712     7-23-83    5:39p
FH        COM    14036     7-23-83    5:39p
FILEFIX   COM     7287     7-23-83    5:39p
FILESORT  COM     6924     7-23-83    5:39p
HL        COM    35607     7-23-83    5:39p

Strike a key when ready . . .
```

```
BLOAD     COM    17685    7-23-83    5:39p
SM        COM    19168    7-23-83    5:39p
DISKOPT   COM     6245    7-23-83    5:39p
DL        COM    32712    7-23-83    5:39p
FH        COM    14036    7-23-83    5:39p
FILEFIX   COM     7287    7-23-83    5:39p
FILESORT  COM     6924    7-23-83    5:39p
HL        COM    35607    7-23-83    5:39p
Strike a key when ready . . .
HM        COM    21590    7-23-83    5:40p
HU        COM    27490    7-23-83    5:40p
LABEL     COM     8063    7-23-83    5:40p
LPRINT    COM    24125    7-23-83    5:40p
REVERSE   COM     1298    7-23-83    5:40p
SCRATR    COM     3426    7-23-83    5:40p
SSAR      COM    23768    7-23-83    5:40p
TIMEMARK  COM     7045    7-23-83    5:40p
UE        COM    26026    7-23-83    5:40p
FDISK     COM     6177    7-23-83    5:31p
BACKUP    COM     3687    7-23-83    5:31p
RESTORE   COM     4003    7-23-83    5:31p
ASCOM     COM    20096    8-04-83    9:12a
DSORTE    BAT       46    8-08-83   12:50p
        37 File(s)     3809280 bytes free
```

RENAME

The RENAME command, or REN for short, allows you to change the name of a file. DOS will accept either version of this command. RENAME is fairly straightforward.

Old file name ⟶ new file name

(If you have used CP/M, you will notice a big difference between DOS and CP/M. All CP/M commands are backwards, with the new file name first, then the old file name. All DOS commands are the opposite, which is not necessarily good or bad. However, it is easier to use commands that change "what it is now" to "what it will be.")

The syntax for RENAME is

RENAME *d:path***oldfilename.***ext* **newfilename.***ext*

The *d:* for the disk drive name and *path*\ for the directory path to the file name are optional. You can skip them if the file you are renaming is on the current disk drive or in the current directory.

The **oldfilename** is the root name of the file whose name will be changed. If the file has an extension (*.ext*), you must give it.

The **newfilename** is the new root name for the file. You can use the same file extension, change the extension, or drop it if you like.

Wild-card characters are allowed in the root file names and extensions. Obviously, wild cards are not allowed for disk drive names or path names. (I have not yet found a DOS command that uses wild cards for disk drive or path names.)

Notice that you don't give a disk drive or path name with the new file name, only when mentioning the original file. Once DOS knows the old file name and where it is (drive and path), DOS changes the name but does not move the file. That's why you do not need to give (nor does DOS allow) a disk drive or path name with the new name.

DOS protects itself from having two files with the same name. RENAME issues an error message if you try to do this. For example, if you use wild cards in the name, which could produce two files with the same name, DOS will stop and give a Duplicate file name error message. Files before the potential duplicate name are changed, but those after the duplicate name are left unchanged. You must use RENAME again to change the names of the rest of the files.

Remember that RENAME does not touch what is in the file. RENAME changes only the file's name in the appropriate directory. As soon as you change the file name, DOS sees this file as a different file. You can't use the old file name with the new file, unless you change the name again.

Your programs may look for a file with a specific file name. If you change that name, your programs will not be able to find the file. *You* may know that it's the same file, but your programs will not. Be careful when changing file names so as not to confuse your programs.

MODE

This command is unique to PC DOS. MODE has been expanded to serve several purposes. In fact, you could say that MODE is four commands in one. (MODE is treated this way in the Command Summary in this book.)

MODE allows you to customize your computer's setup. The major difference between MODE and the CONFIG.SYS file is that what you do with MODE is lost when you turn off your computer or reboot DOS. The effects of MODE disappear. If you find yourself issuing a MODE command each time you boot DOS, it's time to put this command in the AUTOEXEC.BAT batch file.

MODE handles the printers, serial adapters, and display adapters.

Part I

For printing, MODE sets the lines per inch, characters per inch, and time-out handling, and indicates whether you are using a serial printer. Remember that you can have up to three printers. The first printer is called LPT1: It is the primary printer. (PRN is the pseudonym for whatever printer is LPT1:. When you use PRN, you are telling DOS to use whatever has been assigned as LPT1:.)

The syntax for this part of MODE is

MODE LPT#: *cpl, lpi, P*

where **#** is the number of the printer, 1, 2, or 3; and *cpl* is the number of characters per line, based on an 8-inch wide line. The number can be either 80 (10 characters per inch) or 132 (16.5 characters per inch). The *lpi* stands for lines per inch, which can be either 6 or 8; and *P* means "keep trying" when DOS finds that the printer is not ready. (*Time-out* is the technical name.)

DOS starts with the printer at 80 characters per line and 6 lines per inch. To see how your printer is set up, type:

MODE LPT#:

substituting the number of the printer (usually 1) for the **#**.

This command works best with IBM, Epson, and printers that act like Epson printers. If you don't have this type of printer, MODE will not be able to set the characters per line or the lines per inch. In fact, MODE will give you a printer error message if you try to use some other type of printer.

MODE can be tricky. The colon must always appear with the device name. This means that the first line printer must be called **LPT1:**, not just **LPT1**. Because MODE also does not accept pathed device names, phrases such as *dev**lpt1* cannot be used.

The **P** is the "keep trying" option. If you want DOS to keep trying to send characters to the printer when something is wrong, you must give the full command with the **,P** every time you use MODE LPTx: The first time you give MODE LPTx: without the **,P**, DOS will not retry continuously but will give an error message when the printer "times-out."

If you give the **,P** and your printer hangs up, your computer will lock up. You can get the computer out of this by typing a control-break sequence (Ctrl-Break or Ctrl-C). You'll need to wait almost a minute more for DOS to recognize the control-break.

If you don't want to change the characters per line, the lines per inch, or the continuous retries, either drop the element from the command line or just use the comma and leave out the number.

The following command line

MODE LPT1: 132,8

changes the characters per line to 132 and the lines per inch to 8.

Typing:

MODE LPT1: 80

sets the characters per line to 80, but leaves the lines per inch the same.

The command line

MODE LPT1: ,6

leaves the characters per line unchanged and changes the lines per inch to 6. In all three examples, DOS will not retry on a time-out because the **,P** has been omitted. To get continuous retries with the examples above, add **,P** to the first and third examples, and **,,P** to the second example.

Part II

The second part of MODE also relates to the printer. The syntax is

MODE LPT#: = COMx:

where **#** is the number of the printer you are reassigning, and **x** is the communications adapter for your serial printer. This command tricks DOS into using the serial printer connected to a communications adapter instead of the normal parallel printer. You may need to check what the correct number is for the communications adapter because the number can be either 1 or 2. Use 1 if you have only one communications adapter (serial port). If you have two adapters, check with your dealer or experiment with this command.

Typing:

MODE LPT1: = COM1:

redirects DOS to use the printer that is connected to the first communications adapter.

To reverse this setting, use the **MODE LPT#:** command. You don't have to give any other information.

Before you use this version of MODE, you should set up the asynchronous adapter, using the part of the MODE command covered next.

Part III

This part of MODE sets the communications adapter's characteristics: baud rate, parity, data bits, stop bits, and retries. The syntax is

MODE COMx: baud rate, *parity, data bits, stop bits,* **P**

where **x** is the number of the communications adapter, 1 or 2. The **baud rate** is mandatory: you must indicate a baud rate. It can be 110, 300, 600, 1200, 2400, 4800, or 9600. You can give just the first two numbers of the rate if you like.

Everything else is optional. You can leave it off or use a comma to skip over the characteristic. However, if you use parity, for example, then skip to stop bits, don't forget to use a comma for each one you skip. DOS also expects these parameters to be in order. You must use them in the order shown above.

The *parity* can be *O*dd, *E*ven, or *N*one. It starts as Even.

The number of *data bits* is either 7 or 8. It starts as 7.

The number of *stop bits* is either 1 or 2. If you use 110 baud, 2 stop bits is the default. Any baud rate other than 110 defaults to 1 start bit.

As with MODE LPT#:, the *P* means keep trying. If you don't set *P*, then it is off. It you forget to set it, it is also off. Retry is good for printers but not as good when the adapter is being used with a modem. You can also use a Ctrl-Break or Ctrl-C to get out of a time-out retry loop.

Either one of the following two command lines

MODE COM1: 1200
MODE COM1: 12

sets the baud rate at 1200 for the first communications adapter. Everything but retry remains the same. If retry were on before, it is now off because you didn't give it here.

The command line

MODE COM1: 96,,7

sets the first adapter to 9600 baud and 8 data bits. Everything else but the retry is unchanged. Retry will be turned off.

Typing:

MODE COM1: 48,,,,P

sets the adapter to 4800 baud and continuous retries. As before, nothing else is changed.

Part IV

The last part of MODE handles the video displays. This command was enhanced in DOS V2.0 for those who use monochrome and color monitors attached to the Color/Graphics Adapter and those who used the Monochrome Display and another monitor attached to the C/G Adapter. If you use just the Monochrome Display, this command will not work.

The syntax of this command is

MODE *display type, shift, T*

The *shift* shifts the display left or right by one character position. You would enter either L or R to accomplish this. MODE can be used with either a television set or a monitor to adjust the display. With some monitors, characters "fall off" the edge of the screen. This command lets you shift the line back into position.

T stands for *test* pattern. When you request it, MODE shows a line of characters (40 or 80). Then MODE asks whether the display is okay. You enter **Y** if it is. If you enter **N**, MODE will again shift the display by one character and repeat the process. This way you can adjust your screen without having to use the MODE command over and over again.

The *display type* can be any one of the following. (The *C/G display* refers to the monitor or television attached to the Color/Graphics Adapter.)

40	40-column lines for the Color/Graphics display
80	80-column lines for the Color/Graphics display
BW40	Makes the C/G display the active display, turns off color, and uses 40-character lines
BW80	Makes the C/G display the active display, turns off color, and uses 80-character lines

CO40	Makes the C/G display the active display, turns on color capabilities, and uses 40-character lines
CO80	Makes the C/G display the active display, turns on color capabilities, and uses 80-character lines
MONO	Makes the Monochrome Display the active display

An *active display* is the display that DOS and your programs use to show information. If you have two displays, such as a Monochrome Display and another monitor or TV attached to the C/G board, either one can be used with this command.

Color is arbitrary. Some programs use color; others do not. Specifying CO40 or CO80 does not guarantee that your programs will be in color; the selection merely lets DOS display things in color. It's up to you and your programs to make color appear.

MODE also doesn't seem to affect BASIC. If you use a color command in BASIC, it makes no difference whether you specify BW40, BW80, CO40, or CO80. BASIC still tries to send colors. Whether you see colors or not depends on the monitor or TV you use. However, the size of the screen (40- or 80-column) will remain in effect.

COPY

COPY copies files. You have frequently used this command in the preceding chapters of this book.

Part I

COPY can copy files between disk drives, between devices, or between a disk drive and a device. COPY demonstrates how a file can actually be a device. Instead of copying merely from a disk file to another disk file, we can copy from a disk file to a device, from a device to a disk file, or from a device to another device.

The COPY command must know how much information to copy. That's why COPY uses two special switches:

/A	An ASCII file
/B	A binary file

ASCII files use a special character called the end-of-file marker to signal the end of a file. This character is represented as Ctrl-Z, CHR$(26), or 1A in the hexadecimal numbering system. Every program recognizes that Ctrl-Z marks the end of an ASCII text or data file. Anything in an ASCII text file beyond the end-of-file marker is considered invalid and not used. If you hit the F6 special-function key at the system prompt, you will see a ^Z. That character is Ctrl-Z, the end-of-file indicator.

This system works well for text files because all programs respect it. However, a program or non-ASCII data file may actually use 1A. A program can use 1A as an instruction or a memory location, and a compressed data file (or BASIC random-access file) may use this character for data.

COPY makes one assumption about the files it copies. If the file does not come from a character-oriented device, the file must be a binary file. When DOS copies binary files, it uses the file size from the directory to determine how much information to copy. This means that DOS will copy everything in a disk file.

This also works for ASCII files. The end-of-file marker, which is reflected in the directory size, is copied with the rest of the file's information. Therefore, any programs that use text files will see the end-of-file marker.

Working with nondisk devices is different. DOS has no way of knowing how many characters will be involved with nondisk devices. The indicator is the Ctrl-Z, the end-of-file character. When DOS receives a Ctrl-Z from the console, serial port, or other nondisk device, DOS knows that all information has been received or sent.

When copying files with COPY, you can use switches to force conditions. The **/A** switch makes DOS handle the transfer as ASCII text. For source files, DOS copies all information up to, but not including, the first Ctrl-Z. For a destination file, DOS adds a Ctrl-Z to the end. This ensures that a good end-of-file marker is placed in the file. When you copy from a device other than a disk drive, the **/A** switch is assumed.

/B is the opposite of **/A**. **/B** tells DOS to copy binary (program) files. For source files the file, based on its directory size, is copied ignoring Ctrl-Z. For destination files no Ctrl-Z is added. When you copy from one disk to another, the **/B** switch is assumed.

You cannot force DOS to copy a binary file from a device. DOS will have no way of knowing when the information has ended. If you enter the **/B** with the source device name, DOS will give you an error message and halt the command.

The placement of the switch is also important. A COPY switch affects the file or device name that precedes the switch and all file/device names after it until contradicted by another switch. For example, using a **/A** after the first file/device name will affect the entire line. If, however, you use the **/A** after the second file name, the switch will affect the second file and any other files that follow.

If you are copying files between a disk drive and a device or between disk drives, you can put the switch after the word COPY, the first file or device name, or the second file or device name. When you put the switch after the word COPY (before the first file name) or between the first file/device name and the second file/device name, the switch will affect all files (the file before the switch and all files after it). If you put the switch after the second file/device name, then only the second file/device is affected. (The only file or device name before the switch is the destination file). The first source file is unchanged.

There is a third switch used with COPY: **/V**, for verifying that the copies are correct. We used this switch in the second chapter. When you use the **/V** switch, you must place it after the last file name. **/V** does not affect the **/A** or **/B** switches. It ensures that the copy is correctly made on the diskette.

Part II

COPY does more than copy files. It can also join (*concatenated*) files together. The syntax is

COPY */A/B d1:path1***filename1**.*ext1/A/B*
*+ d2:path2***filename2**.*ext2/A/B +* ...
*d0:path0***filename0**.*ext0 /A/B/V*

where *d1:, d2:,* and *d0:* are valid disk drive names; *path1\\, path2\\,* and *path0* are valid path names; and **filename1**.*ext1,* **filename2**.*ext2,* and **filename0**.*ext0* are valid file names. Wild cards are acceptable.

The . . . represent additional files in the form of *dx:pathx***filenamex**.*extx.*

Numbers also have a special notation. The file names above marked *1* and *2* are the source files. Names marked with a *0* usually represent *destination* files. The *source* files are those you want to join. The destination files (there can be more than one) will hold the product of this concatenation.

Can there be more than one destination? Yes, COPY can produce several destination files. This tricky and potentially dangerous process involves wild-card characters (which are discussed later).

Source files can be binary files (programs or non-ASCII data files) or ASCII files. When you concatenate, COPY assumes ASCII files and issues an invisible **/A** switch. This is the opposite of copying disk-based files. Because non-ASCII files are rarely concatenated, this is a helpful assumption.

The syntax of this command is

   A>**COPY FILE1.TXT + FILE2.TXT + FILE3.TXT FILE.ALL /V**

The contents of FILE1.TXT are moved to a file called FILE.ALL. The contents of FILE2.TXT are added to the end of FILE.ALL, and the contents of FILE3.TXT are also appended to FILE.ALL. The **/V** verifies the concatenation. Because no disk drive name or path names are given, the entire activity will take place on drive A in the current directory.

Each source file name can have a disk drive name and a path name. The normal rules about current disk drives and current directory file names apply.

Wild-card characters are allowed. They force COPY to join any file that matches the given wild-card name. With one file name, you can join several files.

If you must give additional file names, separate each one with a plus sign (+). This tells DOS that you are joining files. Give disk drive names and path names for these additional files as necessary.

The destination file is the last file name on the command line that does not have a plus sign in front of its name. If you look at the previous example, you will see that there is only a space, not a plus sign, between FILE.ALL and the last file for concatenation (FILE3.TXT).

If you don't give an explicit destination file name (using plus signs between each file and the next file name), the same rule applies. The last file name without a + in front of it is the destination file. The first source file name becomes the destination file. DOS will add the second and subsequent files to the end of the first file.

This can be confusing. Just remember that the last file without a plus sign in front of its name is the destination file.

If you use matching wild cards for the root names of both the source and the destination names, you can create multiple destination files. For example, this line from the PC DOS manual:

COPY *.PRN + *.REF,*.LST

takes each root name with a .PRN extension, joins it with a file that has the same root name, but an .REF extension, and places the joined result into a file with the same root name but with a .LST extension. This process allows you to produce multiple destination files. If you use a wild card in the destination name, you will get destination files with the same source root-file name.

Look at the following three sets of files:

MYFILE.LST   APROG.LST   FILE3.LST
MYFILE.REF   APROG.REF   FILE3.REF

The previous command would combine these files this way:

MYFILE.LST   + MYFILE.REF → MYFILE.PRN
APROG.LST   + APROG.REF   → APROG.PRN
FILE3.LST   + FILE3.REF   → FILE3.PRN

Each set of files with matching root names and the extensions .LST and .REF is combined and placed into a .PRN file.

The next example concerns wild cards with a destination file that is also a source file. The following sample list shows the files in order as they appear in the directory:

```
COUNT.C
PREP.C
DSKTIME.C
VERTEST.C
ALL.C
SWITCHAR.C
```

To combine these source program files into one destination file called ALL.C., I used the command:

COPY *.C ALL.C

This will give me an error message, but the message comes too late. COUNT.C has already been placed in the file called ALL.C, followed by PREP.C, then DSKTIME.C and VERTEST.C. Now the error occurs.

Why? The destination file is ALL.C. However, ALL.C is also a source file. Here's the sequence of events.

Because the destination file does not have the same name as the first source file, DOS copies the first source file to the destination file. This is a destructive copy because the contents of the destination file are lost before the copy is made. Each additional source file is appended to the destination file.

DOS now encounters a source file name that is identical to the destination file name. DOS has already destroyed the old contents of the original destination file. There is little sense in copying this file. DOS displays the Contents of destination lost before copy message and proceeds to handle the rest of the source files.

When you use wild-card names, DOS scans the directory from beginning to end. As DOS encounters a file that matches the wild-card name, DOS operates on the matching file. ALL.C was not the first file in the directory. The first file was COUNT.C. DOS saw that this file name was not the same as ALL.C, the destination file, and created a new ALL.C. Four files later, DOS discovers that ALL.C was also a source file. DOS has already altered this file—hence, the error message and the problem. The command used above was not correctly phrased. Unfortunately, the error message comes too late.

The correct way to copy all the .C files into ALL.C is

COPY ALL.C + *.C

The last file without a + in front of it is ALL.C. It becomes the destination file. ALL.C is also the first source file. DOS skips copying ALL.C and begins to append all other .C files to ALL.C. The second time DOS finds ALL.C in the directory, DOS will simply skip this file.

You can also change the date and time of a file when you copy it to a different disk. When you copy a file, DOS preserves the date and time. To change B:ALL.C's date and time, you would type:

A>COPY B:ALL.C+

DOS will then join all the files by the name ALL.C ("all" one of them) on drive B and place the results on drive A, the default disk drive in this case. The date and time are changed because the file on drive A is a "new" file, the product of all the files on drive B named ALL.C. In reality, the contents of the file are unchanged. This is a useful quirk of DOS.

To "copy" the file B:ALL.C without moving it and to change the date and time, you would type:

A>COPY B:ALL.C+,, B:

Two commas are added after the +. You must specify **B:** to keep the file on drive B. **B:** is thus the destination file name. However, there is no source file to join with ALL.C. Using two commas tells DOS that there is no other file name after the plus sign.

With MODE, a comma tells DOS to leave something alone. The two commas used here do almost the same thing. They tell DOS that it has reached the end of the source file name. DOS expects a file name after the + sign. To ensure that DOS does not confuse the destination file name with the nonexistent additional source file name, the two commas are used at the end of the source file name.

The COPY command above appends B:ALL.C to a file by the same name on the same drive. When no file name and extension are used for the destination, DOS will use the same file name as the source. What really happens is that DOS leaves the file in place and just changes the date and time.

If you wish to concatenate program or non-ASCII data files, don't forget to use the **/B** switch. If you try either of these examples on a nontext file, you will not get what you want.

Watch out for wild-card names with this last example. If you type:

COPY B:*.* +,, B:

DOS will combine all of the files on drive B into the first file found on B:! You probably do not want to do this.

The second part of COPY, concatenating files, may seem difficult to comprehend at first. Once you can remember all the quirks and rules, COPY will be easier to use.

PRINT

The PRINT command is the *background* printing facility of DOS V2. PRINT allows you to print a disk file while another program is running. In essence, PRINT is a very primitive form of *multitasking,* having your computer do two or more different things at the same time.

You can print any disk file. The only thing you can background print is a disk file. What you should print are only ASCII text files. Program or non-ASCII data files usually have control characters in them. PRINTing these files is like TYPEing them: the characters in the file appear as nonsense. These control characters can drive your printer crazy. Don't try to PRINT files that contain these characters.

The first time you use PRINT, DOS loads part of the PRINT program into memory and hooks the program into DOS. As a result, PRINT will steal about 3,200 bytes of memory when you use it. When you reboot DOS or turn your computer off and on again, this memory will be freed.

PRINT works by stealing idle time from the CPU. When your programs are running, there are times when the computer is waiting for you. When a program is waiting for your response, the CPU runs in a loop. At this time, you can easily divert the CPU's attention into doing something else while it is waiting.

Actually, PRINT prints during these waiting periods. While the CPU is waiting (looping) for something to happen, DOS sends the characters of the file to the printer. As soon as the CPU finds something to do, DOS stops printing and continues with the program it was running before. This means that PRINT can be slow. If there is little free time for the CPU, little will be printed.

One related term you should know is queue. A *queue* is a line in which one waits for a turn. When you PRINT a file, you place it in a queue to await printing. DOS handles the queue in order, one file after another.

The first file you place in PRINT is put at the front of the queue and is the first file printed. Any files that follow are printed in the order in which they were placed into the line. When we talk about a "queue," we are referring to this lineup of files.

The syntax of the PRINT command is

PRINT *d:filename.ext* /T / C / P ...

where *d:filename.ext* is the name of the file and the optional disk drive that holds the file. You can use wild-card characters in the file name to queue up several files to be printed with only one file name. Notice that path names are not allowed. The file you are going to print must be in the current directory of the disk.

The three switches for PRINT are

/T *Terminate,* stop printing
/C *Cancel* the printing of the file
/P *Print* this file

If you don't give a switch, DOS will assume that you are going to type the /P switch, and will print the files on the line.

The ... in the command represent other files and switches on the command line. You can have several files and switches on the same line.

PRINT's switches work like COPY's. A switch affects the file name given before the switch and all files after it, until DOS finds another switch. For this example, assume that each file is an ASCII file on the current disk drive and in the current directory.

The following line

PRINT MYFILE.TXT /P NEXTFILE.TXT

tells DOS to background print MYFILE.TXT and NEXTFILE.TXT. The /P switch affects the file before the switch (MYFILE.TXT) and the file after the switch (NEXTFILE.TXT).

The command

PRINT MYFILE.TXT /C NEXTFILE.TXT FILE3.TXT /P

cancels the printing of MYFILE.TXT and NEXTFILE.TXT and puts FILE3.TXT in the queue. The /C works on the file names before and after the switch. The /P works on the file name before the switch

(FILE3.TXT). If additional files were typed after the **/P** switch, they would also be printed.

You should familiarize yourself with how these switches are used. The COPY command also has switches that work this way.

There is little sense in giving a file name when you use the **/T** switch. **/T** is the "stop everything you're printing and forget it" switch.

The first time you PRINT a file, DOS will ask:

```
Name of list device [PRN]:
```

DOS is asking you where to print its files. You can give any valid and connected device name, such as LPT2, COM1, etc. If you hit Enter without typing in a name, the usual list device (PRN), which is normally the first parallel printer (LPT1), will be used. Don't give a device that is not on your system. DOS will act erratically if you do.

This printing-destination assignment remains in effect until the queue is empty—that is, when either all the files have been printed or they have been canceled. When the queue empties, PRINT will ask you where you want the files printed the next time you use the command.

Changing directories has no effect on PRINT. You can queue up additional files or cancel them even if you change directories. Remember you can queue up only files that are in your current directory, but you can cancel files from anywhere.

Note some warnings about PRINT. PRINT in DOS V2 can handle a maximum of ten files. Don't exceed this number! PRINT will act erratically if you do. If you have more than ten files, you may lose the ability to cancel files when you change directories. The easiest way to overload PRINT is to use wild-card characters. If more than ten files match the wild-card name, you will have problems.

If you are printing a file on a floppy diskette, don't remove the diskette until PRINT has printed the file. If you remove the diskette prematurely, PRINT will print an error message on the printer and skip the file. Generally, PRINT is more gracious about handling this error than it is about the more-than-ten-files overload problem.

Don't try to use the printer again until PRINT is finished. BASIC will give you a "Device not ready" or similar error message. Print-screening (doing a shift-PrtSC) should produce a similar error. When you get this error from DOS, type **A** to abort, and DOS will continue.

This "lockout" of the printer while PRINT is working does not always work. I have sometimes found that what you are screen-printing can end up in the middle of a current printing job handled by PRINT. If you have exceeded the 10-file limitation of PRINT, DOS may be even more erratic.

PRINT is not a sophisticated function. It is not designed to take a file and do the underscoring, boldfacing, nice margins, and page numbering that a word processor can do. PRINT prints only what is in a disk file, exactly as it is, although PRINT does expand tabs out to every ninth column. (For more information on PRINT, see the Command Summary.)

12

BACKUP, RESTORE, and RECOVER

Most of this chapter is for hard disk users, the people who usually had to do things differently throughout this book. Hard disks present certain problems, one of the biggest of which is backing up the hard disk.

BACKUP

Diskettes

The first step in backing up your hard disk is to format enough floppy diskettes to hold the files. Once BACKUP starts, you don't want to stop it until the process is finished. If you don't have enough formatted DOS diskettes on hand, you will have to stop and format more. Depending on what you are backing up, you may need to start the BACKUP process from the beginning again.

Don't use a switch with the FORMAT command. You want the maximum storage capacity from these diskettes; so don't decrease it by placing DOS on the diskettes, using only 8 sectors, or using only one side. You can use the **/V** switch for a volume label if you like. A volume label does not take any more space on the diskette, and BACKUP handles volume labels correctly. (It ignores them, as it should).

You should also label each diskette as you format it. Start with the number 1 and sequentially number each diskette. If you are using several boxes of diskettes, label each group of ten with a letter. For example, the first group could be A, the second B, etc. Indicate the letter on the label of the diskette as well as on the box or holder in which you keep the diskette. You should always keep a group of diskettes together. It would be very frustrating if you lost the diskette that held the file you needed to restore.

How many diskettes will you need? The only answer is another question. What are you backing up? If you are backing up a full hard disk (10 megabytes worth), you will need twenty-nine 360K floppy diskettes, and more if the diskettes hold less than 360K.

Are you backing up only part of the hard disk? You will need to approximate how many diskettes you will use. If you are backing up just one or two files, or a directory, do a DIR command and add up the amount of bytes for the files. Divide this number by 368,640, if you use double-sided diskettes, and round up. The result indicates about how many diskettes you will need. Because BACKUP stores a little more than just the hard disk files on the diskettes, you may need one more diskette.

If you are backing up most or all of the hard disk, the following formula will help you decide how many diskettes you will need.

First, run CHKDSK to see how full the hard disk is. Subtract the free disk space from the total disk space and divide this figure by the amount each floppy disk holds, rounded up. Pocket calculators make this job easy.

Suppose, for example, that CHKDSK reported:

10592256	bytes total disk space
28672	bytes in 3 hidden files
73728	bytes in 18 directories
4894720	bytes in 331 user files
5595136	bytes available on disk

Because this is an approximation, you would round off each figure to the nearest thousand and divide by 1,000. The total disk space is 10,592, and the bytes available is 5,595. You can divide each figure by 1,024 (1,024 bytes to the K).

For this example, the approximate number of bytes used was

$$
\begin{array}{ll}
10592 & \text{~K bytes total} \\
\underline{-5595} & \underline{\text{~K bytes free}} \\
4997 & \text{~K bytes used}
\end{array}
$$

Because we are using double-sided, DOS V2 diskettes that hold 360K, the number of diskettes needed is

$$
\begin{array}{l}
4997 \\
\underline{/360} \\
13.88
\end{array}
$$

or fourteen 360K floppy diskettes (rounding up the 13.88).

This number is fairly close. This hard disk took 13 diskettes to back up, just one diskette less than the approximation.

The approximation is usually close, and it isn't worth the time to be more accurate by totaling the number of bytes for hidden files, user files, and directories.

Fact one: DOS does not actually back up the directories; it backs up only the *files* in a directory. This means that the space taken by directories should not be counted in your total. The "bytes used" figure is thus too high, but this does not matter.

Fact two: DOS creates a small 128-byte file on each floppy to hold the backup diskette's number, the date of backup, and other information. This file is named BACKUPID.@@@. It occupies one cluster (two sectors, or 1K, of diskette space for double-sided diskette drives) even though it is only 128 bytes in size.

Fact three: DOS adds another 128 bytes of information to the front of each backed-up file. This additional information includes the path name of the file, the file name, an indication whether the file is complete or only a segment, and other information. BACKUP, unlike COPY, will break up a file that is larger than your backup media. This way you can back up and restore files that are larger than the storage capacity of the floppy diskette.

The first "fact" decreases our "bytes-used" figure; the second and third facts increase our bytes-used figure. The formula to handle these almost-offsetting factors is more work than it is worth. The approximation works well enough.

If you are unsure or nervous about the number. produced by the approximation, add one or two more diskettes to the result. Or take the easy way out: have 29 formatted, double-sided diskettes on hand for backup.

Where to Be

When you first BACKUP, back up the entire hard disk. The current directory for the hard disk should be the root directory. Type:

CD C:

to get to the directory. As you become accustomed to the BACKUP command, you can start with a different directory and back up only sections of the hard disk.

For the examples that follow, make the hard disk, drive C, the current drive. It will make the next steps easier.

The Command

The complete syntax for the BACKUP command is

BACKUP *d1:path\filename.ext* **d2:** */S/M/A/D:mm-dd-yy*

where *d1:* is the hard disk to be backed up; *path* is the directory path you want to back up; *filename.ext* is the name of the file(s) you want to back up, with wild cards acceptable; and **d2:** is the floppy disk drive to receive the backup files.

The switches used in this command are

/S   Backs up all *subdirectories*, starting with the specified or current directory on the hard disk and working downward

/M	Backs up all files *modified* since the last time they were BACKed UP
/A	Adds the file(s) to be backed up to the files already on the specified floppy disk drive
/D:mm-dd-yy	Backs up any files that were changed or created on or after the specified date. The *date* is in the form of *mm* for the month, *dd* for the day, and *yy* for the year. You can use the slash (/) in place of the hyphen (-).

The *path*\ you give tells DOS which directory to start with. If you begin with the right directory, you can omit the path name. (This is why I always move to the root directory of the hard disk.)

If BACKUP is stored in a subdirectory and the PATH command does not include this directory, use \ as the path to start the backup at the root directory.

The *filename.ext* is the file or files you want to back up. You can use only one *filename.ext,* but it can contain wild-card characters. If you don't give a file name, DOS will assume ***.*** and will back up all files.

If the hard disk drive is the current disk drive and you have given a path or file name, you can omit the hard disk drive name at the beginning of the command. Otherwise, you must give the hard disk drive name.

You must always give the name of the floppy disk drive that will hold the backup diskettes. DOS makes no assumptions about this name.

Switches

The versatility of BACKUP is shown by its switches. Note that some switches can be used together.

If you have been wondering why you should start at the root directory, the **/S** is the answer. This switch tells DOS to start with the directory indicated. If a directory was not indicated, start with the current one. Back up the files specified in this directory. Move to the subdirectories of this directory and do the same. Keep moving down into other subdirectories on this branch of the directory tree and do the same.

To back up the entire hard disk, you would type:

BACKUP C:\ A: /S

This command tells DOS to back up the files in the root directory, any subdirectories, any subdirectories of these subdirectories, and so forth.

If you start with a subdirectory, you will get all the files in the chain of subdirectories for that side of the directory tree, but you won't get the whole hard disk. For example, look at the sample directory in Appendix B. If you start at the root directory and enter **/S**, you will back up the entire disk. If you start in the WORDS directory, you will back up the files in WORDS, LETTERS, and CONTRACTS, but not the files on the DOS subdirectory side of the tree. If you start with DOS, you will back up all the file on that side of the tree, but the WORDS side of the directory tree will not be backed up.

A common mistake I made when first using this command was to start in a subdirectory, not specify a path, and think that I had backed up the entire disk. I was wrong. DOS started with the directory I was in and usually backed up only about one third or less of the hard disk.

Watch your starting directory with BACKUP and the path name you give, if any. Make sure that you tell DOS what you mean.

The **/M** switch tells DOS to back up any file that has been *modified.* This switch really tells DOS to back up a file you have not BACKed UP before. Remember the *archive attribute*? It is stored in the directory with each file name. When you create or change a file, its attribute is turned on. DOS looks at the archive attribute. When you give the **/M** switch, DOS will back up this file. Otherwise, it will skip the file.

This feature allows you to choose the files you want to back up. There is one hitch, however. For example, suppose that on day one, you back up all of your hard disk. On day two, you use the **/M** switch to back up files selectively. On days three, four, and five, you do the same. Did all of your files get backed up each time? Maybe. If a file changed each day, then it was backed up every day. But what happens if the file changed only on days two and three? It was backed up only on those days.

Did you know that unless you give the **/A** switch, DOS will erase all the files on the backup diskettes before recording the new ones? This is helpful when you have only one or two files to back up. But what if you need to restore a file, after using the same backup diskettes each day and not giving the **/A** switch? Each day you erased the files backed up on the preceding day *before* you backed up the new ones. You would have succeeded in backing up the file twice, but still would have lost the file from the backup diskettes.

To avoid this problem, you should either have two sets of backup diskettes or use the **/A** switch every time. This can still cause problems, however. How will BACKUP know which version is the most recent if you have backed up the file more than once? Which set of backup diskettes has the most recent version of this file? To avoid this situation, don't use either the **/M** or the **/A** switch.

The **/D** switch is an alternative to the switches discussed above. This switch allows you to give a date and tells DOS to back up any file that has changed on or after that date. This is one reason why you should always answer the date and time questions when DOS boots. DOS then uses the date in the directory for this search.

The **/D** switch tells DOS to grab any file that has been created or changed on or after the given date. Although this switch allows you to copy the same files each day, it also makes BACKUP run longer. This increase in time, however, makes restoring the hard disk easier.

The BACKUP Process

First, keep three sets of backup diskettes. Each set should have enough diskettes to hold the entire hard disk and should be kept in a separate box.

Once every month or so, back up the entire hard disk, using the first set of diskettes. Try to do this on the same date each month, such as the 1st or 5th.

Each day, or every couple of days, back up the hard disk, using the **/D** option. The second and third sets of diskettes should be used for this procedure, rotating the sets each time. The date you give BACKUP should be the day you backed up the entire hard disk. That way you will back up each file that has changed since the "master" backup of the hard disk.

The monthly backup takes the most time, although the daily backup takes longer each time. Once you have completed the backup process, the entire hard disk and every file that has changed will be on two sets of diskettes. The third set is for safety. If you have a problem with a "daily" diskette, you can go to the other set. You will lose some work on this file, but that is better than losing a month's work.

To restore the entire hard disk, use the RESTORE program. You should run RESTORE twice, first with the monthly set, then with the daily set. You have now restored the entire hard disk.

If you lose a file or two, try to restore the file from the last daily backup. If the file is not there, it has not changed all month. Using the monthly backup set, run RESTORE again to retrieve the missing file.

Running a backup like this requires a little more work each day, but a lot less work when a crisis comes. A crisis will come some day; all disk drives fail eventually.

When I first used hard disks in 1979, my disk failed after a couple of months. The last good backup copy I had was several weeks old. It took me more than a week to restore most of the files. Some files were lost permanently. Experienced? Yes, I am.

If you use the /A switch, DOS will expect the previously used backup diskettes to be in the floppy disk drive you specify. Otherwise, DOS will prompt you to put a diskette into the disk drive and strike a key to start.

One final note on BACKUP. It follows the status of VERIFY. If VERIFY is OFF, your backup files will not be checked to see if they have been recorded properly. If VERIFY is ON, the files will be checked. Turn VERIFY ON before doing a monthly backup. This will ensure that your backup files are good. Be sure to turn VERIFY OFF afterward. VERIFY slows down DOS more than 90 percent on the floppy disk. That's why you should turn on VERIFY only when necessary. You may occasionally chance it on daily backups because it is usually safe. You will be the best judge of whether you should have VERIFY on or off while you are backing up the hard disk.

Restoring Backup Files

The RESTORE command is the opposite of BACKUP. RESTORE takes the files from your backup diskettes and replaces then on the hard disk.

The syntax for the RESTORE command is very close to BACKUP's:

RESTORE d1: *d2:path\filename.ext* /S/P

where **d1:** is the floppy disk drive holding the backup diskette(s), and *d2:* is the hard disk drive. (If the current disk drive is the hard disk drive, you can omit this.)

The *path* is the optional path to the directory that will receive the restored files. The current directory for the hard disk will be used if you don't specify a path.

The *filename.ext* is the name of the file(s) to restore. Wild cards are permitted. All files (***.***) will be assumed if you don't give a file name.

The switches used with RESTORE are

/S   Restores files in this directory and all other *sub-directories* beyond it. /S is identical to BACKUP's /S switch.

/P   Prompts and asks if this file should be restored when:

1. The file is marked "read-only"

2. The file has been changed since the last backup.

Both of these switches are helpful. If a file is marked "read-only," it has probably not been altered, and probably won't be. The only time you may need to restore a read-only file is some rare occasion when the file somehow becomes erased from the hard disk. IBMBIO.COM and IBMDOS.COM are two examples of read-only files.

If the file has changed since it was last backed up, you probably don't want to restore this file either. The backup copy is probably out-of-date.

Either way, DOS will ask whether you want to restore this file. Just answer **Y** for yes or **N** for no.

As with BACKUP, the starting directory is important. You must be in the right part of the directory tree to restore a file.

When a file is backed up by BACKUP or RESTOREd, the path and the name of the file appear on the screen. This information is stored in each backup file and is used when restoring the files. If you have erased a subdirectory, DOS will recreate it. This is a useful feature when you are trying to restore a faulty section of the disk drive, or if the hard disk has been erased.

You may also notice that some of the names of files stored on the backup diskettes have changed. DOS cannot store two files with the same name in the same directory. If DOS encounters two or more files with the same name, DOS will change the extension on the second and any subsequent files with the same name on the backup diskette.

When RESTOREing, you must always start with the first backup diskette of the set and work sequentially—2, 3, 4, etc.—even if you are restoring only a few files. DOS will prompt you to change diskettes.

BACKUP and RESTORE are two powerful utility programs for the hard disk. Study them carefully and use BACKUP frequently. If you are lucky, you will need to use RESTORE only a few times.

When to BACKUP

The suggestion that you back up your hard disk frequently also applies to floppy diskettes. There are two other times that you should back up your complete hard disk: when you reorganize your hard disk, and when you have heavy fragmentation of the hard disk.

Reorganizing a hard disk involves copying many files to different directories. It may also involve creating new directories, deleting unused directories, and deleting old copies of files. After you have reorganized the hard disk, you will want to *snap-shot* (capture an image of, in this case a binary image) the hard disk, or back it up. By backing up your hard disk, you will not have to repeat the work you did to reorganize the hard disk should the disk "crash."

Fragmentation means that a file is not stored continuously on the surface of the hard disk. After you have deleted and added several files, a new file can be scattered across the entire hard disk. This hurts neither DOS nor your file, but DOS must work longer to retrieve this file. The hard disk's recording heads must move across the disk several times to read your file. As a result, the performance of the hard disk decreases. This can also occur after a major reorganization of the hard disk.

The solution to the fragmentation problem is to back up your entire hard disk, reformat it, then restore your files. Formatting will erase all the files and directories from the hard disk. As you restore each file and subdirectory, the information will be stored on consecutive sectors, which will increase the performance of the hard disk.

To accomplish this task, do the following:

Step 1

Have a diskette that contains the operating system (formatted with the **/S** switch) and the following programs:
>BACKUP.COM
>FORMAT.COM
>RESTORE.COM

If BACKUP.COM and FORMAT.COM are already on the hard disk, you may use these versions instead. You will also need a diskette-based copy of RESTORE.COM.

Step 2

Have a sufficient number of preformatted floppy diskettes. Use the guidelines given earlier to determine the number you will need.

Step 3

Turn VERIFY ON. This will almost double the time required for this backup, but you don't want anything to go wrong. Skipping this step can be risky.

Step 4

Run BACKUP by typing:

```
C>BACKUP C:\ A: /S
```

Notice that in my case, BACKUP is one of the files in the PATH command, allowing me to invoke BACKUP from anywhere. When you put BACKUP in the PATH command, you do not have to give a drive name or move to a different directory to use BACKUP. If this is not the case for you, either move to the directory containing BACKUP, or use the diskette containing BACKUP. If you are using a diskette-based copy, include the drive name before the word BACKUP.

DOS then prompts you to put your first diskette into the A: floppy disk drive, Your insert your 1 backup diskette (the diskette with the number "1" on the label), close the door, and hit a key. Coordinate the numbers on the labels of the backup diskettes with the numbers that DOS assigns. This will make the diskettes easy to store and use.

When DOS prompts for the next diskette, take diskette #1 out of the drive and put it back in the envelope. Then insert diskette #2 and repeat this procedure until you are finished. (You can just stack the diskettes on top of each other at the side of the computer as you use them.)

When you are finished, you will have several diskettes in a stack. Together, they make up the copy of your hard disk.

If you get an error message from the floppy disk drive during the backup, abort the program, then reformat the offending diskette. If any bad sectors show up, retire the diskette, format a new one to replace it, then restart BACKUP. The backup copy of the hard disk must be correct! If errors are allowed, information will be lost.

Step 5

Reformat the hard disk.

This is the point of no return. You must have a good backup copy of the hard disk, or you will lose information.

Put the floppy diskette containing DOS, FORMAT.COM, and RESTORE.COM into the A: disk drive. Make A: the current disk drive (**A:**), then type:

```
A>FORMAT C: /S /V
```

This command reformats the hard disk, takes DOS from the floppy diskette and puts it onto the hard disk, and allows you to put a volume label on the hard disk drive. Remembering the rules for volume labels (see Chapter 5), type your volume label when DOS prompts you.

Step 6

To restore the hard disk, type:

```
A>RESTORE A: C:\ /S
```

This command tells DOS to start at the root directory of the hard disk drive and restore all files in this directory as well as all files in the subdirectories. You do not have to remake (MD) a subdirectory. DOS will do it for you as the first file from an erased subdirectory is restored. That's why the path name is included in each backed-up file.

Remove the DOS and program diskette from drive A:, put in the #1 backup diskette, and hit a key. As DOS prompts you, take the next diskette from the pile and restore the next series of files. Continue this process until the system prompt reappears.

Step 7

Turn VERIFY OFF. (This is optional.)

Now you are done! You have backed up the entire hard disk, erased it, and restored it. This procedure takes from thirty minutes to an hour, depending on how full your hard disk is.

If you get a diskette out of order while using RESTORE, it will prompt you to put the correct diskette into the disk drive. If you number your diskettes, you should not have this problem. You can tell by the label whether the diskettes are in the correct numerical sequence.

Store your backup diskettes in a safe place. You have just done a complete backup of your hard disk, and the diskettes will be your monthly backup until the next time you back up the entire hard disk. If you use a monthly and a daily backup procedure with the **/D** switch, change the **/D** date to today's date.

Two Disk Drives in One

If you have an XT, you know that it comes with one floppy disk drive and one hard disk. But did you know that you have two floppy disk drives? The second floppy disk drive is hidden in the first one.

PC DOS knows how many disk drives you physically have. If you have only one physical floppy disk drive, DOS will make it two *logical* (apparent) disk drives. The A: drive is also the B: drive.

If you have an XT, or a similar computer with one floppy disk drive, put a floppy diskette into the disk drive and type:

DIR B:

The following message will appear:

```
Insert diskette for drive B: and strike any key when
ready
```

Press a key. You will see the directory of the diskette. Now type:

DIR A:

The message

```
Insert diskette for drive A: and strike any key when
ready
```

will appear. If you press a key, the same directory will appear. There is one difference. The first line of the directory states that it is the directory of A:\ rather than B:\.

You have two floppy disk drives even though you have only one physical disk drive. This stretching of the one disk drive can be used with COMP (compare files), COPY, DISKCOPY, DISKCOMP, FORMAT, and other floppy disk commands. When you specify the A: and the B:, DOS will prompt you to change diskettes at the appropriate time.

This "two-drives-in-one" system works best with FORMAT. You get one more message to change diskettes before you format. If you **DISKCOPY A: B:** or **DISKCOMP A: B:**, you will also get these messages. If you use DISKCOPY, remember to write-protect the original diskette in case you don't have the correct diskette in the disk drive at the right time.

The worst case for "two-drives-in-one" is COPY. You must change diskettes for each file that is copied between drive A and pseudodrive B. To copy 10 files between the floppy diskettes, you must make 20 diskette changes.

The best way to copy between floppy diskettes on an XT is to create a new subdirectory on the hard disk. COPY the files to this new subdirectory from the first floppy diskette. Then change diskettes and COPY from the subdirectory back to the floppy diskette. Erase these files from the hard disk but keep the subdirectory for the next time you need to copy floppy diskette-based files between diskettes.

RECOVER

RECOVER works with either one file at a time or a complete disk. The part that works with a complete disk is *dangerous* and should not be run unless you have read and heeded the precautions. This form of RECOVER works with the directory of the diskette. Don't run this part of RECOVER unless you have no alternative. Once DOS has "fixed" the directory, you may spend hours trying to recover from RECOVER. The other part of RECOVER is not risky.

For previous versions of DOS, if a disk developed a bad sector where a file was recorded, you had a major problem. To bypass the bad sector, you had to copy the file to another diskette and answer "I," for ignore when DOS gave an error message as the bad sector was encountered. The alternative was to copy the other files to a new diskette and reformat or retire the old diskette. You would then copy the file you need from your backup diskette. This method was inconvenient, but it worked.

Hard disks and hierarchical directories are a new problem. There is no backup copy of a hard disk in the physical sense. You don't have a second set of hard disk platters that you can install. (However, you hopefully have a backup copy of the files; that's what the BACKUP command is for.)

How do you recover a file with a defective sector on the hard disk? RECOVER is the program to use. RECOVER can make a new copy of a file, minus the data held in the bad sectors. A bonus is that the bad sectors are marked as "in-use" so that they will not be used again.

The syntax for using this form of RECOVER is

    RECOVER *d:path***filename**.*ext*

where *d:* is the optional disk drive name if the file is not on the current disk drive. The *path* is the optional path name to the file if it is not in the current directory. The **filename** is the root name of the file to RECOVER, and *.ext* is the extension name if the file has an extension. You may use wild cards in the file name, but only one file can be recovered at a time. If you use a wild card, DOS will use the first file in the directory that matches the wild-card name.

After RECOVER has finished, the file you were recovering will have the same name as before. The bad sectors on the diskette have been "removed" from use, but the material in them is still lost. This means that the total capacity of the disk is decreased by the number of bad sectors.

The only files that you should recover are text and data files. Don't bother recovering program files. Because information has been lost from these files, a program may not run at all, or worse, run erratically when you recover it. Use a backup copy of the program instead.

Text or data files will need some editing. For text or ASCII-stored data files, use a text editor to get rid of any garbage or add any lost information. For non-ASCII data files, you may need to write special programs to restore the file to its original state.

There is little excuse for having to recover a file with RECOVER. If you make daily backup copies of your diskettes and hard disk, you can usually restore your files easily from the backup copies and add or re-edit them. However, you should run RECOVER to "hide" the bad sectors from the disk.

The only way to remove bad sectors is to reformat the disk. If the disk is damaged (a physical problem with the disk's magnetic coating), formatting will not help. If the disk is a floppy diskette, it should be retired. Hard disks, however, are difficult to retire. You'll have to live with any flaws.

Bad sectors are a bad sign. Either the magnetic coating on the disk is damaged, or you have an electronics problem. The most likely reasons—in order—are mishandling of the diskette or hard disk; physical wear from normal use of the diskette (seldom applicable to hard disks because the recording heads do not touch the surface when the drive is in use); mechanical or electronic failure of the disk drive; electronic failure of the disk interface or controller card (the board inside your computer); a damaged disk drive cable; or bad RAM memory in the computer.

The latter cause (bad RAM memory) is infrequent with the Personal Computer. If the memory holding DOS were to go bad, the machine-language instructions that the CPU executes would change. This change could cause erratic or disastrous disk performance. The best you can hope for is that nothing will happen—that DOS will just go "dead in the water." The worst that can happen is that DOS reformats the disk or makes garbage of directories. That's why a memory parity error makes your computer "lock up." IBM wisely chose to stop your computer dead in the water so that only the work in progress is destroyed rather than some or all of the previous work and programs stored on the disks.

If the diskette is physically worn, it's time to retire it. Look at the diskette's surface through the access holes. Dark grooves indicate wear. Dark or dull splotches can indicate spots where the diskette has been mishandled or contaminated. If you see a fold or crease, retire the diskette.

Mechanical or electronic problems are more difficult to analyze. Run your diagnostics. For floppy disk drives, use a diskette formatted on a known good disk drive. If the problem is the hard disk, back it up now!

If problems show up when you run the diagnostics, get your computer or disk drive repaired now before other diskettes are harmed. If a disk drive problem shows up in the diagnostics, the entire computer should be suspected. The problem might be caused by the disk drive, the interface board inside the computer, the cable that connects the board and the disk drive, the power supply of the disk drives, or possibly something else in the computer's main circuitry. Whatever the problem, have it repaired immediately.

You seldom damage electronically a diskette or hard disk when you read information from it. If the problem is not in the diskette itself and you have not written information to it, the diskette and its file are probably still intact. There is always a small chance that the disk drive wrote some garbage instead of reading information. Check out all the diskettes that you used since you first detected a problem. Make sure that the information is intact.

What about bad sectors that develop in directories? This is a major problem. If it is in the root directory, the problem is grave. The root directory is located on a fixed part of the diskette or hard disk. DOS cannot relocate the root directory. For either diskettes or hard disks, this condition can be fatal. The second part of RECOVER is used to recover damaged root directories.

If the bad sector is in a subdirectory, the problem is serious, but not fatal. CHKDSK can cope with this. (For more information about CHKDSK, read the Command Summary.) Before you run CHKDSK, follow the steps below for copying your disk or diskette. If CHKDSK does not work, RECOVER is you final choice.

First, COPY and/or BACKUP all the files you can. Use a different set of diskettes from your last backup copies. Keep your last backup diskette or diskettes intact. You may need to use them if all else fails.

If the defect is in the directory on a floppy diskette, use a different floppy from the last backup copy of the floppy diskette. Use COPY to copy each file to a second separate diskette. Then DISKCOPY the bad diskette to a third diskette.

If the offender is the hard disk, use a different set of backup diskettes. Run BACKUP, keeping your master and last daily backup intact.

Since the cause of the bad sectors is unknown at this point, you should suspect the BACKUP or COPYed files that you have just made. Whatever caused the directory to develop bad sectors may have damaged other areas on the disk or diskette. You should ensure that the files you just copied or backed up are correct before you fully trust them.

(If the problem is a subdirectory, stop and use CHKDSK now. If this does not work, use RECOVER. Either way, read the rest of the section.)

The next step is RECOVER. The syntax for this form of RECOVER is

RECOVER *d:*

The *d:* is the optional disk drive name. If the current disk drive is *not* the disk or diskette to recover, give the appropriate disk drive name.

DOS will now run through the File Allocation Table. Remember that the FAT knows the disk clusters (sectors) where the files are stored; but it does not know the previous file name, its characteristics (system, hidden, etc.), and the file's date and time.

First, DOS creates a new root directory. Then DOS begins to create files in the root directory with the name FILEnnnn.REC. The "nnnn" is a number from 0000 to 9999. Each file created by DOS represents one of the recovered files from the disk. Every file on the disk becomes a FILEnnnn.REC file. This includes program files, data files, and subdirectories.

Now the detective work begins. Each FILEnnnn.REC can be anything, a normal file or a subdirectory. You must now find which FILE-nnnn.REC holds the information you need to keep and which FILEnnnn.REC holds information that you can discard (such as subdirectories). The previous names of the files are lost. Their dates and times are also lost. The major clue to what is in a file is the file itself.

You will need several tools to help you. TYPE can type the characters in a file. This command will help you locate ASCII text files. Program files and subdirectories are different. Most of their information is displayed as gibberish. You will need DEBUG, or a similar program, to display the contents of these files.

Using these tools, locate the files you were not able to COPY or BACKUP. COPY these files to another diskette and change their names back to what they were. Make sure that the files are intact. There is a small chance that whatever caused the directory to develop bad sectors might have affected other areas of the disk or diskette, making these files bad also.

The task of identifying each file is difficult. For practice, I took a backup copy of a good diskette and ran RESTORE on the diskette. (I had another backup copy.) I then tried to locate the files, typing and using DEBUG to identify them. This tedious task took several hours even though I wrote a utility or two to help.

RECOVERing a diskette or disk is very, very difficult. It should be a last-resort measure. Unless your backup copies are extremely out-of-date, recreating or re-editing files is better than trying to RECOVER a disk or diskette.

Before you use RECOVER on a disk, practice on a copy of a diskette. This will help you gain the knowledge you will need to RECOVER the real thing, a damaged directory. If you botch up the copy, nothing is really lost.

When you try to recover a diskette with a flawed directory, use a copy. If you make a mistake with the copy, you can make another copy of the original, flawed diskette. If you work with the flawed diskette and don't have a copy, a mistake can be costly.

Remember that this discussion does not apply to RECOVER *filename,* where RECOVER is used on a single file. Because this process works on one file at a time, the worst that can happen is that you will lose part of the file.

When you have recreated your files, reformat your diskette or hard disk. FORMAT gives a message when it cannot properly format any system area, including the areas for the boot record, the root directory, and the FAT. If you format with the **/S** switch, the areas for IBMBIO.COM and IBMDOS.COM are also checked, and error messages are given if these areas are bad. The error messages indicate that the diskette or hard disk is currently unusable. You can retire a diskette, but hard disks must be repaired.

Remember to back up frequently. You will have less work, frustration, and anxiety if you back up your diskettes and hard disk rather than try to recreate them, using RECOVER.

13

Final Thoughts

This book covered most DOS commands, features, and functions. You have learned how to use DOS effectively, had some hands-on experience, and should now feel comfortable with your system.

No book on DOS can cover everything about it. This book is no exception. For example, we did not examine:

- The COMP command, which compares disk files (COMP is covered, however, in the Command Summary.)
- How to use the ANSI terminal code for DOS
- The DOS system calls
- Some technical details of DOS
- All of the switches (options) available for all DOS programs

The ANSI terminal codes were briefly mentioned in Chapter 10 on configuring your computer. These codes are for programmers and are listed in the DOS manual. The codes do not work with Disk or

Advanced BASIC. The following is a hint for those using the codes in programs: when you give a number, give the ASCII, not the binary. If you want to print 42, print "42," not the equivalent of CHR$(42).

DOS system calls and the more technical information are inappropriate for a user's guide. Programmers (but usually not BASIC programmers) use these calls to control DOS. You can find additional information on DOS system calls in your DOS manual.

Some additional switches are covered in the Command Summary at the end of this book. Read this section and return to it when you are stuck on a command. Many helpful hints are listed in this section.

Dangerous Commands

Several times in this book, commands were labeled as "dangerous." These commands are not dangerous to you personally, but to the data recorded on your disk. If not properly used, the commands can erase or destroy files.

It takes time and work to record anything on a disk. The data may take only seconds to copy or change, but it could represent the heart of your business or personal livelihood. Common sense should tell you that this data must be protected. By applying that common sense to the operation of your computer, you should have few problems.

FORMAT and DISKCOPY are the two most "dangerous" commands. If you FORMAT or DISKCOPY the wrong diskette, you can destroy many files in just a few seconds. ERASE is also dangerous because it deletes files. Although these three commands appear to do the same thing, there are differences among them.

When you ERASE a file, you don't remove it from the disk. DOS simply marks the directory entry holding this file name as "erased" and frees the sectors that held this file in the FAT. With the proper programs, you can unERASE a file if you have not added anything else to the disk. Once you add or extend a file, it can take the directory entry for your erased file or use the sectors that held your file. If you inadvertently erase a file, you can use program tools to recover it. Just don't put anything else on this diskette until you run the unERASE program.

FORMAT and DISKCOPY record new information on the entire diskette. When you format a diskette, dummy information is recorded. When you DISKCOPY, every bit of information from the first diskette is copied to the second one. If you use either FORMAT or DISKCOPY on a diskette that has useful information, the previous information will no longer be usable; it is lost.

If you run FORMAT while the hard disk is the current disk drive and don't give a disk drive name to FORMAT, you will have problems. The message:

```
Strike any key to begin formatting drive C:
```

will appear. If you hit a key, you can lose up to 10 megabytes of information. If you want to lose the information, hit that key. If this is not what you want, carefully press either Ctrl-C or Ctrl-Break to stop the command.

COPY can be troublesome. If you COPY an old version of a file to the diskette holding a newer version and don't change the file name, you will be in trouble. You have just destroyed the new version of your file. Be cautious when you COPY.

The RECOVER command can also be troublesome. For a single file, RECOVER is easy and simple to use. When RECOVER is used to recover a complete disk, however, you may need hours or days to recover. Practice before using RECOVER on "live" disks.

Knowing the Secret

Hierarchical directories and I/O redirection are difficult concepts to grasp at first. With a little practice, these facilities are easily mastered once "you know the secret."

A professional magician appeared on television commercials all over the United States for a product called "TV Magic Cards." He'd perform a few tricks, then tell us that it was easy to do these tricks with TV Magic Cards "once you know the secret."

I feel the same way about computers and DOS. Once you know how a command operates, you know "the secret." Learning the secrets of computers is easy. Once you've learned how to use the commands and a little more about how the computer operates, you can imagine what actually goes on when you invoke and use DOS and its commands. Computers are only "mystical" when no one bothers to explain what really happens inside them. I trust that you have gotten some ideas of how your computer operates from this book.

DOS is really a friendly operating system. You can learn by doing. Just be sure to watch *what* you are doing.

After a while, you will develop *advanced user's syndrome.* Your fingers will fly across the keyboard. You know exactly what you want to do before you do it. And then you will make an "experienced mistake." You will FORMAT or DISKCOPY the wrong diskette, or COPY the wrong files over good ones. The list goes on.

Even the most experienced users make mistakes. Mistakes occur when you get overconfident or sloppy. You don't check that the proper diskettes are in the disk drives. You don't read the messages completely, or you make a typing error and don't see it. You'll get so good at things that you won't notice a mistake until it's too late.

To avoid some of these problems, always proofread your typing and and check your messages. Take the time to be certain. Make sure that the correct diskettes are in the right disk drive. Write-protect important diskettes, even if you plan to remove the tab after you have FORMATted or DISKCOPYed them. Do a DIR to be certain that no useful files will be destroyed with COPY, DISKCOPY, or FORMAT. Label diskettes.

Forgetting to save frequently while you revise a copy of documentation, a spreadsheet, or a program can also be an "experienced mistake." You can feel confident that you will not forget to save your information before you are finished, so you keep adding, editing, or revising the document, spreadsheet model, or program without saving even though the last time you saved a revision to the disk might have been over an hour ago. A troublesome feeling that you should save your revision gnaws at you, but you carry on. This is the time that Murphy strikes.

I worked on a spreadsheet model for more than an hour and continued to refine it. Several times I felt the nagging of my subconscious to save my work. I ignored the feeling and kept on refining the model.

True to Murphy's never-ending mischievousness, a one-half second loss of power destroyed the model I was working on. It took only a half hour to restore the model, but this half hour would not have been wasted if I had only taken ten seconds to save the model. Save frequently and often.

Finally, always back up your hard disk and diskettes. It's a cheap form of insurance.

For More Information

User groups are invaluable resources. You may find that you're not the first person to have a problem with a program. Members of user groups can often help each other with problems or projects. Find a group in your area and join it. It will be worth the money.

If you are looking for other programs to use on your computer, catalogs, magazines, and Que's book, the *IBM PC Expansion & Software Guide,* can help you discover what is available in hardware and software products.

Finally, try and enjoy. You learn by doing, as well as from friends, classes, a user group, or a book.

Best wishes to you on using your computer and PC DOS. I hope the time you have spent with this book was both useful and enjoyable.

Command Summary

Introduction

This section discusses all of the PC DOS commands. Each command is presented in the same format.

The command name appears first, followed by the version of DOS it applies to. Two asterisks (**) indicate that the command's functions are different for the older and newer versions of DOS.

"Internal" and "External" indicate whether the command is built into DOS (internal) or is disk-resident (external).

The purpose of the command is discussed, followed by the syntax required to invoke the command. The exit codes for the command are listed if there are any.

The rules governing the use of the command are also listed. A single asterisk (*) designates a warning.

Examples or sample sessions demonstrate the use of the command. The Sample Session shows the exact dialogue between the operator and the computer during a session. Comments appear on the right-hand side of the page.

The Notes section contains additional comments, information, hints, or suggestions on the use of the command.

The Messages section is an alphabetical listing of the messages produced by the command. The following three types of messages may occur:

1. INFORMATIONAL - which simply informs or prompts the operator for a response

2. WARNING - which warns the operator of a possible problem

3. ERROR - which informs the operator that an error has occurred; a program terminates after issuing an ERROR message.

In the command summaries that follow, note that certain message designations, such as filename and dirname, will vary as each specific file name and directory name is used.

The common notation used to represent file specifications is

d:path\filename.ext

in which

d: is the name of the disk drive holding the file.

path is the directory path to the file.

filename is the root name of the file.

.ext is the file name extension.

If any part of this notation does not appear in the file specification (in the Syntax section), the omitted part is not allowed with this command. For example, the notation **d:filename.ext** indicates that path names are not allowed in the command.

In most cases, a device name may be substituted for a full file specification.

If a notation in the Syntax section appears in **this type face,** it is mandatory and must be entered. If a notation appears in *this type face,* it is optional and is entered only when necessary.

Upper and Lower Case

Upper-case words in the Syntax section must be typed as they appear. Words that appear in lower case are variables. Be sure to substitute the appropriate disk drive letter or name, path name, file name, etc., for the lower-case variable when you type in the command.

Commands, all parameters, and switches typed with the command may be entered in either upper or lower case. The exceptions are SORT and batch commands where the case of the letters of certain parameters may be important. (See the batch and SORT command sections for further information.)

PC DOS Commands by Purpose

Note: Names in parentheses are CONFIG.SYS commands.

To execute automatically a batch file:	AUTOEXEC.BAT
To back up the hard disk:	BACKUP
To background print:	PRINT
To concatenate files:	COPY
To change the active display:	MODE
To change the active console:	CTTY
To change the baud rate:	MODE
To change the current directory:	CHDIR
To change the current disk drive:	**d:**
To change the date:	DATE
To change the display characteristics:	MODE
To change the environment:	SET
To change the name of a file:	RENAME
To change the name/location of the command interpreter:	(SHELL)
To change the number of disk buffers:	(BUFFERS)
To change the number of UNIX/XENIX handles:	(FILES)
To change the time:	TIME
To compare disks:	DISKCOMP
To compare files:	COMP
To control Ctrl-Break:	BREAK, (BREAK)
To control the verification of files:	VERIFY
To convert an .EXE file to .COM:	EXE2BIN
To copy between devices:	COPY
To copy diskettes:	DISKCOPY, COPY

To display the amount of RAM memory:	CHKDSK
To display the contents of a file:	TYPE
To display the date:	DATE
To display the environment:	SET
To display the files on a disk:	DIR, CHKDSK, TREE
To display the free space on a disk:	CHKDSK, DIR
To display the subdirectories on a disk:	TREE, CHKDSK
To display the time:	TIME
To display the version of DOS:	VER
To enable the printing of graphics:	GRAPHICS
To execute a series of commands:	batch
To fix a damaged diskette, hard disk:	CHKDSK, RECOVER
To locate a string in a file:	FIND
To make a new subdirectory:	MKDIR
To move files:	COPY
To pause the display:	Ctrl-NumLock, MORE
To place the operating system on a disk:	SYS, FORMAT
To pipe the output between programs:	I
To prepare new diskettes:	FORMAT
To prepare the hard disk:	FDISK, FORMAT
To print the video screen:	Prt-Sc, >, >>
To reassign the printer(s):	MODE
To reassign the disk drives:	ASSIGN
To redirect the input of a program:	<, I
To redirect the output of a program:	>, >>, I
To remove a file:	ERASE
To remove a subdirectory:	RMDIR
To restore a backed-up hard disk file:	RESTORE
To restore a damaged directory:	CHKDSK, RECOVER
To restore a file with a bad sector:	RECOVER
To set the alternative directories for commands and batch files:	PATH
To set the system prompt:	PROMPT
To sort a disk file:	SORT
To use a new/changed device:	(DEVICE)

Other DOS Messages

When DOS detects an error while reading or writing to a device, including disk drives, the following message appears:

    type error reading device

or

    type error writing device

where `type` is the type of error, and `device` is the device at fault.

Do not remove the diskette from the disk drive. Read the possible causes and actions at the end of this section.

Error Types

The types of errors include the following:

    Bad format call

An incorrect header length was passed to a device driver. The device driver software is at fault. Contact the dealer who sold you the device driver.

    Bad command

The device driver issued an invalid command to `device`. The problem may lie with the device driver software or with other software trying to use the device driver.

    Bad unit

An invalid subunit number has been passed to the device driver. The problem may lie with the device driver software or with other software trying to use the device driver. Contact the dealer who sold you the device driver.

Data

DOS could not correctly read or write the data. Usually the disk has developed a defective spot.

Disk

This is a catch-all error message not covered elsewhere. The error usually occurs when you use an unformatted diskette or disk, or if you leave the disk drive door open.

No paper

The printer is either out of paper or is not turned on.

Non-DOS disk

The FAT has invalid information. This diskette is unusable.

Not ready

The device device is not ready and cannot receive or transmit data. Check the connections, that the power is on, and whether the device is ready.

Read fault

DOS was unable to read the data successfully, usually from a disk or diskette.

Sector not found

The disk drive was unable to locate the sector on the diskette or hard disk platter. This error is usually the result of a defective spot or defective drive electronics.

Seek

The disk drive could not locate the proper track on the diskette or hard disk platter. This error usually results from a defective spot on the diskette or disk platter, your using an unformatted disk, or drive electronics problems.

Write fault

DOS could not successfully write the data to this device.

```
Write protect
```

The diskette is write-protected.

Possible Actions

In every case, DOS will display an error message, followed by the line:

```
Abort, Retry, Ignore?
```

You may type one of the following:

A for abort. DOS will end the program that requested the read or write condition.

R for retry. DOS will try the operation again.

I for ignore. DOS will skip this operation, and the program will continue.

The order of responses should be **R, A,** then **I.** You should retry the operation at least twice. If the condition persists, you must decide whether to abort the program or ignore the error. If you ignore the error, data may be lost. This is why **I** is the least desirable option.

ASSIGN
(Assign disk drive)   V2 - External

Purpose: Instructs DOS to use a disk drive other than the one specified by a program or command

Syntax: To reroute drive activity:

    ASSIGN d1=d2 ...

d1 is the letter of the disk drive that the program or DOS normally uses.

d2 is the letter of the disk drive that you want the program or DOS to use instead.

To clear the reassignment:

    ASSIGN

Exit Codes: None

Rules:
1. Any valid DOS drive may be reassigned to any other drive, but not to itself.

2. Do not use a colon after the disk drive letter, or spaces between the drive letters and the equal sign.

3. More than one assignment can be given on the same line. Use a space between each set of assignments (**ASSIGN B=C A=C**).

4. Some programs, such as DOS' DISKCOMP and DISKCOPY and Lotus' 1-2-3, completely or partially ignore the ASSIGN command.

*5. Do not use ASSIGN with the DOS V2 PRINT command.

6. Use ASSIGN only when necessary.

*7. Do not assign a disk drive to a drive that is not on your system. DOS will give an error message only when you attempt to use the improperly assigned drive.

Examples: A.   **ASSIGN A=C**

tells DOS to reroute activity for drive A to drive C.

B.   **ASSIGN A=C B=C**

tells DOS to reroute requests for activity for drives A and B to drive C.

C.   **ASSIGN**

clears any previous drive reassignment.

Notes: ASSIGN is included in DOS V2 for programs that do not allow you to specify the disk drive to be used. Some accounting and word-processing programs assume that only two disk drives are possible: the minifloppy disk drives A: and B:. Because the hard disk is drive C, the ASSIGN command is used to "trick" programs into using the hard disk rather than the floppy disk drive. This command will be used less frequently as newer versions of programs allow the user to specify which disk drive the program should use.

The ASSIGN command does not work with all programs. Some programs make a special request to DOS to read a specific part of the diskette in the floppy disk drive. ASSIGN cannot intercept and reroute these special requests. In these cases, your only choice is to have the floppy, which the program wants, in the disk drive.

Don't ASSIGN a real disk drive to a nonexistent disk drive. ASSIGN will assume that you are giving it the correct information and will not give an error message. DOS, however, will give an error message when you attempt to use the improperly assigned drive. If you have only three disk drives on your system and type the line

ASSIGN A=D

DOS will issue an Invalid drive specification message when you attempt to use drive A. Use the ASSIGN command again to specify the correct disk drive.

Message: Invalid parameter

ERROR: You did one of the following: (1) put a colon after one or more drive letters; (2) used a space between the drive letter and the equal sign; (3) did not type all the information that ASSIGN wanted; or (4) did not correctly phrase the command.

BACKUP
(Back up the hard disk)   V2 - External

Purpose: Backs up one or more files from a hard disk onto one or more floppy diskettes

Syntax: **BACKUP d1:***path\filename.ext* **d2:** */S/M/A/D:mm-dd-yy*

d1: is the hard disk to be backed up.

path is the starting directory path for backup.

filename.ext is the name of the file(s) you want to back up. Wild cards are allowed.

d2: is the floppy disk drive that will receive the backup files.

Switches: */S* Backs up all *subdirectories*, starting with the specified or current directory on the hard disk and continuing down

/M Backs up all files that have been *modified* since the last time you backed up. This switch backs up any file that has been changed or created since the last time you used BACKUP.

/A *Adds* the file(s) to be backed up to the files already on the specified floppy disk drive. Without this switch, DOS will erase the files on the floppy diskette. DOS expects the correct diskette to be in the drive when a */A* option is used

/D Backs up any file that was changed or created, on or after the specified *date*. The *date* appears in the following form:

mm = month
dd = day
yy = year

Use a colon after the */D* and a minus sign (-) or a slash (/) between the numbers in the date, but do not put spaces between the switch (*/D:*) and the date.

Exit Codes: *0* = Successful backup
1 = No files found to be backed up

2 = Aborted by the user (Ctrl-Break or Ctrl-C)

3 = Aborted because of an error

Rules:

1. You must give both a source and a destination for backup.

2. If the hard disk is not the current drive, the source must start with the hard disk drive name.

3. Whether or not you give a disk drive name, the source may be the following:

   A. A file name with appropriate extensions, if desired. Wild cards are permitted.

   B. A valid directory path

   C. Both of the above

4. The destination is any valid floppy disk drive name.

5. If you do not give:

   A. A source drive name, the current disk drive will be used. If it is not the hard disk, DOS will give you an error message and end the BACKUP command.

   B. A source directory path, the current directory will be used.

   C. A source file name, all files in the specified directory will be backed up.

   D. Any of the above, an Invalid parameters error message will be given.

6. You must have a sufficient number of floppy diskettes formatted before you invoke the BACKUP command. BACKUP will not work on nonformatted or non-DOS diskettes. If you do not have enough formatted diskettes, you will have to restart BACKUP after formatting more of them.

7. To keep the files on a previously backed-up diskette, use the /A option. If you do not use this option, anything previously stored on the diskette(s) will be destroyed. To use the /A option, start with a diskette that contains the special file created by BACKUP: BACKUPID.@@@. Otherwise, BACKUP will give you an error message and abort.

8. If you do not use the /A option, DOS will prompt you to insert the first backup diskette. If you *do* use this option, the backup diskette must be

in the correct drive before you enter the command line. DOS will not wait for you to put a diskette into the drive when you use the /A switch.

9. DOS prompts you to change diskettes. Make sure that you insert the correct diskette into the disk drive when you are prompted.

10. You can only retrieve BACKed UP files with the RESTORE command.

11. BACKUP follows the VERIFY command. For example, if VERIFY is off, the newly created BACKUP files on the floppy diskette are not checked to see if they were recorded correctly. If VERIFY is on, DOS will check to ensure that the files are correctly stored.

*12. The switch character SWITCHAR must not be set. If it is, you will not be able to restore the backed-up files. (See Chapter 10 on the CONFIG.SYS file.)

Examples: Refer to the Sample Hierarchical Directory in Appendix B. Suppose that this sample directory is the directory of the hard disk. This figure is used here to show the effects of the different commands. For each example, the current directory appears before the command line.

A. root

	Command	What It Backs Up
(1)	BACKUP C: A:	IBMBIO.COM, IBMDOS.COM,
(2)	BACKUP C:*.* A:	AUTOEXEC.BAT, CONFIG.SYS
(3)	BACKUP C:\ A:	VDISK.SYS
(4)	BACKUP C:*.* A:	

These four commands all have the same effect. They back up only the files in the root directory.

B. LETTERS

	Command	What It Backs Up
(1)	BACKUP C: A:	IBM.BAK, IBM.TXT
(2)	BACKUP C:*.* A:	JACK.BAK, JACK.TXT
(3)	BACKUP C:.*.* A:	DOUG.LET
(4)	BACKUP C:\WORDS\LETTERS A:	
(5)	BACKUP C:\WORDS\LETTERS*.* A:	
(6)	BACKUP . A:	

These six commands also have the same effect. They back up all files in the directory LETTERS.

Both Examples A-1 and B-1 tell DOS to back up to drive A all the files in the currently used directory on drive C. These examples assume that you are currently using the directory you want to back up. Because a file name is not given, BACKUP assumes that all files should be backed up.

The only difference between A-1/B-1 and A-2/B-2 is that in the latter, the *.* wild card was given. In this instance, giving an *.* is the same as not giving a file name. If you do not give a drive or path name, you must use **BACKUP *.* A:** because BACKUP must have a source name.

The third example line, B-3, and its counterpart, A-3, are phrased differently, and each has a different meaning, although the apparent effect is the same. Example A-3 explicitly tells DOS to back up all files in the root directory. A backslash (\) at the beginning of a path name tells DOS to start with the root directory of the disk. Because the root directory is the only specified directory on the path, only its contents are backed up.

Example B-3 tells DOS to back up the files in the current directory. When a period (current directory symbol) is used as a path name, the effect is the same as giving no path at all.

The major difference between A-3 and B-3 is that A-3 is an absolute path reference, whereas B-3 is relative. No matter what directory you are using on drive C, A-3 will always back up the root directory, and B-3 will always back up the current directory.

Example A-4 is the same as A-3, except that in the former the *.* wild-card file name was used.

Examples B-4 and B-5 are also the same. Both back up all files in the LETTERS subdirectory on the disk. Similar to A-3, Examples B-4 and B-5 will have the same effect because these commands explicitly state the directory to be used for the backup (the last named directory in the chain, or path).

Example B-6 has the same result as B-3. The period (current directory symbol) in B-6 is used without a file name. Because BACKUP assumes that you mean all files if no file name is given, the form in B-6 has the same effect as that in B-3. Since no file name is given in Example B-3, the backslash (\) after the path name is not given.

C. LETTERS

Command	What It Backs Up
(1) **BACKUP C:*.LET A:**	IBM.LET, JACK.LET
(2) **BACKUP C:\WORDS\LETTERS*.LET A:**	DOUG.LET

Examples C-1 and C-2 back up all files ending with the extension .LET in the subdirectory LETTERS. The difference between C-1 and C-2 is that C-2 can be given while you are using a directory other than LETTERS; but to use C-1, however, the current directory must be LETTERS.

D. root

Command	What It Backs Up
(1) **BACKUP C: A: /S**	All files on C:
(2) **BACKUP C:\ A: /S**	

These examples use the **/S** switch. It tells DOS to start with the directory indicated and continue downward through all of its subdirectories. Examples D-1 and D-2 do the same thing: they back up all files on drive C. There is one major difference, however. Example D-2 will work the same way regardless of the directory you are using. But Example D-1 will back up all the files on C only if the current directory is the root directory.

E. DOS

Command	What It Backs Up
(1) **BACKUP C:\ A: /S**	All files on the disk
(2) **BACKUP C: A: /S**	All files in the DOS, BASIC, UTIL, HARDDISK, SAMPLES, and TEST directories

Examples D-2 and E-1 are identical, as are Examples D-1 and E-2. D-2 and E-1 back up all the files on the disk. The key is the indicated path. In D-2 and E-1, the root directory symbol is given for the path. No matter which directory is the current one on C:, BACKUP will start at the root directory.

This condition is not true in Examples D-1 and E-2. Because no path is given, BACKUP starts with the current directory and works downward through any additional subdirectories. A common mistake is to be in a subdirectory and use Example D-1/E-2 when you really want to back up the entire disk. To back up the entire disk, use Example D-2/E-1.

F. root

Command	What It Backs Up
(1) **BACKUP C:\ A: /S /D:8/21/83**	All files that have been changed
(2) **BACKUP C:\ A: /S /D:08-21-83**	or created since August 21, 1983

This command directs BACKUP to back up all files that have been created or changed since August 21, 1983. Examples F-1 and F-2 say the same thing. They show that slashes and minus signs are acceptable between the numbers in dates, and that leading zeros are not necessary with one-digit months or days. Note that no spaces can exist between the starting slash of the switch and the ending number for the year.

G. root

Command	What It Backs Up
BACKUP C:\ A: /S /D:08-21-83 /A	All files that have been created or
	changed since August 21, 1983

Similar to Example F-1, this command also backs up all hard disk files that have been changed or created since the given date. The difference here is that the **/A** switch directs BACKUP to add these files to the backup diskette without deleting the old files. Without the **/A** switch, any files on the diskette will be erased.

When you give the **/A** switch, you must have a backup diskette in the diskette drive. BACKUP does not prompt you to put a diskette into the drive but immediately attempts to use the diskette in the specified drive. The diskette you use must also be a backup diskette. BACKUP will check the diskette for the special file BACKUPID.@@@. If this file is not on the diskette, BACKUP will tell you that you have the wrong diskette and will abort.

H. root

Command	What It Backs Up
BACKUP C:\ A: /S /M	All files that have been changed or
	created since the last time you ran
	BACKUP or that were not BACKed
	UP before

The **/M** switch tells BACKUP to back up any files that do not have the *archive bit* set. An archive bit is a special area kept in the directory for each file. When you create or modify a file, the archive bit is off. When you back up a file, BACKUP turns on the archive bit.

When you use the **/M** switch, BACKUP will skip any file whose archive bit is turned on. This means that BACKUP will back up any file or version of a file you have not backed up before.

Naturally, if you create a file, BACKUP will select this file for backup. If you change a file, BACKUP will also select it. However, backing up a portion of a hard disk may cause some confusion later on. Suppose you BACKUP part of a disk and later BACKUP the complete disk with the **/M** switch. In this case, BACKUP will back up the following:

1. All files in the portion of the disk you had not backed up earlier

2. All files in the previously backed-up portion that have been modified or created since your first BACKUP

The second running of BACKUP will probably select more files than the first running. This selection should not alarm you; BACKUP is simply doing what you requested.

(For some hints and more information on the BACKUP command, see Chapter 12.)

Messages:
1. ✱✱✱ Backing up files to diskette xx ✱✱✱

   INFORMATIONAL: BACKUP gives this message as it archives the files from the hard disk to the floppy diskettes. xx is the number of the backup diskette—a sequential number starting with 1. After this message, you will see a list of the files that are being backed up. The complete path name and file name will be displayed for each file.

2. Diskette is not a backup diskette

   ERROR: The diskette that you inserted into the drive was not created by BACKUP. This message occurs only with the first diskette when you use the **/A** (add) switch. BACKUP aborts after displaying this message.

   Check the diskette in the drive you have specified. Remember that BACKUP does not wait for you to insert a diskette into the floppy disk drive when you have given the **/A** switch. The first file in the diskette's directory should be BACKUPID.@@@. Place the proper diskette into the disk drive and try BACKUP again.

3. `Insert backup diskette xx in drive d:`
    `Warning! Diskette files will be erased`
    `Strike any key when ready`

    INFORMATIONAL AND WARNING: This message appears during
    the BACKUP process. The message should not appear on the first
    backup diskette if you used the /A (add) switch, but will appear for the
    second, and every subsequent, backup diskette.

    This message warns you that any information on the diskette will be
    erased before the BACKed-UP files are added.

    Insert the proper diskette into the drive and strike a key to continue
    BACKUP.

4. `Invalid date`

    ERROR: You gave a space between the /D switch and the date, or you
    gave an impossible date.

5. `WARNING! No files were found to back up`

    WARNING: No files on the fixed disk matched the file specification
    you gave to BACKUP. Check the spelling of the path and file names,
    then do a directory of the hard disk to see whether the files you want to
    back up are located there.

Batch Command   V1** and V2** - Internal

Purpose: Executes one or more commands contained in a disk file

Syntax: *d:* **filename** *parameters*

                  d: is the name of the disk drive holding the batch file.

                  filename is the root name of the batch file.

                  parameters are the optional parameters to be used by the batch file.

Exit Codes: None

Rules for Executing Batch Files:

1. A batch file must have the extension .BAT.

2. If you do not give a disk drive name, the current disk drive will be used.

3. If the batch file is not in the current directory of the disk drive, DOS will search the directory(ies) specified by the PATH command to find the batch file.

4. To invoke a batch file, simply type its name. For example, to invoke the batch file OFTEN.BAT, type **OFTEN**.

5. DOS will execute each command one line at a time. The specified parameters will be substituted for the markers when the command is used.

6. DOS recognizes a maximum of ten parameters. You may use the SHIFT subcommand to get around this limitation.

7. If DOS encounters an incorrectly phrased batch subcommand when running a batch file, a Syntax error message will be displayed. DOS will ignore the rest of the commands in the batch file, and the system prompt will reappear.

8. You can stop a running batch file by typing Ctrl-Break, and DOS will display this message:

   Terminate batch job (Y/N)?_

If you answer **Y** for "yes," the rest of the commands will be ignored, and the system prompt will appear.

If you answer **N** for "no," DOS will skip the current command but will continue processing the other commands in the file.

9. DOS remembers which disk holds the batch file. If you remove the diskette that holds the batch file, DOS will prompt you to place that diskette into the original drive to get the next command.

10. DOS remembers which directory holds the batch file. Your batch file may change directories at any time.

11. You can make DOS execute a second batch file immediately after finishing the first one by entering the name of the second batch file as the last command in the first file.

12. Batch subcommands are only valid for batch files. The batch subcommands cannot be executed as normal DOS commands. (See Notes.)

Rules for the AUTOEXEC.BAT File:

1. The file must be called AUTOEXEC.BAT and reside in the root directory of the boot disk.

2. The contents of the AUTOEXEC.BAT file conform to the rules for creating batch files.

3. When DOS is booted, it automatically executes the AUTOEXEC.BAT file.

4. When AUTOEXEC.BAT is executed after DOS is booted, the date and time are not requested automatically. To get the current date and time, you must put the DATE and TIME commands into the AUTOEXEC.BAT file.

Rules for Creating Batch Files:

1. A batch file contains ASCII text. You may use the DOS command COPY; EDLIN, the DOS line editor; or another text editor to create a batch file. If you use a word processor, make sure that it is in the programming, or nondocument, mode.

2. The root name of a batch file can be one to eight characters long and must conform to the rules for file names.

3. The file name extension must be .BAT.

4. A batch file should not have the same root name as a program file (a file ending with .COM or .EXE) in the current directory. Nor should an internal DOS command, such as COPY or DATE, be used as a root name. If you use one of these root names, DOS will not know whether you want to execute the batch file, the program, or the command.

5. Any valid DOS commands that you can type at the keyboard may be entered. You may also use the parameter markers (%0-%9) and the batch subcommands.

6. You may enter any valid batch subcommand. (Batch subcommands are listed in this section.)

7. To use the percent sign (%) in a command for a file name, enter the percent symbol twice. For example, to use a file called A100%.TXT, enter A100%%.TXT. This does not apply to the parameter markers (%0-%9).

Notes: Two batch subcommands, ECHO and PAUSE, are accepted by DOS as system commands. However, the usefulness of these two commands at the command level is uncertain.

(For further information on batch files and subcommands, see Chapter 9.).

Batch Commands
ECHO subcommand   V2 Only

Purpose: Displays a message and allows or inhibits the display of batch commands and messages by other batch subcommands as the commands are executed by DOS

Syntax: To display a message:

ECHO *message*

To turn off the display of commands and messages by other batch commands:

ECHO OFF

To turn on the display of commands and messages:

ECHO ON

message is the text of the message to be displayed on the video display.

Rules:
1. To display unconditionally a message on the video screen, use **ECHO** *message*.

2. When ECHO is on, all commands in the batch file are displayed as each line is executed. Any messages from the batch subcommands are also displayed.

3. When ECHO is off, the commands in the batch file are not displayed as they are executed by DOS. In addition, messages produced by other batch subcommands are not displayed. The exceptions to this rule are the Strike any key when ready message by the PAUSE subcommand and any **ECHO** *message* commands.

4. A batch file starts with ECHO ON.

5. An ECHO OFF command is active only while the batch file executes. If one batch file invokes another, ECHO will be turned back on by DOS when the second batch file is invoked.

6. ECHO affects only messages produced by batch subcommands. It does not affect messages from other DOS commands or programs.

Note: The ECHO message is not the same as the REM message. REM is affected by an ECHO OFF command. The message with the REM subcommand will not be displayed if ECHO is off. The message on the line with ECHO will always be displayed.

Batch Commands
FOR..IN..DO subcommand

V2 Only

Purpose: Allows iterative (repeated) processing of a DOS command

Syntax: **FOR %%variable IN (set) DO command**

variable is a single letter.

set is one or more file specifications in the form *d: filename.ext*. Wild cards are allowed.

command is the DOS command to be performed for each file in the **set**.

Rules:

1. You may have more than one full file specification in the **set**. Each file specification should be separated by a space.

2. **%%variable** becomes each full file specification in the **set**. If you use wild-card characters, FOR..IN..DO will execute once for each file that matches the wild-card file specification.

3. Path names are not allowed. Each file for the **set** must be in the current directory of the disk drive, on either the current or the specified disk drive.

4. FOR..IN..DO subcommands cannot be nested, and you cannot put two of these subcommands on the same line. You may use other batch subcommands with FOR..IN..DO.

Batch Commands
GOTO subcommand   **V2 Only**

Purpose: Jumps (transfers control) to the line following the label in the batch file and
continues batch file execution from that line

Syntax: **GOTO label**

label is the name used for one or more characters, preceded by a colon. Only
the first eight characters of the label name are significant.

Rules: 1. The **label** must be the first item on a line in a batch file and must start
with a colon (:).

2. When the GOTO label is executed, DOS jumps to the line following the
label and continues execution of the batch file.

3. A label is never executed. DOS only uses the label as the jump-to
marker for the GOTO subcommand.

4. If you attempt to GOTO a nonexistent label, DOS will issue an error
message and stop processing the batch file.

Message: Label not found

ERROR: DOS could not find the specified label in a GOTO command. The
batch file is aborted, and the system prompt will reappear.

Batch Commands
IF subcommand   V2 Only

Purpose: Allows conditional execution of a DOS command

Syntax: **IF** *NOT* **condition command**

NOT tests for the opposite of the **condition** (executes the command if the condition is false).

condition is what is being tested. It may be one of the following:

ERRORLEVEL number—where DOS tests the exit code of the program. If the exit code is greater than or equal to the **number**, the condition is true.

string1==string2 —where DOS tests whether the two alphanumeric strings, **string1** and **string2**, are identical

EXIST *d:* **filename.***ext*—where DOS tests whether the file *d:* **filename.***ext* is current on the specified drive (if *d:* is given) or current disk drive

command is any valid command for a DOS batch file.

Rules:
1. For the IF subcommand, if the condition is true, the command is executed. If the condition is false, the command is skipped, and the next line of the batch file is immediately executed.

2. For the IF NOT subcommand, if the condition is false, the command is executed. If the condition is true, the command is skipped, and the next line of the batch file is immediately executed.

3. At present, only BACKUP and RESTORE use exit codes. Using ERRORLEVEL with a program that does not leave an exit code is meaningless.

4. In **string1==string2**, DOS makes a character-by-character comparison of the two strings, based on the ASCII character set.

5. When using **string1==string2** with the parameter markers (%0-%9), both strings must not be nulls (empty or nonexistent strings). DOS will give a Syntax error message and abort the batch file.

Batch Commands
PAUSE subcommand   V1 and V2
(Pause execution)

Purpose: Suspends batch file processing until a key is depressed and optionally displays the user's message

Syntax: **PAUSE** *message*

message is an optional message to be displayed.

Rules:
1. *message* is a series of up to 121 characters. It must be on the batch file line with the word PAUSE.

2. When DOS encounters a PAUSE subcommand in a batch file, DOS displays the optional *message* if ECHO is on. If ECHO is off, the optional *message* will not be displayed.

3. Regardless of ECHO's setting, DOS will display the message Strike a key when ready ....

4. DOS will suspend the processing of the batch file until any single key is depressed. After the key is depressed, DOS will continue processing the lines in the batch file. You may enter Ctrl-Break or Ctrl-C to end batch processing.

Batch Commands
REM subcommand   **V1 and V2**
(Show remark)

Purpose: Displays a message within the batch file

Syntax: **REM** *message*

message is an optional string of up to 123 characters.

Rules:
1. REM must be the last batch file command on the line when used with the IF or FOR..IN..DO subcommands.

2. The optional *message* can contain up to 123 characters and must immediately follow the word REM.

3. When DOS encounters a REM subcommand in a batch file, DOS will display the optional *message* if ECHO is on. If ECHO is off, the optional *message* will not be displayed.

4. The difference between the **ECHO** *message* and the **REM** *message* is that with ECHO, the message is always displayed. IF ECHO is off, the message with REM will not be displayed.

Batch Commands
SHIFT subcommand   V2 Only
(Shift parameters)

Purpose: Shifts one position to the left the parameters given on the command line
                   when the batch file was invoked

Syntax: **SHIFT**

Rules: 1.   When you SHIFT, the command line parameters are moved one
                        position to the left.

                   2.   When you SHIFT, DOS discards the former first parameter (%0).

BREAK
(Control Break)   V2 - Internal

Purpose: Tells DOS when to look for a Control Break to stop a program (Ctrl-C for MS-DOS and Ctrl-Break for PC DOS)

Syntax: To turn on BREAK:

BREAK ON

To turn off BREAK:

BREAK OFF

To find out whether BREAK is on or off:

BREAK

Rules:
1. BREAK is always either on or off.

2. If BREAK is on, DOS will look for the Control Break when performing any operation.

3. If BREAK is off, DOS checks for the Control Break only when performing operations with the following equipment:

   A. The terminal or keyboard/screen

   B. The printer

   C. The RS-232 (asynchronous) adapters

4. When you successfully set BREAK, no other message is displayed.

Notes: The BREAK command tells DOS when to check for Control Break. (Control Break aborts, or stops, the currently running program.) With programs that do very little input and output to the keyboard, screen, or printer (computation-bound programs), you may not be able to stop the program if something goes wrong. BREAK ON tells DOS to check for the Control Break before any DOS operation, including using the disk drives.

BREAK ON has little effect on disk performance. DOS works only 1 to 2 percent slower with BREAK on.

It is usually safe to have **BREAK** off, unless you are running long programs with little display, keyboard, or printer activity. In these cases, turn **BREAK** on before running the program and turn **BREAK** off after the program is finished.

The Ctrl-Break (or Ctrl-C) command does not work while the computer is "number crunching" but does work when a program is interacting with DOS. Using **BREAK ON** will not allow Ctrl-Break to stop a CPU-intensive, computative task.

This command is the same as the **BREAK** command in the configuration file in Chapter 11.

Message: Must specify ON or OFF

WARNING: You gave the **BREAK** command with some word other than ON or OFF.

CHDIR or CD
(Change directory)   V2 - Internal

Purpose: Changes the current directory or shows the path of the current directory

Syntax: To change the current directory:

    CHDIR *d:* **path**

or

    CD *d:* **path**

To show the current directory path on a disk drive:

    CHDIR *d:*

or

    CD *d:*

d: is a valid disk drive name.

path is a valid directory path.

Rules:
1. If you do not indicate a disk drive, DOS will use the current disk drive.

2. When you give a path name, DOS will move to the last directory specified in the **path**.

3. To start your move with the root directory of the disk, the first character in the path must be \; otherwise, DOS assumes that the path starts with the current directory.

4. If you give an invalid **path**, DOS will display an error message, and you will remain in the current directory.

Exit Codes: None

Examples: (Refer to Appendix B, the Sample Hierarchical Directory.)

To move from root to DOS, use

    CHDIR DOS

To move from root to UTIL, use

CHDIR DOS\UTIL

To move from UTIL back to DOS, use

CHDIR ..

or

CHDIR \DOS

These examples illustrate two different ways to move between directories. The first example shows how to move up to a parent directory. DOS does not permit movement by parent-directory name when you are in a subdirectory. Therefore, you cannot move up a level from UTIL to DOS by typing the line

CHDIR DOS

In this case, DOS will think that you are trying to move to a subdirectory of \UTIL with the name DOS, instead of trying to move up a level. The only way you can move up one level is by using the parent-directory symbol (..).

The second example illustrates how to move from the root directory of the disk to the correct directory. Notice that the first character in the directory name is the path character, the backslash (\). When a backslash is the first character in the path name, DOS returns to the root directory to begin its movement. In this example, we return to the root directory, then move down one level to the DOS subdirectory.

To move from UTIL to BASIC, use

CHDIR ..\BASIC

or

CHDIR \DOS\BASIC

The first example moves you up to the parent directory of UTIL, which is DOS, then down to the BASIC subdirectory. The second example begins the movement at the root directory, then moves down through DOS to BASIC. Although either method can be used, the first method may be easier to remember.

To move from UTIL to WORDS, use

CHDIR ..\..\WORDS

or

CHDIR\WORDS

This example is almost the same as the preceding one. Notice that we move up two directories (DOS and the root), then move down to WORDS. The second method, returning to the root directory and moving down one level, is the easier way because it involves typing fewer characters and is easier to remember.

To move from LETTERS to SAMPLES, use

CHDIR ..\..\DOS\BASIC\SAMPLES

or

CHDIR \DOS\BASIC\SAMPLES

These two examples do the same thing, but the second method is simpler.

Notes: CHDIR, or the shorthand CD, is the command used to maneuver through the hierarchical directories of DOS V2. The command is identical to the UNIX/XENIX command in name and use, except for the path separator. (UNIX and XENIX use the slash, /, rather than the backslash, \.) CD can always be typed in place of CHDIR.

There are two ways to maneuver through the hierarchical directories: (1) you can start at the root (top) directory of the disk and move down, or (2) you can start with the current directory and move up and/or down.

To start at the root directory of a disk, the path must begin with the path character (\), such as \ or **B:**\. When DOS sees the \ as the first character in the path, DOS will start with the root directory. Otherwise, DOS will assume that you start with the current directory.

To start forcibly the move with the current directory, use one of the subdirectory names or a parent-directory symbol (..). DOS will know that you are starting with your current directory. To move one level up, use the double period (..). DOS will move to the *parent directory* (the directory that holds the name of the current directory). A disk drive name can also precede the (..). Otherwise, use a subdirectory name that appears in the current directory.

To move more than one directory at a time, separate each directory name with the the path character (\). You can have as many directories chained together as you wish, provided that the total number of characters for the path is not more than 63.

You are not restricted to changing directories only on the current disk. For example, if the current drive is A: and your example directory disk is in drive B:, you can add **B:** in front of each path name, and your examples will work the same way.

Message: Invalid directory

ERROR: A directory you specified does not exist. This error can occur for one of several reasons: (1) your spelling of the directory name may be incorrect; (2) you forgot or misplaced the path character (\) between the directory names; or (3) the directory does not exist in the path you specified.

CHDIR will abort and remain in the current directory.

CHKDSK
(Check disk)   V1** and V2** - External

Purpose: Checks the directory and file allocation table (FAT) of the disk and reports disk and memory status. CHKDSK can also repair errors in the directories or FAT.

Syntax: **CHKDSK** *d:filename.ext/F/V*

 d: is the disk drive name to analyze.

 filename.ext is a valid DOS file name. Wild cards are allowed.

Switches: */F*   Fixes the file allocation table and other problems if errors are found

 /V   Shows CHKDSK's progress and more detailed information about the errors it finds (*Verbose*)

Rules: 1.   If no disk drive name is given, CHKDSK will use the current disk.

 2.   To check a diskette, make sure that the diskette you want to analyze is in the drive before you run CHKDSK.

 If you have a one-drive system and want to analyze a diskette that does not have CHKDSK on it, specify the tandem drive (that is, B: instead of A:).

 3.   CHKDSK V1.x automatically repairs the FAT. CHKDSK V2.x must be directed to make this repair with the */F* switch. CHKDSK V2.x will ask you to confirm the repairs before proceeding.

 4.   If you give a file name, with or without wild cards, CHKDSK will check the file(s) for continuity.

 *5.   Do not use a different version of CHKDSK with a different version of DOS (for example, V1.1 of CHKDSK with DOS V2.0). You can lose files if you do.

Examples: A.   **CHKDSK**

 analyzes the disk or diskette in the current drive.

B. **CHKDSK B:**

analyzes the diskette in drive B:.

C. **CHKDSK A: /F**

analyzes the diskette in drive A: and asks permission to repair the file allocation table (FAT) if a flaw is found. In case of a flaw, one of the messages may be the following:

```
xxx lost clusters found in xxx chains
Convert lost chains to files (Y/N)?_
```

If you answer **Y** for "yes," CHKDSK will convert the lost areas of the disk into files. These will appear in the root directory of the disk with the name *FILExxxx.CHK*, where *xxxx* is a consecutive number between 0000 and 9999. If these files do not contain anything useful, you may delete them.

D. **CHKDSK /V**

is the verbose mode, which lists each directory and subdirectory on the disk and each file in the directories. This output can be redirected to a file or printer.

E. **CHKDSK *.***

checks all files in the current directory on the current drive to see if they are stored contiguously on the disk. If the message

```
All specified file(s) are contiguous
```

appears, you are getting good disk performance. If the message

```
d:path\filename.ext
Contains xxx noncontiguous blocks
```

appears, the specified files are not stored contiguously on the disk. This message will appear for each file. If many files appear, you will probably want to COPY (not DISKCOPY) the files from the analyzed floppy diskette to another one, or, in the case of the hard disk, BACKUP your entire hard disk, reformat it, and RESTORE it.

What CHKDSK shows:

A. Volume name and creation date (only V2 disks with volume label)
B. Total disk space

C.   Number of bytes used for hidden or system files
D.   Number of bytes used for directories (V2.0 only)
E.   Number of bytes used for user (normal) files
F.   Bytes used by bad sectors (flawed disk space)
G.   Bytes available (free space) on disk
H.   Bytes of total memory (RAM)
I.   Bytes of free memory

CHKDSK shows that the sample directory diskette (in Appendix B) has the following:

Volume EXAMPLE DSK created Jun 23, 1983 11:36a

```
362496    bytes total disk space
 25528    bytes in 3 hidden files
  9216    bytes in 9 directories
323504    bytes in 30 user files
  7160    bytes available on disk

262144    bytes total memory
225280    bytes free
```

Because this diskette had no bad sectors, the Bytes in bad sectors message was not displayed.

Notes: CHKDSK checks the directory(ies) on the disk and the file allocation table. The command also checks the amount of memory in the system and how much of that memory is free. If CHKDSK finds any errors, it will report them on the screen before making a status report.

CHKDSK *filename* also checks to see if the specified file or files are stored contiguously on the disk. When you first use a disk, the individual 512-byte sections of the program or data files are stored in contiguous sectors (one after the other). After files have been erased and others added, DOS will attempt to store a new file in any open spot. This means that a large file may be stored in several noncontiguous places on the disk. DOS will slow down when reading this file because DOS must move the disk's recording head many times to read the entire file.

When CHKDSK *filename* is used, DOS reports whether any programs are stored noncontiguously and how many different sections the file or files are in.

If CHKDSK reports that many files on a floppy diskette are noncontiguous, you should format a new floppy diskette. Use the COPY *.* (not DISKCOPY) command to consolidate your files from the old diskette to the new one.

Read the chapter on disk storage (Chapter 4) for further information.

Messages: 1. `All specified file(s) are contiguous`

INFORMATIONAL: The files you specified are stored in contiguous sectors on the disk, and you are getting the best performance from this diskette.

2. `filename`
    `Allocation error for file, size adjusted`

WARNING: The file `filename` has an invalid sector number in the file allocation table (FAT). The file has been truncated by CHKDSK at the end of the last valid sector.

You should check this file to ensure that all information in the file is correct. If there is a problem, use your backup copy of the file. This message is usually displayed when the problem is in the FAT, not in the file. Your file should still be good.

3. `filename`
    `Contains invalid cluster, file truncated`

WARNING: The file `filename` has a bad pointer to a section on the disk in the FAT. If the /F (fix) switch was given, the file will be truncated at the last valid sector. Otherwise, no action will be taken.

You should check this file to see if all information is intact. If it is, CHKDSK can usually safely correct this problem without any loss of information in the file.

4. `filename`
    `Contains xxx noncontiguous blocks`

This message informs you that the file `filename` is not stored contiguously on the disk but in xxx number of pieces. If you find a large number of files in noncontiguous pieces, COPY the floppy to another one to increase performance. If you are using the hard disk, BACKUP the hard disk, format it, then RESTORE it.

5. `dirname`
    `Convert directory to file (Y/N)?`

    WARNING: The directory `dirname` contains so much bad
    information that it is no longer usable as a directory. If you respond **Y**,
    CHKDSK will convert the directory into a file so that you can use
    DEBUG or another tool to repair the directory. If you respond **N**, no
    action is taken.

    Respond **N** the first time you see this message. Try to copy any files you
    can from this directory to another disk. Check the copied files to see if
    they are usable. Then rerun CHKDSK to convert the directory into a
    file and try to recover the rest of the files.

6. `Disk error writing FAT x`

    WARNING: This message warns that a disk error was encountered
    while CHKDSK was attempting to put information into FAT 1 or FAT
    2 (as shown by the number x).

    If this message appears for either FAT 1 or FAT 2 on a floppy diskette,
    copy all your files from this diskette to another one. Then retire or
    reformat the bad diskette. If this message appears for the hard disk,
    BACKUP all files on the hard disk, reformat the hard disk, then
    RESTORE it.

    If this message appears for both FAT 1 and FAT 2, the diskette is
    unusable. Copy any files you can to another diskette and retire or
    reformat the diskette after you have taken off all the information you
    can from the diskette.

7. `.`

    or

    `..`
    `Entry has a bad attribute`

    or

    `Entry has a bad size`

    or

    `Entry has a bad link`

WARNING: The link to the parent directory (..) or the current directory (.) has a problem. If you gave the /F switch, CHKDSK will attempt to repair the problem. This procedure is normally a safe one, which does not carry the risk of losing files.

8. `Error found, F parameter not specified`
`Corrections will not be written to the disk`

INFORMATIONAL: An error has been found by CHKDSK. This message tells you that CHKDSK will go through the steps to repair (fix) the disk but will not actually make any changes to it because you did not give the /F switch.

If you see this message, you can freely answer **Y** to any CHKDSK message, knowing that the disk or diskette will not be changed. You will see what possible actions CHKDSK will take to correct the error it found. However, this message also means that your diskette still has problems. You will have to run CHKDSK with the /F switch to fix the disk.

9. `filename1`
`Is cross linked on cluster x`
`filename2`
`Is cross linked on cluster x`

WARNING: Two files—`filename1` and `filename2`—have an entry in the FAT that points to the same area of the disk (cluster). In other words, the two files "think" that they own the same piece of the diskette.

CHKDSK will take no action on this problem. You will have to handle it yourself. You should do the following:

A.   Copy both files to another diskette
B.   Delete the files from the original diskette
C.   Edit the files as necessary

Each file may have some garbage in it.

10. `filename`
`First cluster number is invalid,`
`entry truncated`

WARNING: The file `filename`'s first entry in the FAT refers to a nonexistent portion of the disk. If you gave the /F switch, the file will become a zero-length file (truncated).

Try to copy this file to another diskette before CHKDSK truncates the file. You may not get a useful copy, however, and the original file will be lost.

11. `Insufficient room in root directory`
    `Erase files from root and repeat CHKDSK`

    ERROR: CHKDSK has recovered so many "lost" clusters from the disk that the root directory is full. CHKDSK will abort at this point.

    Examine the FILExxxx.CHK files. If there is nothing useful in them, delete them. Then rerun CHKDSK with the /F switch to continue recovering "lost" clusters.

12. `dirname`
    `Invalid subdirectory`

    WARNING: The directory `dirname` has invalid information in it. CHKDSK will attempt to repair this directory. For more specific information about the problem with the directory, do *one* of the following:

    A.   Enter

    CHKDSK /V

    B.   Move into the faulty directory, if you can, and enter

    CHKDSK *.* /V

The verbose mode will tell you more about what is wrong.

13. `Probable non-DOS disk.`
    `Continue (Y/N)?_`

    WARNING: The special byte in the FAT indicates that your diskette is a DOS diskette, but the diskette was either not formatted, was formatted under a different operating system, or is badly damaged.

    If you used the /F switch, answer **N**. Recheck the diskette without the /F (fix) switch, then answer **Y** to the question. See what action DOS takes. Then, if your diskette is a DOS diskette, run CHKDSK again with the /F switch.

    If you did not use the /F switch, answer **Y** and see what action DOS takes. Then decide if you want to rerun CHKDSK /F to correct the diskette.

14. Processing cannot continue, message

ERROR: This error message indicates that CHKDSK is aborting because of an error. message will tell you what the problem is. The likely culprit is lack of enough RAM memory to check the diskette. This message occurs most often with 64K systems.

You may have to increase the amount of memory in your computer or "borrow" another computer to check the diskette.

15. Tree past this point not processed

WARNING: CHKDSK is unable to continue down the indicated directory path because of a bad track.

Copy all files from the disk to another floppy. The original diskette may not be usable any more, and you may have lost some files.

16. xxxxxxxxxx bytes disk space freed

INFORMATIONAL: CHKDSK has regained some disk space that was improperly marked as *in use*. xxxxxxxxxx will tell you how many additional bytes are now available. To free this disk space, review and delete any *FILExxxx.CHK* that does not contain useful information.

17. xxx lost clusters found in yyy chains

INFORMATIONAL: Although CHKDSK has found xxx blocks of data allocated in the FAT, no file on the disk is using these blocks. They are lost clusters, which normally may be safely freed by CHKDSK if no other error or warning message is given.

See the message Convert lost clusters to files and the examples in the Notes section for additional information.

CLS
(Clear screen)   V2 - Internal

Purpose: Erases the display screen

Syntax: **CLS**

Rules:
1. All information on the screen is cleared, and the cursor is placed at the home position (upper left-hand corner).

2. This command affects only the currently active video display.

3. If you have used the ANSI control codes to set the foreground and background, the colors will remain in effect.

4. If you have not set the foreground/background color, the screen will revert to light characters on a dark background.

5. CLS does not affect memory, disk storage, or anything else.

COMP
(Compare files)   **V1 and V2 - External**

Purpose: Compares two sets of disk files to see if they are the same or different

Syntax: **COMP** *d1:path1\filename1.ext1 d2:path2\filename2.ext2*

d1: is the drive containing the first set of files to be compared.

path1 is the path to the first set of files.

filename1.ext1 is the file name for the first set of files. Wild cards are allowed.

d2: is the drive containing the second set of files to be compared.

path2 is the path to the second set of files.

filename2.ext2 is the file name for the second set of files. Wild cards are allowed.

d1 and *d2* may be the same.

path1 and *path2* may be the same.

filename1.ext1 and *filename2.ext2* may also be the same.

Special Terms: *d1:path1\filename1.ext1* is the *primary* file set.

d2:path2\filename2.ext2 is the *secondary* file set.

Rules:
1. If you do not give a drive name for a set, the current disk drive is used. (This rule applies to *d1:* and *d2:*).

2. If you do not give a path for a set, the current path for the drive is used.

3. If you do not enter a file name for a set, all files for that set (primary or secondary) will be compared (same as entering ***.***). However, only files in the secondary set whose names match files in the primary set will be compared.

4. If you do not enter a drive name, path name, and file name, COMP will prompt you for the primary and secondary file sets to compare.

5. Only normal disk files are checked. Hidden or system files and directories are not checked.

6. Files with matching names, but different lengths, are not checked. A message is printed to indicate that these files are different.

7. After ten mismatches (unequal comparisons) between the contents of two COMPed files, COMP automatically ends the comparison between the two files and aborts.

Examples: A.   **COMP A:IBM.LET C:IBM.LET**

compares the file in the current directory on drive A:, IBM.LET, with the file in the current directory on drive C:, IBM.LET.

B.   **COMP *.TXT *.BAK**

compares files with the extension .TXT with files that end with the extension .BAK on the current disk in the current directory.

C.   **COMP A:\WORDS\LETTERS\DOUG.LET B:DOUG.LET**

compares the file DOUG.LET on drive A: in the subdirectory LETTERS with the file DOUG.LET in the current directory on drive B:.

D.   **COMP C:\WORDS\DAVID C:\WORDS\MIKE**

compares all files in the subdirectory DAVID on drive C: with the subdirectory MIKE, also on drive C:. Note that DAVID and MIKE must be directories, not files, and that by not giving a file name, COMP assumes *.* (all files).

Sample Session

This example first compares one file with another, then compares a set of files on one disk to a set of files with the same names on the hard disk.

A>**COMP**

Enter primary file name
FIXIT.C   {I enter the first file name.}
Enter 2nd file name or drive id
FIXIT1.C   {Then enter the second name, or disk name.}

A:FIXIT   .C and FIXIT1   .C   {DOS gives the file names.}

Compare error at offset 36A
File 1 = 78
File 2 = 62

{There was a mismatch. The offset is the number of bytes into the file where the mismatch occurred. The displayed differences are in hexadecimal format (base 16). 78 hex is the letter X; 62 hex is the letter B. These are the only differences between the two files.}

Compare more files (Y/N)? **Y**
Enter primary file name
*.C
Enter 2nd file name or drive id

{Now compare all files that end with .C against the files on drive C: with the same names.}

C:

A:FIXIT   .C and C:FIXIT   .C

Files compare ok.

A:TEST87 .C and C:TEST87 .C

Files compare ok

A:CHECKSUM.C and C:CHECKSUM.C

Files compare ok
Compare more files (Y/N) **N**
A>

{All files match.}
{So we'll quit.}

Notes: COMP is the utility used in comparing files. Its ideal use is to ensure that the files you have just COPYed are correct, or to check a known good copy of a program against a questionable copy. If you have a program that formerly functioned properly but is now acting strangely, check a good backup copy of the file against the copy you are currently using. If there are differences, copy the good program onto the diskette you are using.

Don't try to use a copy of the program that has been archived with the BACKUP program. You will find differences because BACKUP adds additional information to the front of the file. If your only backup copy of a program is on a BACKed UP diskette, use RESTORE to place the file in a directory, then COMPare the files. If the program still resides in the same directory as its BACKUPed copy, first copy the program to a different directory, then RESTORE the BACKed-UP version. If you do not do this, the current copy of the program will be replaced by the BACKed-UP version.

When you are trying to find the last revision of a file, look at the date and time stamp in the directory instead of using COMP. Often you can identify much faster the most recent revision of a file through this method rather than by using COMP. If you wish to compare two entire diskettes that have been DISKCOPYed, use DISKCOMP instead of COMP.

Messages: 1.   Compare error at offset xxxxxxxx

INFORMATIONAL: The files you are comparing are not the same. The difference occurs xxxxxxxx bytes from the beginning of the file. (The number given is in hexadecimal, base 16.) The different values for the two bytes in the files are also displayed in hexadecimal format.

2.   EOF mark not found

INFORMATIONAL or WARNING: This message is informational if the files you are comparing are program files. The message is a warning if the files you are comparing are text files. The message indicates that COMP could not find the customary end-of-file (EOF) marker (a Ctrl-Z, 1A hex). COMP got to the end of the file before it found the end-of-file marker.

This is not a problem for program files and some data files, but it is a problem for text files. COMP always compares the files based on each file's length in the directory. Sometimes files are saved with extraneous information after the end-of-file marker. As a result, you may get a compare error for the extra bytes. Check that the text files are intact. If the file is okay, COMP was comparing the extraneous part of the file.

3.   Files are different sizes

WARNING: COMP will compare only files that are the same size. You have asked COMP to compare two files that are of different lengths. COMP will skip the comparison.

4.   10 Mismatches-ending compare

Warning: COMP found ten mismatches between the two files you were comparing. COMP, therefore, assumes that there is no reason to continue and aborts the comparison between these two files.

COMMAND
(Invoke secondary command processor)   V2 - Internal

Purpose: Invokes a second copy of COMMAND.COM, the command processor

Syntax: **COMMAND** *d:path* */P* */C string*

           d: is the drive name where DOS can find a copy of COMMAND.COM.

           path is the DOS path to the copy of COMMAND.COM.

Switches: */P*   Keeps this copy *permanently* in memory (until the next system reset)

           /C   Passes this set of *commands* (the *string*) to the new copy of COMMAND.COM. A *string* is the set of characters you pass to the new copy of the command interpreter.

Rules: 1.   You may load only additional copies of COMMAND.COM.

           2.   The *string* in the */C* option is interpreted by the additional copy of COMMAND.COM as if you typed it at system level (A>). The */C* must be the last switch used on the line. Do not use the form **COMMAND /C string /P**.

           3.   You can exit from the second copy of the command processor by issuing the command, **EXIT**, if you have not used the */P* option (permanent).

Note: COMMAND is an advanced DOS command that is not recommended for use by newcomers or novices. Consult the DOS manual for more information on this command.

COPY
(Copy files)   V1** and V2** - Internal

Purpose: Copies files between disk drives and/or devices, either keeping the same file name or changing it. COPY can join (concatenate) two or more files into another file, or append one or more files onto another file. Options allow special handling of text files and verification of the copying process.

Syntax: To copy a file:

    COPY /A/B d1:path1**filename1**.ext1/A/B
      d0:path2\\filename0.ext0/A/B/V

or

    COPY /A/B d1:path1**filename1**.ext1/A/B/V

To join several files into one file:

    COPY /A/B d1:path1**filename1**.ext1/A/B +
      d2:path2**filename2**.ext2/A/B + ... d0:path0**filename0**.ext0 /A/B/V

d1:, d2:, and d0: are valid disk drive names.

path1\\, path2\\, and path0\\ are valid path names.

filename1.ext1, **filename2**.ext2, and **filename0**.ext0 are valid file names. Wild cards are allowed.

The three dots (...) represent additional files in the form dx:pathx**filenamex**.extx.

Special Terms: The file that is being copied from is the *source* file. The names above with *1* and *2* are the source files.

The file that is being copied to is the *destination* file. It is represented by a *0*.

Switches: **/V**   Verifies that the copy has been recorded correctly

The next two switches have different effects for the source and the destination.

With the source file:

/A   Treats the file as an *ASCII* (text) file. The command copies all the information in the file up to, but not including, the end-of-file marker (a Ctrl-Z). Anything after the end-of-file marker is ignored.

/B   Copies the entire file (based on its size, as listed in the directory) as if it were a program file *(binary)*. The switch treats any end-of-file markers (Ctrl-Z) as normal characters and copies them.

With the destination file:

/A   Adds an end-of-file marker (Ctrl-Z) to the end of the file after it is copied. This ensures that the *ASCII* text file has a good end-of-file marker.

/B   Does not add the end-of-file marker to this *binary* file

Note: The meanings of the **/A** and **/B** switches come from their position in the line. DOS will use the **/A** or **/B** switch on the file that immediately precedes the switch and on all files after the switch *until* another **/A** or **/B** is encountered. When one of these switches is used before a **filename**, the switch will affect all files *until* another **/A** or **/B** is encountered.

Exit Codes: None

Rules: When you are copying files, if you give both the source and the destination, the following rules apply:

1.   The source name will come first, followed by the destination name.

2.   If you do not give a drive name, the current drive will be used.

3.   If you do not give a path, the current directory for the disk drive will be used.

4.   The following applies to the file name:

   A.   You must give a file name for the source. Wild cards are permitted.

   B.   If you do not give a destination file name, the copied file(s) will have the same name as the source file(s).

5.   You may substitute a device name for the complete source or destination name.

6. When copying between disk drives, COPY assumes that binary files are being copied (as if a */B switch* were given).

7. When copying to or from a device other than a disk drive, COPY assumes that ASCII files are being copied (as if the */A* switch were given).

8. A */A* or */B* switch will override the default COPY settings (Rules 5 and 6).

When you are copying files, if you give only one file specification, the following rules apply:

1. The file specification you give (*d1:path1***filename1**.*ext1*) is the source. It must have the following:

    A. A valid file name. Wild cards are permitted.

    B. A drive name, a path, or both. The drive name, path name, or both must be different from the respective current drive and current path.

2. The source cannot be a device name.

3. The destination is the current drive and current directory.

4. The copied file(s) will have the same name as the source file(s).

5. COPY assumes that binary files are being copied (as if a */B* switch were given).

When you are joining (concatenating) files, the following rules apply:

1. The destination file is the last file in the list, if there is no plus sign (+) before the file name. If you do not specify a destination file name, the first source name becomes the destination name.

2. If you do not give a drive name, the current drive is used.

3. If you do not give a path, the current directory is used.

4. The following applies to source files:

    *A. You must give a valid file name. Wild cards are permitted but can be dangerous. (See the discussion on COPY in Chapter 11.)

    B. After the first file name, any additional source file specifications must be preceded by a plus sign (+).

5. The following applies to the destination file:

    A. There can be only one destination. If you give a destination without wild cards, only one destination file is used. If you give a destination file name with wild cards, one or more destination files will be used.

    *B. If you do not give a destination, the first source file will also be used as the destination, resulting in:

        i.   The first file that matches the wild-card file name will be used as the destination file if you gave a wild card as part of the first source file name.

        ii. The files to be joined are appended to the end of the first source file.

(See Chapter 11 for examples of how the COPY command is used.)

Messages: 1. Cannot do binary reads from a device

ERROR: This message tells you one of two things:

    A. You have used a /B switch while attempting to copy something from a binary device. When copying from a device, DOS must have some way of determining where the information to be transferred ends. This indication is made with an end-of-file marker, the Ctrl-Z. DOS is acting intelligently. If there were no end-of-file marker, DOS would have no way of knowing when to complete the transfer and would wait forever.

    B. You have used a /B (binary) switch somewhere on the command line in front of the device name, probably just after the word COPY. Use the /B switch after the file name instead, or just omit the /B completely.

2. Invalid path or file name

ERROR: You gave a directory name or file name that does not exist, used the wrong directory name (a directory not in the path), or mistyped a name. COPY will abort at this point. If you used a wild card for a file name, COPY will transfer all valid files before issuing the error message.

Check to see which files were already transferred. Then check whether the directory and file names are spelled correctly and whether the path is correct, and try again.

3. Content of destination disk lost before copy

WARNING: A destination file was not the first source file. The previous contents have been destroyed. COPY will continue concatenating the remaining files, if any.

For more information see COPY in Chapter 11.

CTTY
(Change console)   V2 - Internal

Purpose: Changes the standard input and output device to an auxiliary console and/or back from an auxiliary console to the keyboard and video screen

Syntax: **CTTY device**

                 device is the name of the device you want to use as the new standard input and output device. This name must be a valid DOS device name.

Exit Codes: None

Rules: 1. **device** should be a character-oriented device capable of both input and output.

                 2. Do not use a colon after the device name.

                 3. Programs that are designed to work with the video display's control codes may not function properly when redirected.

                 4. CTTY does not affect any other form of redirected I/O or piping. For example, the <, the >, and the | work as usual.

Examples: A. **CTTY COM1**

                 makes the device attached to COM1 the new console. The peripheral connected to COM1 must be a terminal or a teleprinter (printer with a keyboard). After this command is given, DOS expects normal input to come from COM1 and puts anything for the video display to COM1.

                 B. **CTTY CON**

                 makes the keyboard and the video display the console. In effect, this command cancels the first example but must be typed on the currently active console.

Notes: The CTTY command was designed so that a terminal or teleprinter, rather than the IBM PC's keyboard and video screen, can be used for console input and output. This added versatility has little effect on most Personal Computer users.

You must specify a device that can both input and output characters with the computer system. Using CTTY with a normal printer (one that is output only) is a mistake. DOS will patiently wait forever for you to type commands on the printer's nonexistent keyboard. In other words, the computer will "go west" and will have to be reset before it can be used again.

Message: Invalid device

ERROR: You specified an invalid device name. Your spelling may be incorrect, or DOS does not "know" the device. Perhaps you specified a device that is not character oriented or added a colon (:) after the device name.

DATE
(Set/show date)   V1 and V2 - Internal

Purpose: Displays and/or changes the system date

Syntax: **DATE** *mm-dd-yy*

or

DATE *mm-dd-yyyy*

mm is a one- or two-digit month (1 to 12).

dd is a one- or two-digit day (1 to 31).

In the first option:

yy is a one- or two-digit year (80 to 99—the 19 is assumed).

In the second option:

yyyy is a four-digit year (1980 to 2099).

Exit Codes: None

Rules:
1. When you enter a correctly phrased date with this command, DOS will set the date and return to the system prompt.

2. If you do not enter a date, DOS will display a date that may or may not be correct. You can then do the following:

    A.   Enter a correctly phrased date, which DOS will use as the new date, and hit the Enter key.

    B.   Hit the Enter key, and

    DOS will continue to use the same date.

3. You may use either the minus sign (-) or the slash (/) between the month and day and between the day and year.

4. Entering an incorrectly phrased or nonsense date (such as 02/29/85, 06/31/83, or 06:03:1983) will cause DOS to display an error message and a request to try again.

Sample Session: _____

A> **DATE 07/31/83**   {The DATE command was run with a
                                        correctly phrased date, July 31, 1983.
A>   DOS accepts the date and returns to the
                                        system prompt.}

A> **DATE**   {DATE is invoked, shows the current date, and
                                        allows you to reset the date. When a new
Current Date is Sun 7-31-1983   date is entered, DOS returns to the system
                                        level.}
Enter new date: **8/1/83**

A>**DATE**   {Check to see if DOS did use the new date.}

Current Date is Mon 8-01-1983

Enter new date: **<Enter>**

{In this case, DATE displayed the correct date, so hit <Enter>. DOS will not change the date
but will return to the system prompt.}

A>

Notes: When you boot DOS, it issues the DATE and TIME commands to set
                correctly your system clock. If the AUTOEXEC.BAT file is on the boot
                diskette, DOS will not ask for the date or time. You may include the DATE
                or TIME command if you want these functions to be set when DOS is
                booted.

                Every time you create or update a file, DOS updates the directory with the
                date you enter. The date stamp lets you see which copy is the last revision of
                the file. The DOS BACKUP command will use the date stamp in selecting
                files to back up.

                The day-of-year calendar uses the time-of-day clock. If you leave your system
                on overnight the day will advance by one at midnight. DOS also knows about
                leap years and appropriately adjusts its calendar. However, you must access
                this clock once each day, or DOS will not advance the date properly. If you
                leave your computer on over the weekend and return Monday, DOS will be
                one day behind.

The time-of-day clock built into most computers is a software clock. Its accuracy can vary. If you leave your system on constantly and do not reset it (system boot), the date will usually be accurate, but the time may not be.

Message: `Invalid date`

ERROR: You gave an impossible date or used the wrong type of character to separate the month, day, and year. This message will also occur if you enter the date with the Personal Computer's keypad when it is in the cursor-control mode rather than the numeric mode.

DEL
(Delete files)   V1 and V2 - Internal

Purpose: Deletes files from the disk

DEL is the shorthand form of ERASE. (See ERASE for a complete description.)

DIR
(Directory)   V1 and V2 - Internal

Purpose: Lists any or all of the files and subdirectories in a disk's directory

The DIR command shows the following:

Disk volume name (if any)
Name of the directory (its complete path)
Name of each disk file or subdirectory
Number of files
Amount, in bytes, of free space on the disk

The DIR command, unless otherwise directed, also shows the following:

Number of bytes occupied by each file
Date/time of the file's creation/last update

Syntax: **DIR** *d:path\filename.ext/P/W*

d: holds the disk you want to examine.

path is the path to the directory you want to examine.

filename.ext is a valid file name. Wild cards are allowed.

Switches: */P*   Pauses when the screen is full and waits for a keypress

/W   Gives a *wide* (80-column) display of the names of the files. The information about file size, date, and time is not displayed.

Rules: 1.   If you do not give a drive name, the current drive is used.

2.   If you do not give a path, the current directory is used.

3.   If you do not give a file name, all files in the directory will be displayed.

4.   The DIR command shows the contents of only one directory at a time.

Exit Codes: None

(For more information on DIR, see Chapter 11.)

Notes: The DIR command finds the disk files or subdirectories on the disk. This command shows only the files and subdirectories in the specified (or default) directory. To see a list of all the files on a disk, use either the CHKDSK /F or TREE /F command.

If you use the /W (wide) option, the file names and directory names will be listed with five names on a line. The file date and size are not printed, nor is the <DIR> for subdirectories. When you give the **DIR /W** command, you may have trouble deciding which file names refer to actual files and which refer to directories.

Message: File not found

ERROR: The path or file name you gave does not exist. The path may be incorrect, the file may not exist in the directory, or your spelling may be incorrect.

If you were doing a directory of another directory, you might move to the other directory (CHDIR) and try the command again.

If you still believe that the file should be in the directory, enter **DIR /P** to get the complete directory and check for the file.

Hints:

1. Before you ERASE files, using a wild-card character or characters, do a DIR with the same file name. If files that you do not want to erase are displayed, don't use that file name. Keep experimenting with the DIR command until you get the correct file name for the ERASE command, or issue separate ERASE commands without a wild-card character.

2. I/O redirection is easy with the DIR command. You can print the directory by typing **DIR >PRN**; or you can put a copy of the directory into a file by typing **DIR >filename**, where **filename** is the name of the file to hold the directory.

DISKCOMP
(Compare diskettes)

V1 and V2 - External

Purpose: Compares two diskettes on a track-for-track, sector-for-sector basis to see whether their contents are identical

Syntax: **DISKCOMP** *d1: d2: /1 /8*

d1: and *d2:* are the disk drives that hold the diskettes to be compared. (These drives may be the same disk drive or different drives.)

Switches:

/1 Compares only the *1*st side of the diskette, even if the diskette or disk drive is double-sided

/8 Compares only *8* sectors per track, even if the first diskette has nine sectors per track (DOS V2.0 format)

Rules:

1. If you do not give a drive name, the first floppy disk drive (usually drive A:) will be used.

2. If you give only one valid floppy disk drive name, it will be used for the comparison.

3. Giving the same valid floppy disk drive name twice is the same as giving only one disk drive name.

4. If you give a valid hard disk drive name, DOS will use the first floppy disk drive (same as Rule 1).

5. When using one disk drive (Rules 1-4), DOS will prompt you to change diskettes.

6. Only compatible diskettes should be compared. The two diskettes must be formatted with the same number of tracks, sectors, and sides.

Exit Codes: None

Examples:

A. **DISKCOMP A: B:**

compares the diskette in drive A: with the diskette in drive B:.

B. **DISKCOMP A: A:**

and

DISKCOMP

perform a single-drive comparison on drive A:. DOS will ask you to insert and change diskettes at the appropriate times. Then DOS will wait for you to hit a key before continuing.

C.   **DISKCOMP A: B: /1**

forces DOS to compare only the first side of the diskette in drive A: with the first side of the diskette in drive B:.

D.   **DISKCOMP A: B: /8**

forces DOS to compare only 8 sectors per side of the diskette in drive A: with 8 sectors of the diskette in drive B:.

Sample Session: —————————————————————————

This session demonstrates both a successful comparison and a failed comparison by DISKCOMP. In this example, a diskette is DISKCOPYed, then COPYed. The original diskette is then compared to the two copies. It has been in use for some time, and several BASIC programs have been added and deleted.

A>**DISKCOPY A: B:**   {First copy the diskette.}

```
Insert source diskette into drive A
Insert destination diskette into drive B
Strike any key when ready <Enter>

Copying 9 sectors per track, 2 side(s)        {It's a DOS V2.0 diskette.}
Copy complete
Copy another (Y/N)? N
```

A>**COPY A:*.* B:**   {Now I put a formatted diskette into drive B and copy the files.}

```
. . .
. . .
. . .

x file(s) copied
```

A>**DISKCOMP A: B:**   {Now I put the DISKCOPYed diskette back into drive B.}

```
Insert first diskette into drive A
Insert the second diskette into drive B
Strike any key when ready <Enter>
```

```
Comparing 9 sectors per track, 2 side(s)

Diskettes compare OK

Compare more diskettes (Y/N)? Y

Insert first diskette into drive A
Insert the second diskette into drive B        {I put the COPYed diskette into
                                                drive B.}
Strike any key when ready <Enter>

Compare error(s) on Track 9, side 1


  .  .  .
  .  .  .
  .  .  .

Compare more diskettes (Y/N)? N
A>
```

This session shows that the destination diskette made with DISKCOPY is identical to the original diskette. The message Diskettes compare OK indicates that the two diskettes are identical. Note that the destination diskette made with COPY failed the DISKCOMP. This was expected. When you COPY files from one diskette to another, they may not be placed in the identical spots on the new diskette. For this reason, DISKCOMP indicated that the diskettes were different. This message does not mean that the files on the destination diskette are bad or damaged, but that they are not in the same place on the two diskettes.

To compare files that have been COPYed, use COMP rather than DISKCOMP.

If DISKCOMP reports any differences between newly DISKCOPYed diskettes, then the destination diskette is faulty. If this happens, DISKCOPY the diskette again. If DISKCOPY or DISKCOMP shows that the destination diskette is still faulty, it is bad and should be discarded.

The next example is a single-drive comparison involving the original diskette and the destination diskette created by DISKCOPY. Drive A: is used for the comparison.

```
A>DISKCOMP A:
Insert first diskette into drive A
Strike any key when ready <Enter>

Comparing 9 sectors per track, 2 side(s)
```

```
Insert second diskette into drive A
Strike any key when ready <Enter>

Insert first diskette into drive A
Strike any key when ready <Enter>

Insert second diskette into drive A
Strike any key when ready <Enter>

Diskettes compare OK

Compare more diskettes (Y/N)? N
A>
```

The number of times you change diskettes depends on how much memory you have and the type of diskette (8 versus 9 tracks, 1 versus 2 sides). The more RAM memory you have in your system, the less often you will have to change diskettes. You will also change single-sided diskettes less often than double-sided ones, and 8-sector diskettes less often than those with 9 sectors.

Notes: DISKCOMP compares the contents of two compatible diskettes. The command does a track-for-track comparison of the files. Although you can use this command with any two compatible (or nearly compatible) diskettes, its most effective use is in comparing original and duplicate diskettes that have been DISKCOPYed.

DISKCOMPing an original diskette with a duplicate that has been COPYed can be meaningless. COPY copies files one at a time. This means that the copied files may not reside in exactly the same spots on the duplicate diskette as on the source diskette. This kind of comparison seldom works because DOS will report that the contents of the tracks of each diskette are not the same when, in fact, the files are identical. To compare diskettes that have been COPYed (not DISKCOPYed), use the COMP command.

The switches, /1 for one-side comparison and /8 for 8-sector (DOS 1.x) comparison, affect only how much of the diskette the program will compare. If you try to compare two different types of diskettes, DOS will either abort the comparison or give a number or a message indicating that the two diskettes are not the same.

Interestingly, DOS will attempt to compare incompatible diskettes only if the first diskette is smaller than the second one. For example, DOS will attempt to compare a single-sided diskette with a double-sided diskette. DOS will state that almost every track on the first diskette does not match the second diskette, but it will compare them.

The reverse does not work, however. If you try to compare a double-sided diskette with a single-sided diskette, DOS will tell you that the diskettes are incompatible and abort the program.

Remember, compare only DISKCOPYed diskettes.

Messages: 1.   Incompatible diskette or drive types

ERROR: The diskettes or drives used for the comparison are different. The first diskette was successfully read on both sides. However, the second diskette may be single-sided; the disk drive for the second diskette may also be single-sided; or the first diskette uses nine sectors, whereas the second uses eight.

Do a CHKDSK on both diskettes, using a double-sided drive, if possible. Look at the number on the line bytes total disk space for both diskettes.

If the number is different for each diskette, then you can't compare them. If the number is the same, the disk drive holding the second diskette in the comparison either is single-sided or has a hardware problem.

If the number is the same, compare both diskettes on the same diskette drive. If this message appears again, you are using a bad copy of DISKCOMP, or the second diskette is faulty. If this message does not appear again and the second drive is double-sided, you have a hardware problem.

2.   Incompatible drive types

ERROR: The source diskette and disk drive are double-sided, but the destination disk drive is single-sided.

Do a single-drive DISKCOMP, using the double-sided drive.

3.   Invalid drive specification

ERROR: You gave an illegal drive name for the comparison.

4. Invalid parameter

    ERROR: You have given on the command line a switch that DISKCOMP does not recognize.

5. Not ready error reading drive x
    Correct, then strike any key

    WARNING: DISKCOMP is having difficulty reading the diskette in drive x. The disk drive door may be open, a nonformatted or non-DOS diskette may have been placed in the drive, or the diskette is not properly inserted in the disk drive. Check these conditions, and then strike a key for DISKCOMP to retry the comparison.

6. Unrecoverable read error on drive x
    Track tt, side s

    WARNING: Four attempts were made to read the data from the diskette in the specified drive. The error is at track number tt, side s. If drive x is the diskette holding the destination (copied) diskette, the copy is probably bad. (The diskette has a "hard" read error.)

    If drive x holds your original diskette, either the diskette had a flaw when it was formatted, or it developed a flaw.

    Run CHKDSK on the original diskette and look for the line bytes in bad sectors. If this line exists, the original diskette may actually be good. When FORMATting a diskette, FORMAT will detect bad sectors and "hide" them. However, DISKCOMP does not check for bad sectors and will attempt to compare the track even if bad sectors are present. If CHKDSK shows that the original diskette has bad sectors, the destination may actually be good in spite of this message. Either way, you will want to retire the original diskette eventually.

    If CHKDSK doesn't show anything for bad sectors, then the original diskette has a bad spot, or the disk drive that held the diskette is faulty. The diskette is the likely source of the error. Run the diagnostics on your disk drive. If it passes this test, your diskette is faulty and should be retired.

DISKCOPY
(Copy entire diskette)   V1** and V2** - External

Purpose: Copies the entire contents of one diskette to another on a track-for-track basis (carbon copy); works only with floppy diskettes

Syntax: **DISKCOPY** *d1: d2: /1*

d1: is the floppy disk drive that holds the source (original) diskette.

d2: is the floppy disk drive that holds the target diskette (diskette to be copied to).

Switch: */1*   Copies only the *1*st side of the diskette

(See Advanced User Notes.)

Special Terms: The diskette you are copying from is the *source* diskette.

The diskette you are copying to is the *target* diskette.

Rules: *1.   If you do not give a drive name, the default disk drive will be used. If this is the hard disk drive, DISKCOPY will attempt to copy the hard disk drive to itself and not give an error message.

2.   If you give only one valid floppy disk drive name, it will be used for the copy (for single floppy disk drive computers). If your system has two physical floppy disk drives, giving only one valid disk drive name results in an `Invalid drive specification` error.

3.   Giving the same valid floppy disk drive name twice is the same as giving only one disk drive name.

4.   If you have a single floppy drive system, drive A: will be used no matter what drive you give.

5.   When copying on one floppy disk drive (Rules 2-4), DOS will prompt you to insert the appropriate diskette, then wait for a keystroke before continuing.

6.   If you give a valid hard disk drive name or an invalid disk drive name, DOS will issue an error message and abort.

7. After copying, DISKCOPY prompts with the following:

    `Copy another (Y/N)?_`

    Answer **Y** to copy another diskette, **N** to stop the program. If you
    answer **Y**, the next copy will be performed on the same disk drive(s) as
    before.

8. If the target diskette is either not formatted or formatted differently
    from the source diskette, DISKCOPY will format it for you. The target
    diskette will be formatted identically to the source diskette. This
    formatting does not apply, however, to copying a double-sided diskette
    on a single-sided drive with the */1* switch.

*9. DISKCOPY destroys any information previously recorded on the target
    diskette. Don't use as the target diskette a diskette containing
    information you want to keep.

10. To ensure that the copy is correct, run DISKCOMP on the two
    diskettes.

Exit Codes: None

Sample Session: ―――――――――――――――――

This session involves a two-drive, double-sided system. First, a double-sided, V2.0 diskette will
be copied, then a single-sided, V1.x diskette. In both cases, two double-sided diskettes were
formatted on the system.

A>DISKCOPY A: B:
```
Insert the source diskette in drive A:      {Change diskettes before hitting
Insert the target diskette in drive B:       <Enter>.}
Strike any key to begin.
Copying 9 sectors per track, 2 side(s)
```

{Copying process continues ....}

`Copy another(Y/N)?` **Y**

```
Insert the source diskette in drive A:      {Change the diskettes before hitting
Insert the target diskette in drive B:       <Enter>.}
Strike any key to begin.

Copying 8 sectors per track, 1 side(s)
```

```
Formatting while copying

Copy another(Y/N)? N
A>
```

Notes: DISKCOPY makes identical copies of a diskette. The command automatically "sizes" the source diskette and makes an exact copy of it on another disk drive. If the target diskette was not previously formatted or is formatted differently, DISKCOPY reformats the diskette to the same "size" as the source diskette. This means that if the source diskette is single-sided with 9 sectors per track and the target diskette is double-sided with 8 sectors per track, DISKCOPY will reformat the target diskette to be single-sided with 9 sectors per track before copying the information to the target diskette.

Always format your diskettes ahead of time. If FORMAT reports any bad sectors on a diskette, you will not be able to use it as the target with DISKCOPY. The command will still attempt to write to the bad sectors and will not give you a good copy.

Users of computer systems with a hard disk should always give at least one floppy disk drive name with DISKCOPY. If the current disk is the hard disk drive, and you type the line

C>DISKCOPY

you will see the following:

```
Insert formatted target diskette into drive C
Press any key when ready.
```

Hit Ctrl-C or Ctrl-Break!

DISKCOPY will attempt to copy the hard disk to itself. I did this once and aborted the program just a few seconds into the DISKCOPY. I didn't lose anything, but I don't want to find out if this is a safe mistake. If you always give a floppy disk drive name with DISKCOPY, you shouldn't have a problem.

Hints: 1. Write-protect your source diskette.

This is particularly important when you make a copy of a diskette by using only one floppy disk drive. DOS will periodically prompt you to change the diskette. If the source diskette is write-protected, you cannot damage it if you put it into the drive when DOS tells you to put in the target diskette.

This advice can also be important for a two-floppy disk drive system in a case where you specified the wrong drives for the copy. An infrequent but fatal mistake is to put the source diskette in drive B:, the target diskette in drive A:, then type the following:

DISKCOPY A: B:

Now the intended source and target diskettes are reversed. If DISKCOPY is not stopped in time, the information on the intended source diskette is destroyed and replaced by whatever (if anything) is on the old target diskette.

For peace of mind, write-protect the source diskette.

2. If you have a two-floppy disk drive system and didn't write-protect your diskette, watch the disk drive lights and be ready to flip open a disk drive door.

    If you don't write-protect your diskette on a two-drive system, watch to see which floppy disk drive light comes on first when the copying starts. The disk holding the source diskette should be the first light to come on. If the wrong disk drive light comes on, **immediately flip the drive door open on the intended source diskette** and let DOS error out (abort). If DOS starts to write to the wrong diskette, it's too late!

    Typing the control-abort keystroke(s) does not always work because DOS may not check for this action in time. Nor does flipping the drive door open on the "new" source diskette always work because DOS may have already read enough information on this diskette and may be on its way to copying on the wrong diskette.

    Flipping open the disk drive door does not hurt either diskette. When DOS starts its copying process, only information from the first diskette is read. It is difficult to damage a diskette from which you are only reading.

3. Have as much free RAM memory available as possible.

    When DISKCOPYing, DOS reads into memory as much information from the source diskette as possible. Then DOS copies this information to the target diskette and reads the next batch of information from the source diskette. The more free memory you have, the less time is required to copy a diskette.

4. If you have used a diskette for a long time and have created and deleted many files on it, use COPY *.* rather than DISKCOPY.

DISKCOPY makes a "physical" image (exact copy) of a diskette. One that has had many files created and deleted on it becomes *fragmented,* meaning that a file is stored all over the diskette. This fragmentation frequently happens with word-processing programs that automatically create a backup copy of files.

The result of this fragmentation is that DOS slows down when using the file because DOS must read your file from all the different places. CHKDSK *.* tells you if this condition is true for a particular diskette.

If CHKDSK *.* tells you that several files are noncontiguous, format a diskette and COPY *.* from the old floppy to the new one to make the files contiguous and speed the search for the file. If you have subdirectories on a diskette, be sure to make the same subdirectories (MD or MKDIR) on the new copy, and copy their contents.

**Advanced
User Notes:**

1. SWITCHAR for this command is always the slash (/).

2. */1* does not work in DOS V2.0.

Messages:

1. `Incompatible drive types`

ERROR: You have attempted to use a single-sided disk drive to copy a double-sided diskette. (See this message under DISKCOMP for remedial action.)

2. `Invalid drive specification`

ERROR: You have given an invalid disk drive name (the corresponding disk drive does not exist), or you have forgotten to place a colon after the disk drive name.

3. `Unrecoverable format error on target`

`Unrecoverable read error on source`

`Unrecoverable write error on target`

`Unrecoverable verify error on target`

```
track tt side s
target diskette may be unusable
```

WARNING: Each of the four messages indicates that the source diskette, destination diskette, or disk drives used for the DISKCOPY are flawed. Several of these messages show that the error occurs at track tt on side s. Most messages also warn that the destination (target) diskette may not be an exact copy of the original and is therefore unusable.

If the message indicates a read error, the source diskette and the source drive are suspect. If you have not experienced any difficulties with the disk drive, the source diskette may have a bad sector or track. If other messages appear, the target diskette or disk drive holding the target diskette is suspect. If no other problems have surfaced in previous use of the disk drive, the diskette is bad.

A read error will occur on source diskettes with any bad sectors. Diskettes that have been formatted and have shown bytes lost to bad sectors will also produce a read error when the diskette is DISKCOPYed. DISKCOPY attempts to copy the bad sectors, although no useful information resides in them. In this case, the target diskette is good and may be used. However, some disk space on the target diskette is still lost to the "bad sectors" on the source diskette. This loss occurs because the FAT of the source diskette, which has the bad sectors marked out, is copied to the target diskette. Thus, good sectors on the target diskette are lost.

If the source diskette does not show bad sectors when CHKDSK has been run, a recent flaw in the source diskette has caused the bad sector. The target diskette is probably unusable.

Source diskettes that have bad tracks should usually be COPYed rather than DISKCOPYed.

If the problem is a format, verify, or write error and if the disk drive is in good working condition, the problem lies with the target diskette. Exit DISKCOPY and then FORMAT the intended target diskette. If bad sectors show when FORMAT analyzes the diskette, this diskette cannot be used for DISKCOPYing. If FORMAT does not show any bad sectors, repeat the DISKCOPY. If further problems exist, try to DISKCOPY from drive B to drive A and suspect that one disk drive may be at fault.

4. Not ready error reading drive d
    Not ready error writing drive d

    WARNING: DISKCOPY is having difficulty reading or writing the
    diskette in drive d. Either the diskette is not properly inserted, the
    source diskette is not formatted or is a non-DOS diskette, or the drive
    door is open. Check each of these possibilities.

5. Target diskette write-protected
    Correct, then strike any key

    WARNING: The target diskette has a write-protect tab on it (for 5 1/4-
    inch minifloppies) or is missing the write-enable tab (for 8-inch
    floppies).

    Before removing or adding the tab, make sure the correct diskettes are
    in the disk drives and check how you have invoked the DISKCOPY
    command. If you used the write-protect notch to protect the wrong
    diskette from being destroyed, make sure you DISKCOPY the intended
    source diskette to the right target diskette.

ERASE
(Erase files)

V1 and V2 - Internal

Purpose: Removes one or more files from the directory

Syntax: **ERASE** *d:path\filename.ext*

or

DEL *d:path\filename.ext*

d: is the name of the disk drive holding the files to be erased.

path is the directory of the files to be erased.

filename.ext is the name of the file(s) to be erased. Wild cards are allowed.

Rules:
1. If you do not give a disk drive name, the current disk drive will be used.

2. If you do not give a path name, the current directory on the disk drive will be used.

3. If you give a disk drive name and/or a path name but no file name, DOS assumes the file name is *.* (all files). If you do not give a disk drive, path, or file name, DOS issues an Invalid number of parameters error and aborts.

4. If you specify *.* or no name (when you have given a disk drive name and/or path name) for the file name, DOS will prompt with the following:

   Are you sure (Y/N)?_

   If you answer **Y**, all files in the specified directory will be erased.

   If you answer **N**, the files will not be erased.

5. You cannot erase a directory, including the . (current directory) and the .. (parent directory) from a subdirectory.

Notes: ERASE, or its shorthand form DEL (delete), removes files. The entry in the directory is altered to mean "not in use," and the space occupied by the file on the diskette or disk is freed.

This activity means that as long as you do not place any more information on that diskette, the file can be recovered by special utility programs not provided with DOS. One such utility is provided with the Norton Utilities. However, IBM's RECOVER is not designed for this use and will not recover erased files. Remember, you may not be able to recover erased files if you put any more information on (write to) the diskette.

Hints:

Wild cards are useful when you erase a group of files, but inadvertently erasing the wrong file or files is easy to do. Use the DIR command and your intended wild-card file name to test which files will be erased. If a wrong file or files show up, you must use a different file name. In other words, experiment with the DIR command to find the right file name before you ERASE.

Erasing the wrong file is much easier than recovering the erased file, even if you have the right utility program.

You should also check your typing before you hit Enter. It is very easy to make a typographical error and erase the wrong file.

Messages:

1. `File not found`

   ERROR: The file name you gave does not exist on the current or specified disk drive or directory. Check your typing of the names, ensure that the correct diskette is in the drive, and try again.

2. `Invalid number of parameters`

   ERROR: You did not specify a disk drive name, path name, or file name; you have spaces in the file specification; or you have extraneous characters on the command line.

EXE2BIN
(Change .EXE file into a
.BIN or .COM file)

V1.1 and V2 - External

Purpose: Changes suitably formatted .EXE files into .COM files

Syntax: **EXE2BIN** *d1:path1***filename1**.*ext1 d2:path2\\filename2.ext2*

d1: is the name of the disk drive holding the file to convert.

path1 is the directory of the file to convert.

filename1 is the root name of the file to convert.

.ext1 is the extension name of the file to convert.

d2: is the name of the disk drive for the output file.

path2 is the directory of the output file.

filename2 is the root name for the output file.

.ext2 is the extension name of the output file.

Special Terms: The file to convert (*d1:path1***filename1**.*ext1*) is the *source* file.

The output file (*d2:path2\\filename2.ext2*) is the *destination* file.

Exit Codes: None

Rules:
1. If you do not specify a drive:

    A.   For the source file (*d1:*), the current drive will be used as the source file.

    B.   For the destination file (*d2:*), the source drive will be used.

2. When you do not specify a path (*path1* or *path2*), the current directory of the disk will be used.

3. You must specify a root file name for the source file to be converted (**filename1**).

4. If you do not specify a root file name for the destination file (*filename2*), the root file name of the source will be used (**filename1**).

5. If you do not specify an extension:

   A. For the source file (*.ext1*), the extension .EXE will be used.

   B. For the destination file (*.ext2*), the extension .BIN will be used.

6. The .EXE file must be in the correct format (following the Microsoft conventions).

Note: EXE2BIN is a programming utility that converts .EXE (executable) program files to .COM or .BIN (binary image). The resulting program takes less disk space and loads faster. However, this conversion may be a disadvantage in future versions of DOS. Unless you are using a compiler-based language, you will probably never use this command. For further information on EXE2BIN, see your DOS manual.

FIND
(Find string filter)

V2 - External

Purpose: Displays all the lines from the designated files that match/do not match the specified string. This command can also display the line numbers.

Syntax: **FIND** */V/C/N* **string** *d:path\filename.ext ...*

string is the set of characters for which you want to search. The characters in **string** must be enclosed in quotation marks (").

d: is the name of the disk drive for the file.

path is the path to the *filename.ext*.

filename.ext is the file you want to search.

Switches: */V*   Displays all lines that do *not* contain **string**

               /C   Counts the number of times **string** occurs in the file but does not display the actual lines where **string** occurred

               /N   Displays the line *number* (number of the line in the file) in front of each line that matches **string**

Rules: 1.   You may use more than one file specification. Each file specification should be separated by a space. All file specifications must appear after **string**.

           2.   For each file specification:

                A.   If you do not give a disk drive, the current drive will be used.

                B.   If you do not give a path name, the current directory will be used.

           3.   If you do not give any file specifications, FIND will look for information from the keyboard (standard input).

           4.   Switches, if given, must be typed between the word **FIND** and **string**. (Most DOS commands require that switches be placed at the end of the line.)

Sample Session:

For this example, two files were created: MEN.TXT and GETTY.TXT.

C>**dir**

```
Volume in drive C is QUE_DISK
Directory of C:\test

.                <DIR>        8-01-83    10:27a
..               <DIR>        8-01-83    10:27a
MEN      TXT        72        8-05-83     3:29p
GETTY    TXT       180        8-05-83     3:31p
     4 File(s)   3981312 bytes free
```

C>**type men.txt**   {Show what's in the file.}
```
Now is the time for all good
men to come to the aid of
their party.
```

C>**type getty.txt**   {Show what's in this file.}
```
Fourscore and seven years ago, our
fathers brought forth upon this
continent a new nation conceived in
liberty and dedicated to the proposition
that all men are created equal.
```

C>**find "men" men.txt**   {Now find the word "men"
                                                        in MEN.TXT.}

```
---------- men.txt                                    {The file name}
men to come to the aid of                             {The lines from the file}
```

C>**find "men" getty.txt**   {Now do the same thing
                                                        for GETTY.TXT.}

```
---------- getty.txt
that all men are created equal.
```

C>**find "men" men.txt getty.txt**   {Now find "men" in both files.}

```
---------- men.txt
men to come to the aid of

---------- getty.txt
that all men are created equal.
```

C>find /v "men" men.txt getty.txt

{Now show which lines don't have "men."}

```
---------- men.txt
Now is the time for all good
their party.

---------- getty.txt
Fourscore and seven years ago, our
fathers brought forth upon this
continent a new nation conceived in
liberty and dedicated to the proposition
```

C>find /c "men" men.txt getty.txt

{Now count the lines that have "men" in them.}

```
---------- men.txt: 1
```

{The file name and the count}

```
---------- getty.txt: 1
```

{The file name and the count}

C>find /v/c "men" men.txt getty.txt

{Count the number of lines that don't have "men."}

```
---------- men.txt: 3
```

```
---------- getty.txt: 5
```

C>find /n "men" men.txt getty.txt

{Number the lines with "men."}

```
---------- men.txt
[2]men to come to the aid of
```

{Notice that the count is always relative to the file.}

```
---------- getty.txt
[5]that all men are created equal.
```

C>find /v/n "men" men.txt getty.txt

{Same thing, but lines without "men"}

```
---------- men.txt
[1]Now is the time for all good
[3]their party.
[4]
---------- getty.txt
[1]Fourscore and seven years ago, our
[2]fathers brought forth upon this
```

```
[3]continent a new nation conceived in
[4]liberty and dedicated to the proposition
[6]
C>find /n "t" men.txt getty.txt
```
{Now let's search for any line with the letter "t."}

```
---------- men.txt
[1]Now is the time for all good
[2]men to come to the aid of
[3]their party.

---------- getty.txt
[2]fathers brought forth upon this
[3]continent a new nation conceived in
[4]liberty and dedicated to the proposition
[5]that all men are created equal.

C>find /n "th" men.txt getty.txt
```
{I got too many lines. I was actually looking for lines with "th."}

```
---------- men.txt
[1]Now is the time for all good
[2]men to come to the aid of
[3]their party.

---------- getty.txt
[2]fathers brought forth upon this
[4]liberty and dedicated to the proposition
[5]that all men are created equal.

C>find /n "the" men.txt getty.txt
```
{Now I'll look for the word "the."}

```
---------- men.txt
[1]Now is the time for all good
[2]men to come to the aid of
[3]their party.

---------- getty.txt
[2]fathers brought forth upon this
[4]liberty and dedicated to the proposition

C>find /n "THE" men.txt getty.txt
```
{How about "THE"?}

---------- men.txt

---------- getty.txt   {Not in either file}

The last example shows one problem you may encounter when trying to find a string. FIND looks for the exact match to your search string. Upper- and lower-case letters are treated differently. FIND will not locate a lower-case word if it has any capital letters. That's why "the" was found in the file, but "THE" was not found.

Notes:	FIND is one of several filters provided with DOS V2. This command can find lines that contain **string** and those that do not. It can also number lines and count lines rather than display them.
	This filter is useful when combined with the I/O redirection of DOS V2. The output of FIND can be redirected into a file with the > character. Because FIND lets you name a sequence of files to search, you do not have to redirect the input to FIND.
Messages:	1. FIND: File not found filename
	WARNING: FIND could not find the file named filename. The file does not exist, the file is not where you said it should be (wrong drive or path), or the spelling is incorrect. If you give a switch after **string**, FIND will think that the switch is a file name and will give you this warning message. After issuing the message, FIND continues to process any subsequent files you have specified.
	2. FIND: Invalid number of parameters
	ERROR: You didn't give FIND enough information. You must type at least the following:
	FIND "string"
	You probably didn't give a string to search for.
	3. FIND: Invalid parameter x
	WARNING: You gave FIND an incorrect switch. FIND only recognizes /C, /N, or /V. FIND will print this warning message and continue.
	4. FIND: Syntax error
	ERROR: You did not phrase the command correctly. You probably didn't put quotation marks around the string for which you were searching.

FORMAT
(Format disk)

V1** and V2** - External

Purpose: Initializes the disk to accept DOS information and files. The command also checks the disk for defective tracks and optionally places DOS on the diskette.

Syntax: **FORMAT** *d:* /S/1/8/V/B

d: is a valid disk drive name.

Switches:

/S Places a copy of the operating *system* on the disk, which makes the diskette bootable

/1 Formats only the 1st side of the diskette

/8 Formats an 8-sector diskette (V1)

/V Writes a *volume* label on the disk (PC DOS)

/B Formats an 8-sector diskette and leaves the proper places in the directory for the operating system, *but* does not place the operating system on the diskette

Rules:

1. If you do not give a disk drive name, the current disk drive will be used.

2. Before a new diskette can be used, it must be FORMATted. The only exception is when you use a new diskette as the target for DISKCOPY (because DISKCOPY also formats diskettes).

3. DOS will check the floppy disk drive and format the diskette to its maximum capacity (both sides if a double-sided drive is used, with 9 sectors per track), unless otherwise directed through a switch.

Some switches do not work together. For example, you cannot do the following:

A. Use /V or /S with /B.

B. Use /V with /8.

C. Use /1, /8, or /B with the hard disk

*4.   FORMAT destroys any information previously recorded on the diskette. Do not FORMAT a diskette with any useful information on it.

5.   To make a diskette usable with all versions of DOS and IBM computers, use the /B/1 switches. (Format the diskette for any DOS and format only one side.)

6.   If you give a volume name, it can be one to eleven characters long and contain any character that is legal in a file name.

7.   If you use the /S switch (place the operating system on the disk) and the current directory does not have a copy of DOS, DOS will prompt you to place a DOS diskette into drive A to get the copy of DOS before formatting the diskette.

Exit Codes: None

Sample Session: ———————————————————

This session covers the formatting of four diskettes. The first two will only be formatted, the third will have the operating system added (/S switch), and the last diskette will have a volume label added.

A>**FORMAT A:**

```
Insert new diskette for drive A:
and strike any key when ready
```
{I put a diskette in A: and hit <Enter>.}

```
Formatting...Format complete

   362496 bytes total disk space
   362496 bytes available on disk
```

```
Format another (Y/N)?Y
```
{Now the second diskette}

```
Insert new diskette for drive A:
and strike any key when ready
```

```
Formatting...Format complete

   362496 bytes total disk space
    15360 bytes in bad sectors
   347136 bytes available on disk
```
{This diskette had several bad sectors. I can use it for most operations, but not for DISKCOPY and DISKCOMP.}

```
Format another (Y/N)?N
```
{To put the operating system on the next diskette, I must exit FORMAT and run the program again.}

A>FORMAT A: /S

Insert DOS disk in drive A:
and strike any key when ready

{Now run the program with the */S* switch.}
{This message appears only when you give the */S* switch; the current disk does not have the operating system on it.}

Insert new diskette for drive A:
and strike any key when ready

Formatting...Format complete
System transferred

  362496 bytes total disk space
   40960 bytes used by system
  321536 bytes available on disk

Format another (Y/N)?**N**

A>FORMAT A: /V
Insert new diskette for drive A:
and strike any key when ready

Formatting...Format complete

Volume label (11 characters, ENTER for none)? **ACCOUNT DSK**

  362496 bytes total disk space
  362496 bytes available on disk

Format another (Y/N)?**N**
A>DIR A:

Volume in drive A is ACCOUNT DSK
Directory of A:\

File not found

A>

Notes: Every diskette and hard disk must be formatted before it is used. The FORMAT program actually performs several tasks. It sets up each track and sector on the disk to accept information. Special information is recorded, such as track headers (one for each track), sector headers (one for each sector), and CRC bits (cyclic redundancy check) to ensure that the recorded information is accurate.

DOS V2 always records nine sectors per track. If you have used the /B or /8 option for eight sectors per track, DOS will simply record the FAT making the ninth sector "invisible" and unusable.

As DOS completes the formatting of each track of the disk, DOS tests the track. If the track passes the test, DOS moves to the next track. If the track is bad, DOS remembers and marks the track as "reserved" in the FAT. No useful information will be recorded on bad tracks.

DOS then establishes the area for the disk's root directory and file allocation table (FAT). If any bad tracks were found, the FAT is marked appropriately.

Hints:
When you use a one-floppy disk drive system, use drive B for formatting and/or write-protect the diskette holding the FORMAT program. Either will prevent the accidental erasure of a good diskette that was inadvertently left in drive A. As you become accustomed to operating your computer, use drive A for formatting, but always check that the proper diskette is in the drive before pressing the key to begin formatting.

With the XT, always give FORMAT a drive name. If you don't, you may inadvertently reformat the hard disk drive. If the hard disk is the current disk drive, then

```
C>FORMAT
Press any key to begin formatting drive C.
```

DOS is telling you that when you strike any key, DOS will start formatting the hard disk! Type Ctrl-C or Ctrl-Break immediately, or you will lose all the information on the hard disk! Once FORMAT begins, it is too late. Your information is lost. This possibility necessitates backing up your hard disk frequently.

Messages:
1. Attempted write-protect violation

   WARNING: The diskette you are trying to format is write-protected. Covering the write-protect notch on minifloppy diskettes with a tab protects the diskette. To write-protect 8-inch diskettes, do not cover the write-protect notch (a procedure opposite from that used with minifloppy diskettes).

Check the diskette in the drive. If this is the diskette you want to format, remove the write-protect tab (for minifloppies) or put a write-protect tab over the notch (for 8-inch floppies). If the diskette in the drive was the wrong diskette, put the correct diskette in the drive and try again.

2. Disk not compatible

ERROR: The disk drive or pseudodisk (RAM disk) drive cannot be used by the DOS FORMAT command. This error should not occur if you are using IBM disk drives or most RAM-disk programs.

If you are using an IBM-compatible disk drive, run a different copy of FORMAT. If this message reappears, reboot your system and try again. You may have a hardware problem if the message appears a third time.

If your drive is not compatible, use the format program provided by your drive's vendor or simply use a different disk drive for FORMAT.

3. Disk unsuitable for system disk

WARNING: FORMAT detected one or more bad sectors on the diskette where DOS normally resides. Because DOS must reside on a specified spot on the disk and this portion is unusable, the diskette cannot be used to boot (load and start) DOS.

You might try to reformat this diskette. Some diskettes format successfully the second time but not the first. If FORMAT gives this message a second time, the diskette cannot be used as a boot diskette.

4. Format failure

ERROR: FORMAT encountered a disk error that it could not handle. This message usually comes after another error message and indicates that FORMAT has aborted.

One cause of this error may be a diskette that has bad sectors where the boot sector, FAT, or root directory is normally recorded. A diskette or disk with flaws in any of these areas is unusable.

5.   Insert DOS disk in d: and strike any key when ready

INFORMATIONAL: Before formatting a diskette with the /S switch, FORMAT reads into memory the DOS system files IBMBIO.COM, IBMDOS.COM, and COMMAND.COM. However, DOS cannot find these files. To solve this problem, put a DOS diskette containing these three files into drive d: and hit any key to continue.

6.   Invalid characters in volume label

WARNING: One or more of the characters in the label name you gave are invalid. Give the name again, making sure that the characters are appropriate for a volume name. The most common mistake is using a period (.) in the volume name. DOS will ask you to try again.

7.   Invalid parameters

ERROR: You have given an invalid disk drive name or a nonrecognized switch.

8.   Parameters not compatible

ERROR: You gave two or more switches that are not compatible. Check the rules in this section to see which switches can be used together and try running FORMAT again.

9.   Parameter not compatible with fixed disk

ERROR: You gave the /1 or /8 switch when you were trying to format the hard disk. Check to be sure you are formatting the correct disk drive. If you are formatting the hard disk, don't use either switch.

10.   Track 0 bad - disk unusable

WARNING: Track 0 holds the boot record, the FAT, and the directory. This track is bad, and the diskette is unusable. Try formatting the diskette again. If the error recurs, the diskette is bad and cannot be used.

11.   Unable to write BOOT

WARNING: Either the first track of the diskette or the DOS portion of the hard disk is bad. The bootstrap loader (BOOT program) cannot be written to the diskette or disk. The diskette or DOS portion of the hard disk cannot be used. Reformat, and if the error recurs, the diskette or hard disk drive is completely unusable.

GRAPHICS
(Graphics screen print)   V2 - External

Purpose: Allows the graphics screen to be printed on a suitable printer

Syntax: **GRAPHICS**

Exit Codes: None

Rules:

1. After the GRAPHICS command is invoked, you can print the graphics screen by pressing the Shift and PrtSc (print screen) keys.

2. To print the graphics screen, your printer must be compatible with the IBM Graphics Matrix Printer.

3. If you are in text mode, screen printing will take less than thirty seconds. If you are in graphics mode, screen printing will take up to three minutes.

4. If you are in the 320 x 200 (medium-resolution) mode, the printer will print in four shades of gray, corresponding to the four possible colors. If you are in the 640 x 200 (high-resolution) mode, the printer will print in black and white, but the printout will be rotated 90° to the left. (The upper right-hand corner of the screen is placed on the upper left-hand corner of the printout.)

5. Once the GRAPHICS command has been given, do not reinvoke it until after your next system reset or power up. The GRAPHICS command increases the size of DOS by at least 688 bytes. Each time you invoke GRAPHICS, it will waste at least an additional 688 bytes.

6. Once GRAPHICS is invoked, the only way to deactivate the command is to reset your computer.

Notes: The GRAPHICS command replaces many graphics screen-printing programs written for earlier versions of DOS. This command allows you to "dump" the graphics screen to the printer. Although GRAPHICS has no effect on systems that do not have the Color/Graphics Adapter, the command still increases the size of DOS by at least 688 bytes, if invoked. The exact size of the increase varies, depending on your type of computer (PC versus XT), use of device drivers, and other DOS features.

GRAPHICS affects only the graphic screen dumps. If your display is in text mode (A/N), the print-screen function will not act any differently. Only when medium- or high-resolution graphics are active will GRAPHICS print the screen differently.

If you frequently use this command, make it part of the AUTOEXEC.BAT file for your DOS boot diskette.

MKDIR
(Make directory)

V2 - Internal

Purpose:	Creates a subdirectory
Syntax:	**MKDIR** *d:path***dirname**

or

MD *d:path***dirname**

d: is the name of the disk drive for the subdirectory.

path is a valid path name for the path to the directory that will hold the subdirectory.

dirname is the name of the subdirectory you are creating.

Exit Codes: None

Rules:

1. If you do not specify a disk drive name, the current disk drive is used.

2. If you do not specify a path name, the subdirectory will be established in the current directory of the specified drive if you gave a disk drive name, or the current disk drive if you did not give a disk drive name.

3. If you use a path name, separate it from the **dirname** with a path character, the backslash (\\).

4. You must specify the new subdirectory name (**dirname**). The **dirname** must be between one and eight characters long with an optional extension, and conform to the rules for directory names.

5. You cannot use a directory name that is identical to a current file in the parent directory. For example, if you have a file named MYFILE in the current directory, you cannot create the subdirectory MYFILE in this directory. However, if the file is named MYFILE.TXT, there is no conflict between the names, and the MYFILE subdirectory may be created.

Notes: MKDIR, or the shorthand form MD, makes subdirectories. You can make as many subdirectories as you like, but there is one caution. DOS provides only 63 characters for the path name, including the backslashes. It is possible to make so many levels of subdirectories with long directory names that the path to a directory exceeds the 63-character limit.

You are not restricted to creating subdirectories in the current directory you are using. By adding a path name, DOS will establish a new subdirectory wherever you direct it.

Message: Unable to create directory

ERROR: The directory you were going to create already exists, one of the path names you gave is incorrect, the root directory of the disk is full, the disk is full, or a file already exists by the same name.

Check the directory in which the new subdirectory was to be created. If a conflicting name exists, change the file name or use a new directory name. If the disk or the root directory is full, delete some files, create the subdirectory in a different directory, or use a different disk.

MODE
(Change/set mode)   V1** and V2** - External

Purpose: Sets the mode of operation for the printer(s) and printing, the video display, and the Asynchronous Communications Adapter.

Notes: The MODE command is actually four commands in one. MODE sets and controls (1) the printer characteristics; (2) the redirection of printing between the parallel and serial printers; (3) the characteristics of the video display, which display to use (when more than one display is in a system); (4) and the characteristics of the Asynchronous Communications Adapter.

Because of its versatility, MODE is treated here as four separate commands.

MODE
(Parallel printer characteristics)   V1 and V2 - External

Purpose: Sets the IBM printer characteristics

Syntax: **MODE LPT#:** *cpl, lpi, P*

is the printer number (1, 2, or 3).

cpl is the characters per line (80 or 132).

lpi is the line spacing (6 or 8 lines per inch).

P specifies continuous retries on time-out errors.

Exit Codes: None

Rules:

1. You must give a printer number, followed by a colon.

2. All other parameters are optional. If you do not want to change a parameter, simply give a comma for that parameter.

3. This command cancels the effect of **MODE LPT#: = COMx**.

4. If you enter an invalid parameter or skip a parameter (other than the printer number), the parameter will not be changed.

5. If you give a *P* for continuous retries, the only way to cancel it is by repeating the MODE command without the *P*.

6. The characters-per-line and lines-per-inch portions of the command affect only IBM, Epson, and other printers with Epson-compatible control codes.

Notes: This command controls the IBM Matrix and Graphics printers, all Epson printers, and Epson-like printers. It may work partially or not at all on other printers.

When you change the column width, MODE sends the special printer control code to use the normal font (80) or the condensed font (132) on the printer. When you change the lines per inch, MODE sends the special printer control code to print either 6 or 8 lines per inch. The printer is also set to use the appropriate lines per page for line spacing, based on an 11-inch sheet of paper. The printer will print 88 lines per page in the 8-lines-per-inch mode and 66 lines per page in the 6-lines-per-inch mode.

If you issue the *P* option in an attempt to send continuously characters to a deselected printer, the computer will not give you a time-out error. Instead, the computer will continue to loop until the printer is ready (printer turned on, connected to the PC, and selected). During this time, approximately one minute, the computer will appear to be "locked up." Then to abort the retry, press Ctrl-Break.

MODE
(Set display adapter/display characteristics)   V2 - External

Purpose: Switches the active display adapter between the Monochrome Display and the Color/Graphics Adapter on a two-adapter system and sets the characteristics of the Color/Graphics Adapter

Syntax: **MODE dt**

or

MODE dt, s, T

dt is the display type. (See below.)

s shifts the display right (*R*) or left (*L*) one character.

T requests alignment of the screen with a one-line test pattern.

dt may be one of the following:

40	Sets the display to 40 characters per line for the Color/Graphics Adapter
80	Sets the display to 80 characters per line for the Color/Graphics Adapter
BW40	Makes the Color/Graphics Display the active display and sets the mode to 40 characters per line, black and white (color disabled)
BW80	Makes the Color/Graphics Display the active display and sets the mode to 80 characters per line, black and white (color disabled)
CO40	Makes the Color/Graphics Display the active display and sets the mode to 40 characters per line (colors enabled)
CO80	Makes the Color/Graphics Display the active display and sets the mode to 80 characters per line (colors enabled)
MONO	Makes the Monochrome Display the active display

Exit Codes: None

Rules:
1. You must enter the display type (**dt**). All other parameters are optional.

2. If you do not have the correct display on your system, an `Invalid parameter` message will appear.

3. If you use the **CO40** or **CO80** parameter, color will not be displayed immediately. However, programs that use color will be able to display color.

4. When any valid form of the command is given, the display is cleared.

5. The shift (R or L) parameters work with only the Color/Graphics Adapter. If you use this command with the Monochrome Display, the display will not shift.

6. The T command (test pattern) works with either adapter. However, you cannot shift the display of the monochrome adapter (Rule 5).

MODE
(Set Asynchronous Communications
Adapter characteristics)

V1.1 and V2 - External

Purpose: Controls the protocol characteristics of the Asynchronous Communications
Adapter

Syntax: **MODE COMn: baud,** *parity, databits, stopbits, P*

n is the adapter number (1 or 2).

baud is the baud rate (110, 150, 300, 1200, 2400, 4800, or 9600).

parity is the parity checking (*None, O*dd, or *E*ven).

databits is the number of data bits (7 or 8).

stopbits is the number of stop bits (1 or 2).

P represents continuous retries on time-out errors.

Rules:
1. You must give the number of the adapter, followed by a colon, a space,
   and a baud rate. All other parameters are optional.

2. If you do not want to change a parameter, enter a comma for that
   value.

3. If you give an invalid parameter, no action will take place, and an
   `Invalid parameter` message will be displayed.

4. You may enter the first digits for the baud rate in shorthand form (for
   example, 11 for 110 baud, 96 for 9600 baud).

5. If you want continuous retries after a time-out, the *P* must be entered
   every time you use the **MODE COMn:** command.

6. If the adapter is set for continuous retries (*P*) and the device is not
   ready, the computer will appear to be "locked up." You can abort this
   loop by pressing Ctrl-Break.

MODE
(Redirect printing from a parallel to a serial printer)

V2 - External

Purpose:	Forces DOS to print to a serial printer rather than a parallel printer
Syntax:	**MODE LPT#: = COMn:**

is the parallel printer number (1, 2, or 3).

n is the Asynchronous Communications Adapter number (1 or 2).

Exit Codes: None

Rules:
1. You must give a valid number for both the parallel printer and the serial printer.

2. After the command is given, all printing to the parallel printer goes to the designated serial printer.

3. This command can be canceled with the **MODE LPT#:** command.

4. The colon (:) in **LPT#:** is mandatory. The colon in **COMn:** is optional.

Notes: This command is useful for systems that have only a serial printer. By typing the line

MODE LPT1: = COM1:

all output that would normally be sent to the system printer is sent to the serial printer (assuming that the printer is connected to the first Asynchronous Communications Adapter). This output includes the screen print (Shift-PrtSc) function.

The serial adapter used for the serial printer should be set up with the MODE COMn: command.

MODE
(General)

Messages:

1. `COMn bbbb,p,d,s,t initialized`

    INFORMATIONAL: The Asynchronous Communications Adapter has been successfully initialized. `n` is the adapter number, `bbbb` is the baud rate, `p` is the parity, `d` is the number of data bits, `s` is the number of stop bits, and `t` is the retry on time-out.

2. `Do you see the leftmost 0? (Y/N)`
    `Do you see the rightmost 9? (Y/N)`

    INFORMATIONAL: You are adjusting the display connected to the Color/Graphics Adapter with MODE. Answer **N** or any other key to shift the display left or right (depending on how you invoked MODE); answer **Y**, if the display is properly centered, to end the MODE command.

3. `Illegal Device Name`

    ERROR: You did not specify a number with the LPT#: or COMn:; you used a number that is not in the correct range (1, 2, or 3 for LPT#:; 1 or 2 for COMn:); you put no spaces between LPT#:, COMn:, and the next parameter; you put more then one space between LPT#: or COMn: and the next parameter; or the specified adapter is not connected to your system. Check each possibility and try the command again.

4. `Invalid baud rate specified`

    ERROR: You gave an incorrect baud rate. The baud rate must be 110, 150, 300, 1200, 4800, 9600, or the first two characters for one of these numbers.

5. `Invalid parameters`

    ERROR: You forgot to give a necessary parameter; the first parameter (for the printer or communications adapter) did not start with an L or C; you gave a wrong parameter with the command; or the display adapter you are referencing is not connected to your system.

6. `LPT#: not redirected`

INFORMATIONAL: The specified printer is getting its own output. Any previous reassignment (LPT#: = COMn:) has been canceled. This occurs when you set or reset the characters-per-line or the lines-per-inch setting of the printer.

7. `LPT#: redirected to COMn:`

INFORMATIONAL: The output that would normally go to the specified printer will now go to the specified communications adapter.

8. `LPT#: set for 80`
   `LPT#: set for 132`

INFORMATIONAL: The specified printer is set for 80 or 132 characters per line.

9. `Printer error`

WARNING: The printer MODE command (MODE LPT#: cpl, lpi, P) was unable to set the printer because of an I/O error; the printer is out of paper, turned off, or not selected; or the printer is not an IBM or IBM-compatible printer. Check these conditions and try the command again.

10. `Printer lines per inch set`

INFORMATIONAL: You have specified a parameter for the lines-per-inch setting (6 or 8). If the attempt to set the lines per inch fails, a `Printer error` message will normally follow this message.

MORE
(More output filter)   V2 - External

Purpose: Displays one screenful of information from the standard input device and
                   pauses for a keystroke while displaying the message -- More --

Syntax: **MORE**

Exit Codes: None

Rules:
1.   MORE displays one screenful of data on the standard output (display).

2.   After displaying a screenful of information, MORE will pause and wait
     for a keystroke. This process is repeated until the input is exhausted.

3.   MORE is best used with DOS V2's I/O redirection and piping.

Examples: A.   **MORE <TEST.TXT**

                   displays a screenful of information from the file TEST.TXT. MORE,
                   then displays the prompt -- More -- at the bottom of the screen and
                   waits for a keystroke. When you press a key, MORE continues this
                   process until all information is displayed. MORE will not display the
                   prompt on the final screenful of information.

                   B.   **DIR | SORT | MORE**

                   displays the sorted output of the directory command, 23 lines at a time.

Notes: MORE is a DOS filter that allows you to display a screenful of information
                   without manually pausing the screen. This command is similar to the TYPE
                   command, except that MORE pauses automatically after each screenful of
                   information.

                   A screenful of information is based on 40 or 80 characters per line and 23
                   lines per screen. This does not mean, however, that MORE will display 23
                   lines at a time from the file. When a line exceeds the display width (40 or 80
                   characters), MORE will display the first 40 or 80 characters (depending on
                   the display width) in a line, move down to the next line on the screen, display
                   the next 40 or 80 characters, and so on, until the complete line from the file is
                   displayed. If one line from the file takes 3 lines to display, MORE will display
                   a maximum of 21 lines from the file. In other words, MORE acts intelligently
                   with long lines.

PATH
(Set directory search order)

V2 - Internal

Purpose: Tells DOS to search the specified directories on the specified drives if a program or batch file is not found in the current directory

Syntax: **PATH** *d1:path1;d2:path2;d3:path3; ...*

d1:, *d2:*, and *d3:* are valid disk drives names.

path1, path2, and *path3* are valid path names to the commands and batch files you want to run while in any directory.

Rules:
1. If you do not enter a disk drive name for a path, the current disk drive will be used.

2. Each path can be any valid series of subdirectories, separated from one another by the backslash.

3. If you specify more than one set of paths, the following applies:

    A. Each path set must be separated by a semicolon.

    B. Do not use spaces in or between the path names.

    C. The search for the program or batch file will be in the order of the path sets given. First, the current directory is searched, then *d1:path1,* followed by *d2:path2,* then *d3:path3,* etc., until the command or batch file is found.

4. If you give invalid information (a bad drive name, bad delimiter, a deleted path, etc.), DOS will not give an error message. When searching the path for a program or batch file, DOS will simply skip a bad or invalid path.

5. If the file cannot be found in the current directory and the given paths, a Bad command or filename message will be given.

6. PATH affects only the execution of a program (.COM or .EXE file) or a batch file (.BAT). This command does not work with data files, text files, or program overlays

Notes:

PATH is a useful command with hierarchical directories. Directories that contain your utility programs, system programs, or batch files can be established and used from anywhere on the disk. PATH will automatically cause DOS to search these directories to find your programs without your having to type the path each time.

Note that only program files and batch files are eligible for PATH. Once you have invoked a program, it is up to the program, not DOS, to look in other directories for data files, text files, or program overlays. Programs like WordStar® need their overlay files in the same directory in which you are working. Future versions of programs will allow you to "install" a path.

To view the current path, use either the PATH or SET commands.

Hint:

Specify an absolute path that starts with the root directory of a disk (\), instead of a relative path that starts with the current directory (.\). By specifying an absolute path, you won't be concerned about which current directory you are in.

For example, I keep my DOS programs for my PC XT in a level 2 directory called BIN and a level 3 directory called UTIL. I set the path to

PATH C:\BIN;C:\BIN\UTIL

This command allows me to invoke a DOS command from anywhere on the hard or floppy disk. If I used the PATH command with a relative directory, starting with the current or parent directory, I would have to change the path almost every time I changed subdirectories. In addition, I can be on any disk drive, not just the hard disk, and invoke the DOS commands in BIN and UTIL.

PRINT
(Background printing)   V2 - External

Purpose: Prints a list of files on the printer, while the computer performs other tasks

Syntax: **PRINT** *d1:filename1.ext1/P/T/C d2:filename2.ext2/P/T/C ...*

d1: and *d2:* are valid disk drive names.

filename1.ext1 and *filename2.ext2* are the names of the files you want to print. Wild cards are allowed.

Switches: */P*   Queues up the file (places the file in the line) for *printing*

        /T   *Terminates* the background printing of any or all files, including any file currently being printed

        /C   Cancels the background printing of the file(s)

Exit Codes: None

Rules:

1. If you do not give a disk drive name, the current disk drive will be used.

2. If you do not give a file name, the status of the background printing will be displayed.

3. You may print files only in the current directory. Paths are not allowed.

4. Do not queue more than 10 files. If you do, PRINT will give you the message `PRINT queue is full` and ignore the command. PRINT will not function correctly until all currently queued files are printed.

5. A switch will affect the file name that precedes the switch and all files that follow until the next switch is found on the line.

6. Entering **PRINT /C** has no effect.

7. The first time you invoke the PRINT command, the message

   `Name of list device [PRN]:`

   will appear. You may do either of the following:

   A. Press <Enter>. This will send the files to LPT1:. If LPT1: is redirected (see MODE command), the files will be redirected.

B.   Enter a valid DOS device name. Printing will be to this device. If you enter a device that is not connected to your system, unpredictable things will happen.

You cannot change the assignment for background printing until the queue (line) is empty; you have changed the current disk drive or directories; and you have issued the PRINT command again.

8.   Files are printed in the order in which they were entered. If wild cards are used in the file name, files are printed in the order they are found in the directory.

9.   If DOS detects a disk error in the file that it is trying to print, DOS cancels the printing of the file and continues with any other files that are in line to be printed.

Notes: PRINT controls the background printing feature of DOS V2.

Background printing is simply the printing of a disk-based file during the computer's free time. This free time occurs when the computer is not performing a CPU-intensive task.

The word *queue* comes from the Old French word for *tail* or *line*. When you invoke the PRINT command to print a file, you queue this file to be printed, or you add this file to the line of files to be printed. DOS will print each file in the line as free time is available.

Background printing is best used with program files stored in ASCII format. The PRINT command will print any disk file. All characters in the file are transmitted to the printer, including control characters. An exception is made for the tab character Ctrl-I or CHR$(9), which DOS pads with spaces to the next 8-column boundary. If you attempt to background print a .COM or .EXE file, your printer will do strange things.

The position of a switch is important because it affects the file preceding and all files following the switch until another switch is encountered. For example, the command

PRINT LETTER.TXT /P PROGRAM.DOC MYFILE.TXT /C TEST.DOC

will result in the following:

1.   Place the files LETTER.TXT and PROGRAM.DOC into the queue to be background printed.

2.   Cancel the background printing of MYFILE.TXT and TEST.DOC.

In this example, the /P switch affects the files before and after it. The /C switch affects the file before it and all files that follow.

If you use the /T switch, all files in the queue, including the file being background printed, will be canceled. Giving the /T switch with a particular file name is unnecessary because all files, including any file names given on the command line, will be canceled.

If you cancel or terminate a file that is being printed, the following occurs:

1. A cancellation message is printed on the printer. If you terminate (/T) all files, the message says: All files canceled by operator. If you cancel (/C) the file currently being printed, the name of the file will appear with the message File canceled by operator.

2. The printer does a form feed.

3. The printer's bell rings.

4. If all files have not been canceled, printing will continue with the next queued file (next file on the list).

If a disk error occurs during the background printing of a file, the following occurs:

1. The current file is canceled.

2. A disk error message appears on the printer.

3. The printer performs a form feed and rings its bell.

4. DOS prints any remaining files in the queue.

Several cautions about the PRINT command should be mentioned. First, when PRINT has control of the printer, don't try to print anything else. Strange things may happen. If you are in BASIC, you will get a printer error message. If you are at the system level or are using some other program, what you attempt to print may be printed in the middle of a background printing task; your output will appear in the middle of the background printout.

Second, if you try to queue more than 10 files, you will not be able to cancel (/C) or terminate (/T) the files if you change to a different directory or to a different disk drive. Once the files have been printed, you may change directories or disk drives without losing the ability to cancel or terminate the print files.

Third, if you are printing files that reside on a floppy disk, don't remove the disk until PRINT is finished printing the files. In addition, don't edit, alter, or erase the files being PRINTed. DOS will skip the file if the disk is removed or deleted (as if DOS had a disk error), or may not print the correct copy of the file (if the file is edited or altered).

Messages:

1. `All files canceled by operator`

   INFORMATIONAL: You have used the */T* switch to terminate all queued files.

2. `Errors on list device indicate that it may be off-line. Please check`

   WARNING: The device used for PRINT is probably not selected, connected, or turned on. Check your printer and cable and check to see that all connections are correct.

3. `File canceled by operator`

   INFORMATIONAL: This message appears on the printout to remind you that the printout is only a partial listing of the file because you canceled the printing of the file.

4. `File is currently being printed`
   `File is in queue`

   INFORMATIONAL: This message tells you what file is currently being printed and what files are in line to be printed. The message is displayed whenever you use PRINT with no parameters or if you queue additional files.

5. `List output is not assigned to a device`

   ERROR: The device you gave PRINT is not a recognized device. PRINT will abort. To solve this problem, reissue PRINT and give a correct device name when DOS requests it.

6. `Print queue is empty`

   INFORMATIONAL: No files are currently in line to be printed by PRINT.

7. `Print queue is full`

   WARNING: You attempted to add too many files to PRINT, exceeding the 10-file limit. Your request to add more files has failed for every file past the 10-file limit in the queue. You must wait until PRINT has processed a file before you can add another one. (See the cautions about PRINT in the Notes section.)

8. `Resident part of PRINT installed`

    INFORMATIONAL: The first time you use PRINT, this message tells you that PRINT has installed itself into DOS and has increased the size of DOS by about 3,200 bytes.

9. `disk-error-type error on file filename`

    WARNING: This message appears on the printer. A disk error (`disk-error-type`) occurred when DOS was trying to read the file `filename`. The procedure for disk errors will be followed.

PROMPT
(Set the system prompt)   Version 2 - Internal

Purpose: Allows the user to customize the DOS system prompt (the A>, or
                 "A prompt")

Syntax: **PROMPT** *promptstring*

                 promptstring is the text to be used for the new system prompt.

Exit Codes: None

Rules: 1. If you do not enter the *promptstring*, the standard system prompt
                     will reappear (A>).

                 2. Any text you enter for *promptstring* will become the new system
                     prompt. You may enter special characters with the meta-strings listed
                     below.

                 3. The new system prompt stays in effect until you reset the computer
                     or reissue the PROMPT command.

                 4. To see the text of PROMPT after it has been set, use the SET
                     command.

                 5. To start the prompt with a character that is normally a DOS
                     delimiter (blank, semicolon, comma, etc.), precede the character with
                     a null meta-string (a character that has no meaning to PROMPT,
                     such as a **$A**).

Meta-strings: A *meta-string* is a group of characters that is transformed into another
                 character or characters. To use certain characters, you must enter the
                 appropriate meta-string to place the desired character(s) in your
                 promptstring. Otherwise, DOS will immediately attempt to interpret the
                 character (for example, the < or > signs).

                 All meta-strings begin with the dollar sign ($) and are two characters in
                 length (including the $).

Character	What It Produces
$	$, the dollar sign
_ (underscore)	Carriage return, line feed (Move to the first position of the next line.)
b	|, the vertical **b**ar
e	The **Esc**ape character, CHR$(27)
d	The **d**ate, like the DATE command
h	The **b**ackspace character, which erases the previous character, CHR$(8)
g	>, the **g**reater than character
l	<, the **l**ess than character
n	The current disk drive
p	The current disk drive and path, including the current directory
q	=, the e**q**ual sign
t	The **t**ime, like the TIME command
v	The **v**ersion number of DOS
All other characters	Nothing or null; the character is ignored

Examples: A.   **PROMPT**

or

B.   **PROMPT ng**

sets the DOS system prompt to the normal prompt (A>). Example A is the default. If you do not specify a prompt string, the standard system prompt is restored. In example B the **$n** is the letter of the current disk drive. The **$g** is the greater than sign (>). The new prompt, if the current disk drive is A:, becomes "A" + ">" or "A>."

C.   **PROMPT The current drive is $n:**

sets the new system prompt to

    The current drive is A:

D.   **PROMPT $p**

sets the system prompt to the current disk drive and the path to the current directory. If you were using the example disk in drive A and were in the SAMPLES directory, the system prompt in example **4** would show the following:

```
A:\DOS\BASIC\SAMPLES
```

E.   **PROMPT $A;$t;**

sets the system prompt to

```
;12:04:12.46;
```

or whatever the system time is. Note that the semicolon is normally used to separate items on the DOS command line. To make the first character of the system prompt a delimiter, a null meta-string must be used. Because "$A" does not have any special meaning for DOS, it ignores this meta-string but allows the semicolon to become the first character for the new prompt.

F.   **PROMPT $$**

sets the next system prompt to imitate the UNIX prompt

```
$
```

Notes: The PROMPT command is a new DOS V2 command that lets users have greater control over their systems—in this case, the system prompt. With the new hierarchical directories, it is helpful to display the current path on your disk drive. For that reason, many DOS V2 users may want to set the system prompt to

   PROMPT $p

to display the current disk drive and the current path.

Any text may be used in the prompt, including text you might not normally think of, such as your name. Because I am conscious of time and forgetful of dates, my normal system prompt is

```
PROMPT $d $t $p $_yes, Chris $
```

which sets the system prompt to the date, time, and current disk drive and path, then moves to the next line and displays "yes, Chris," as in the following:

```
Mon 8-15-1983 9:57:13.11 A:\DOS\BASIC
yes, Chris _
```

I used the last dollar sign to ensure that a space would appear between the "s" in "Chris" and whatever I type at this new system prompt. Some text editors "strip" out any spaces after the last printable character on a line. (IBM's Personal Editor does this.) To force the space, I use the dollar sign, which DOS currently ignores, as the last character. New versions of DOS may force me to use a complete null meta-string like the "$A" instead.

The system prompt has two disadvantages. First, it is a wordy two-line prompt that distracts other people who use my computer. Second, if drive A is the current disk drive, you must always have a floppy in the drive. I use an IBM XT. Normally, the current disk drive is the hard disk, drive C. Whenever I make drive A the current drive, I must have a DOS disk in the drive because every time the system prompt is displayed, DOS reads the disk first to obtain the current path. DOS does this because, when you change diskettes, the current directory you were working with before may not exist on the new diskette. If DOS senses that you are working with a different diskette, DOS resets the current directory of the new disk to the root directory.

Another problem with this prompt is that if the drive door is left open or no diskette is in the minifloppy disk drive, I get a "drive not ready" error. If you use the "$p" (drive/path) meta-string in your prompt, expect DOS to read the current disk drive before DOS displays your customized system prompt.

PROMPT is an enjoyable command with which to experiment. You can try it many times without "hurting" anything. Once you have created a prompt that you like, include it in the AUTOEXEC.BAT file, or create a separate batch file that you can execute once DOS has started. To cancel your new prompt and restore the old A-prompt, just reissue the PROMPT without a *promptstring*.

RECOVER
(Recover files or disk directory)   V2 - External

Purpose: Recovers a file with bad sectors or a file from a disk with a damaged directory

Syntax: To recover a file:

> **RECOVER** *d:path\filename.ext*

To recover a disk with a damaged directory:

> **RECOVER** *d:*

d: is the name of the disk drive holding the damaged file/diskette.

path is the path name of the path to the directory holding the file to recover.

filename.ext is the file to recover. Wild cards are allowed, but only the first file that matches the wild-card file name will be RECOVERed.

Exit Codes: None

Rules: *1.   Do not use this command on files or disks that do not need it!

2.   If you do not give a drive name, the current disk will be used.

3.   If you do not give a path name, the current directory will be used.

4.   If you give a file name, DOS will recover as much information as possible from the file, skipping over the bad sectors.

*5.   If you give just a drive name or do not give any names, DOS will attempt to RECOVER the directory of the disk.

6.   If you give a wild-card character in the file name, RECOVER will work only on the first file it finds that matches the ambiguous name.

7.   RECOVER will not restore erased files.

Notes: RECOVER attempts to recover either a file with a bad sector or a disk whose directory contains a bad sector.

To recover a file with one or more bad sectors, use RECOVER d:filename.ext. (DOS gives you a disk error when you try to use the file). DOS will read the file, one sector at a time. If DOS successfully reads a sector, DOS places the information into a temporary file. If DOS cannot successfully read the sector, DOS skips the sector but marks it in the FAT so that no other program will use the bad sector. This process continues until the entire file is read. The old file is erased, and the temporary file is renamed to the same name as that of the damaged file. The new file will be in the same directory as the old file.

If the damaged file is a program file, chances are that the program cannot be used. If the file is a data or text file, some information can be recovered. Because DOS reads to the end of the file, make sure that any garbage at the end has been edited out with a text editor or a word processor.

To recover a disk, type the disk drive name after the command. DOS will create a new root directory and recover each file and subdirectory, giving them the name *FILEnnnn.REC*. (*nnnn* is a four-digit number.) Even good files will be placed in the *FILEnnnn.REC* files. The only way you can determine which file corresponds to which *FILEnnnn.REC* is to type or dump each file and use the last printed directory of the disk—or to have a good memory. If you have a disk editor that can display the ASCII and hexadecimal characters of a file, the editor will be a big help. If you don't have one, type each file and rename it after you are sure what it is. Then try to guess the remaining files.

Remember that subdirectories will also be RECOVERed into *FILEnnnn.REC* files. If you TYPE the file, the first character will be a period (.). About halfway across the screen you will see a double period (..). When you see these two symbols, you can safely guess that this file is a subdirectory.

RECOVER does not recover erased files. You will need a separate utility program to recover them.

(For more information, see Chapter 12.)

Message: Warning-directory full

ERROR: The root directory on the disk is now full. No more files can be RECOVERed. RECOVER will stop. You should erase or copy the files in the root directory to free more directory space and rerun RECOVER.

RENAME
(Rename file)

V1 and V2 - Internal

Purpose:	Changes the name of the disk file(s)
Syntax:	**RENAME** *d:path***filename1**.*ext1* **filename2**.*ext2*

or

REN *d:path***filename1**.*ext1* **filename2**.*ext2*

d: is the name of the disk drive holding the files to be renamed.

path\\ is the path name of the path to the files to be renamed.

filename1.*ext1* is the current name of the file. Wild cards are permitted.

filename2.*ext2* is the new name for the file. Wild cards are allowed.

Rules:

1. If you do not give a drive name, the current disk drive will be used.

2. If you do not give a path name, the current directory will be used.

3. You can give only a disk name and a path name for the first file name.

4. You must give both the old file name and the new file name with their appropriate extensions, if any.

5. Wild-card characters are permitted in the file names.

6. If a file in the same directory already has the new file name (**filename2**.*ext2*), a Duplicate file name or File not found message is displayed, and no further action is taken.

Notes:

RENAME, or the shorthand form REN, changes the name of files on the disk. The form is simply

    RENAME old name new name

Because you are renaming an established disk file, any drive or path designation goes with the old name. DOS will know which file you are renaming.

Wild-card characters are acceptable in either the old or the new name, but these can be troublesome if you are not careful. For example, suppose that a directory has the following files:

```
LETTER.TXT
LETTER1.TXT
RENAME.DOC
RENAME.TXT
```

If you attempt to rename all .TXT files as .DOC files with the command

RENAME *.TXT *.DOC

RENAME will stop when it encounters RENAME.TXT because a RENAME.DOC already exists. However, all .TXT files preceding RENAME.TXT will be successfully changed to .DOC files.

Messages:

1. Duplicate file name or File not found

   ERROR: You attempted to change a file name to a name that already existed, or the file to be renamed does not exist in the directory. Check the directory for conflicting names. Make sure that the file name does exist and that you have spelled it correctly. Then try again.

2. Invalid number of parameters

   ERROR: You have given too few or too many file names. You must give two file names. Possible causes are that spaces exist between the disk drive name, path name, or file name for the first file; or that you have used an invalid character in the file names.

3. Missing file name

   ERROR: You forgot to enter the new name for the file.

RESTORE
(Restore files to the hard disk)   V2 - External

Purpose: Restores one or more BACKed-UP files from the floppy diskettes to the hard disk. This command complements BACKUP.

Syntax: **RESTORE d1:** *d2:path\filename.ext /S/P*

d1: is the disk drive name that contains the floppy diskette(s).

d2: is the hard disk drive.

path is the path name of the path to the directory that will receive the restored files.

filename.ext is the name of the file you want to restore. Wild cards are allowed.

Switches: */S*   Restores files in the current directory and all other *subdirectories* beyond it

/P   *Prompts* and asks whether a file that has been changed since the last backup or that is marked read-only should be restored

Exit Codes: *0* = Normal completion
1 = No files were found to restore
3 = Terminated by the operator (through a Ctrl-Break or Esc)
4 = Terminated by an encountered error

Rules:
1.   Only files that have been saved on floppy diskettes with the BACKUP command may be RESTOREd.

2.   You must give the floppy disk drive name(**d1:**). If the current disk to be restored is the hard disk, you need not give *d2:*.

3.   If you do not give a path name, the current directory on the hard disk will be used.

4.   If you do not give a file name, all files backed up from this directory will be restored (Not giving a file name is the same as using *.*).

5. RESTORE will prompt you to insert the backup diskettes in order. If you insert a diskette out of order, RESTORE will prompt you to insert the correct diskette.

Notes: If you used the */S* (all subdirectories) switch and removed a subdirectory holding files on the backup diskettes, RESTORE will re-create the subdirectory, then restore the files into it.

(For more information, see Chapter 12.)

Messages: 1. `Backup file sequence error`

ERROR: A file was stored on two or more backup diskettes. The first part of the file was not restored first. You have inserted the diskettes in the wrong order. Rerun RESTORE, starting with the correct diskette.

2. `Insert backup diskette xx in drive d:`
    `Strike any key when ready`

INFORMATIONAL: RESTORE wants the next diskette in sequence. Insert the diskette and press a key.

3. `The last file was not restored`

WARNING: RESTORE was stopped before the current file was fully restored to the hard disk. You aborted RESTORE, or the hard disk is full. In either case, RESTORE deleted the partially restored file.

4. `Warning! Diskette is out of sequence`
    `Replace the diskette or continue`
    `Strike any key when ready`

WARNING: You have a backup diskette that is out of order. Insert the correct diskette in the drive and continue. You may continue with the wrong diskette if you do not want to restore any files on the skipped diskettes or if a partial file was being restored. If a partial file has been restored, RESTORE will want to restore the rest of the file. RESTORE will continue to reissue this message until the right diskette is inserted.

5. `Warning! File filename`
    `is a read-only file`
    `Replace this file (Y/N?)_`

WARNING: This message appears when you give the /P switch. The file (filename) already exists on the hard disk and is marked read-only. Answer **Y** to replace the preexisting file with the backup copy, **N** to
skip it.

6. Warning! File filename
   was changed after it was backed up
   Replace this file (Y/N?)_

WARNING: This message appears when you give the /P switch. The file (filename) already exists on the hard disk and has a later date than the backup copy, meaning the backup copy may be out of date. Answer **Y** to replace the preexisting file with the backup copy, **N** to skip it.

7. Warning! No files were found to restore

WARNING: No files that matched the file specifications you gave were found on the backup diskettes. This message can also occur if you reset SWITCHAR.

8. *** Files were backed up mm/dd/yyyy ***

INFORMATIONAL: RESTORE displays the backup date for these diskettes.

9. *** Restoring files from diskette xx ***

INFORMATIONAL: RESTORE will display a list of the files it is restoring from backup diskette number xx.

RMDIR or RD
(Remove directory)   V2 - Internal

Purpose: Removes a subdirectory

Syntax: **RMDIR** *d:* **path**

                or

                RD *d:* **path**

                d: is the name of the drive holding the subdirectory.

                path is the path name of the path to the subdirectory. The last path name is the subdirectory you want to delete.

Exit Codes: None

Rules: 1. If you do not specify a drive name, the current drive will be used.

                2. You must give the name of the subdirectory to be deleted. If you supply a path, the subdirectory to be deleted must be the last name in the path.

                3. The subdirectory to be deleted must be empty. (The only files allowed are "." and "..".)

                4. You cannot delete the current directory or the root directory of a disk.

Notes: RMDIR, or the shorthand form RD, removes subdirectories from the disk. RMDIR is the complement of the MKDIR command (make directory).

                When you remove a subdirectory, it must be empty, except for the current directory file (".") and parent directory files (".."). The current directory also cannot be the directory you are using. If you attempt to remove a subdirectory that is not empty or is the current directory, DOS will give you an error message and not delete the directory.

Message: Invalid path, not directory
                or directory not empty

                RMDIR did not remove the specified directory because you gave an invalid directory in the path, the subdirectory still has files in it other than the "." and ".." entries, or you misspelled the path or directory name to be removed. Check each possibility.

SET
(Set/show environment)   V2 - Internal

Purpose: Sets or shows the system environment

Syntax: To display the environment:

    SET

To add or alter the environment:

    SET name=_string_

name is the name of the string you want to add to the environme ı٠.

string is the information you want to store in the environment.

Special Terms: _Environment_ is a reserved area in RAM memory for alphanumeric (string) information that may be examined and used by DOS commands or user programs. For example, the environment usually contains _COMSPEC,_ the location of COMMAND.COM; _PATH,_ the additional path to find programs and batch files; and _PROMPT,_ the string that defines the DOS system prompt.

Exit Codes: None

Rules:
1. If you do not specify a **name** or _string,_ SET will display the current environment.

2. To set a string in the environment or to change the string associated with a current name, use **SET name=string.**

3. To delete a **name**, use **SET name=.**

4. Any lower-case letters in **name** will be changed to upper-case letters when placed in the environment.

5. You can also set the system prompt and information for the PATH command with SET, instead of using the PROMPT or PATH commands.

6. You may change the COMSPEC (the location of COMMAND.COM) with SET.

    If you load a resident program (such as MODE, GRAPHICS, or PRINT), DOS cannot expand the environment past 127 characters. If you have not used more than 127 characters, you may add additional information up to that limit. If you have already used 127 characters or more, you cannot add additional information to the envirnoment.

Notes

SET is an advanced DOS command that is seldom used. This command puts information in a safe place in memory for later use by invoked programs. One such use is to store the directory path to some data files or program overlays. When the program is invoked, it can examine the RAM memory where the SET information is stored and issue the proper commands to find the data or program overlays.

SET is a versatile command. It can put almost any information into the RAM memory for the environment. (Remember the restriction stated in Rule 7, however.) Unfortunately, few programs take advantage of the features provided by this versatile command.

SORT
(Sort string filter)   V2 - External

Purpose:	Reads lines from the standard input device, performs an ASCII sort of the lines, then writes the lines to the standard output device. The sorting may be ascending or descending and may start at any column in the line.
Syntax:	**SORT** /R /+c
Switches:	/R Sorts in *reverse* order. This means that the letter Z comes before the letter A.
	/+c Starts sorting with the column number indicated c
Exit Codes:	None

Rules:

1. If you do not give the /R (reverse sort) switch, the file will be sorted in ascending order.

2. If you do not give the /+c switch, sorting will start with the first column (first character on the line).

3. If you do not redirect the input or output, all input will be from the keyboard (standard input), and all output will be to the video display (standard output).

4. SORT uses the ASCII sequence and does not expand any control characters. (See Notes on the significance of this rule.)

5. The maximum file size that SORT can handle is 63K (64,512 characters).

6. SORT sorts the entire physical file, including any information beyond the end-of-file marker.

Examples:

1. **SORT <WORDS.TXT**

   sorts the lines in the file called WORDS.TXT and displays the sorted lines on the video display.

2. **SORT <WORDS.TXT /R**

   reverse sorts the lines in the file WORDS.TXT and displays the lines on the video screen.

3. **SORT/+8 <WORDS.TXT**

starts the sorting at the eighth character in each line of the
WORDS.TXT file and displays the output on the video display.

4. **DIR | SORT /+14**

displays the directory information sorted by file size. (The file size starts
in the 14th column.) Unfortunately, other lines, such as the volume
label, are also sorted starting at the 14th column. (See Notes below on
sorting numbers.)

Notes: SORT is a "dumb" general-purpose sorting program. Don't let the term
"dumb" deceive you. SORT is a powerful filter, but it has some limitations.

First, SORT uses the ASCII sequence for sorting. Look at the ASCII chart in
Appendix C. Note the relative positions of the numbers, punctuation
symbols, and letters. The first limitation of SORT stems from this chart.

Notice that the upper-case A comes before the upper-case Z, but the lower-
case "a" comes after the upper-case Z. SORT respects this difference,
sometimes to the chagrin of the user. For example, the word "TEXT" comes
before the words "text," "TEXt," and "TeXT."

A second limitation is that numbers are treated not as numbers but as
characters. Therefore, 1 will always come before 2, 3, or 9. (The 0 comes
before 1, by the way.) The problem is that 11, 123, and 12576 will all come
before 2, 3, 21, or any other number that does not begin with 0 or 1.

This limitation does not affect numbers stored in strings that are left-padded
with spaces (right justified). When sorting the numbers "   1," " 121," and
"1915," the numbers (actually character strings) are sorted into the proper
order. This is why the previous example that sorts a directory by file size
works. The file size is stored as a left-padded ASCII character string.

For these reasons, SORT is a "dumb" sorting program. The additional
intelligence required to recognize and handle similarly upper- and lower-case
letters and to handle numbers as numbers is not in the SORT filter. Programs
that solve these problems are available. However, these sorting programs are
not provided with DOS. SORT was not intended to handle these problems. It
is simply a good utility program for "standard" sorting and is provided "free"
with DOS.

Control characters are another problem. When you print a Ctrl-I (the tab
character) on the screen or printer, the printer moves out to the next tab

column, usually every ninth character position. Because SORT does not expand tab characters, the output you expect from SORT may not be what you get. Some text editors compress extra spaces into tab characters (Personal Editor, for one). When you sort a file created by Personal Editor, some lines may appear to be out of order. Loading and resaving the file without tab characters (Personal Editor has this option), will give you the correct order when you resort the file.

A thorny problem may arise when you try to sort the output from some text processors or data files created by a few languages. Some text-processing programs (for example, WordStar) put out a series of end-of-file markers, such as Ctrl-Z or CHR$(26), to fill out the last sector when you save a file. Most programs will stop reading more information from the file when they see the end-of-file marker. SORT works with the file's "real" length, the length recorded in the directory. This means that SORT will sort the end-of-file markers.

Look at the ASCII character. The Ctrl-Z comes before any printable characters. Therefore, the first line in the newly sorted file is a series of end-of-file markers. When you attempt to edit or type the sorted file, nothing is there because either the TYPE command or the word-processing program sees the end-of-file marker at the front of the file and thinks that's all there is to the file. Actually, the entire file is there, but it is trapped behind the end-of-file markers.

Some languages store their data in a special, compressed format. When you type a data file, garbage appears on the screen. This kind of file should not be sorted with SORT. The results you get will be unpredictable. The data is not stored as ASCII numbers but as compressed codes, some of which may be control characters. SORT does not have the intelligence to handle these files.

Don't underestimate SORT, however. It can be a very useful filter if you use it correctly. SORT works best when it is used in the "pipeline" with other commands, such as DIR.

SYS
(Place the operating system
on the diskette)

V1 and V2 - External

Purpose: Places a copy of DOS on the specified diskette

Syntax: **SYS** *d:*

d: is the disk drive holding the diskette that will receive a copy of DOS.

Exit Codes: None

Rules: 1.   The disk to be SYSed must be:

      A.   Previously formatted, using the */S* option (DOS V1 or V2).

      B.   Previously formatted, using the */B* option (DOS V2 only).

      C.   Completely empty.

      D.   Formatted with a special program (non-IBM supplied) that reserves the proper disk space for the operating system.

If you attempt to SYStem a disk that is not one of the above, a No room for system on destination disk message will appear, and DOS will not perform the operation.

2.   A copy of DOS (IBMBIO.COM and IBMDOS.COM) must reside on the current disk.

Notes: The SYS command places a copy of IBMBIO.COM and IBMDOS.COM on the targeted disk. To make the disk bootable (able to load and execute the disk operating system), you must also copy COMMAND.COM.

The SYS command puts DOS on application program diskettes sold without DOS. These SYSed diskettes allow you to boot the computer system from diskettes with the application software. A diskette provided by the program publisher must be specially formatted, or SYS will not work. You should check the instructions that come with the applications program to see if you can SYS the diskette.

There is a small difference between V1 and V2 for SYS. SYS V2 checks the destination disk to see if the proper space is available for DOS. If not, an error message is given. SYS V1 places DOS on the diskette anyway, regardless of whether the proper space is available. Running SYS V1 on a diskette with existing files can garbage some files on the diskette.

To load DOS initially into the computer, the first two entries in the root directory of the boot disk must be IBMBIO.COM and IBMDOS.COM (even though these are system files and hidden from the DIR command). IBMBIO.COM also must reside on consecutive sectors. If either of these two conditions is not true, DOS will not load itself properly from this disk.

Messages: 1.   `Insert DOS disk in d: and strike any key when ready`

INFORMATIONAL: DOS tried to load itself into memory but could not find IBMBIO.COM, IBMDOS.COM, and/or COMMAND.COM. Loading these files into memory is a required step before SYS can place the operating system on a diskette or disk. Put the diskette that holds all three programs into drive `d:` and hit a key.

2.   `No room for system on destination disk`

ERROR: The diskette or disk was not formatted with the necessary reserved space for DOS. This diskette cannot be SYStemed.

3.   `System transferred`

INFORMATIONAL: DOS has successfully placed a copy of IBMBIO.COM and a copy of IBMDOS.COM on the target diskette.

TIME
(Set/show the time)

V1.0 - External
V1.1 and V2 - Internal

Purpose: Shows and/or sets the system time

Syntax: **TIME** *hh:mm:ss.xx*

hh is the one- or two-digit representation for hours (0 to 23).

mm is the one- or two-digit representation for minutes (0 to 60).

ss is the one- or two-digit representation for seconds (0 to 60).

xx is the one- or two-digit representation for hundredths of a second (0 to 99).

Exit Codes: None

Rules:
1. If you enter a valid time, it will be accepted, and no other message will appear.

2. If you do not enter the time with the TIME command, the following message will appear:

   ```
   Current time is hh:mm:ss.xx
   Enter new time
   ```

   If you just press Enter, the time will not be reset. If you enter a valid time, the new time will be accepted immediately, and no other message will be displayed.

3. You must enter the correct delimiters between the numbers, as shown above under Syntax (colons between the hours, minutes, and seconds; a period between the seconds and hundredths of a second).

4. You do not have to enter all the information. If you change only the first parts of the time, the remaining portions will be set to 0.

5. If you specify an invalid time or incorrect delimiters, an `Invalid time` message will be displayed, and you will be prompted to enter the time again.

Notes: TIME is used to set the internal, 24-hour software clock of the computer. The time and date are recorded in the directory for every file whenever you create or change it. This directory information can help you locate the most recent version of a file.

The software clock used by the native Personal Computer is based on the 60 Hz power supply. As such, the time usually loses or gains several seconds each day. This inaccuracy is not a fault of the computer, but a minor (and normal) problem with the ac power provided by your power company.

If you don't set the time when you start up your computer, the time defaults to 00:00:00.00.

Message: `Invalid time`

ERROR: You entered a nonsense time or did not punctuate the time correctly. Check your typing and try again.

TREE
(Display all directories)   V2 - External

Purpose: Displays all the subdirectories on a disk; optionally displays all the files in
                 each directory

Syntax: **TREE** *d: /F*

                 d: is the name of the disk drive holding the disk you want to examine.

Switch: */F*   Displays all the *files* in the directories

Rules: 1.   If you do not give a drive name, the current disk drive will be used.

                 2.   All directories, starting with the root directory, are displayed with their
                      full path names. If the */F* switch is used, every file in the directory (with
                      the exception of the "." and ".." entries) will be listed with its full path
                      name.

Notes: The TREE command displays all directories on a DOS V2 disk, freeing the
                 user from having to enter each directory, do a DIR command, and search for
                 each <DIR> file (subdirectory). The */F* option will also display each file in
                 every directory.

                 The tree shows one directory or file on a line and can quickly scroll off the
                 screen. If you want a copy of the entire tree, redirect the output to the printer
                 by typing the line

                 TREE >PRN

                 or

                 TREE /F >PRN

                 The disadvantage to TREE is that the file's date, time, and size are not
                 displayed. You will have to do a DIR command to find this information.

Hint: After you have finished a BACKUP of your hard disk, make a printed copy
                 of the directories with the TREE command by typing the line

                 TREE d: /F>PRN

where **d:** is the name of the hard disk drive. Store the printed copy with the BACKed-UP diskette. You can then quickly locate the files you have backed up.

Messages:

1.   Invalid path

   ERROR: TREE could not use a subdirectory. Something is wrong with the directory file. Run CHKDSK, without the */F* switch, to determine what is wrong with the disk or diskette, then take the necessary corrective actions.

2.   No subdirectories exist

   INFORMATIONAL: The root directory of the disk you specified has no subdirectories. If there should have been subdirectories, DIR the diskette or disk, or run CHKDSK.

TYPE
(Type file on screen)

V1 and V2 - Internal

Purpose: Displays the contents of the file on the screen

Syntax: **TYPE** *d: path***filename.***ext*

d: is the name of the disk drive holding the file to type.

path\\ is the DOS path to the file.

filename.*ext* is the name of the file to type. Wild cards are not permitted.

Exit Codes: None

Rules:

1. If you do not give a drive name, the current drive will be used.

2. If you do not give a path name, the current directory will be used.

3. You must provide a file name that matches the name in the directory.

4. All characters in the file, including control characters, are sent to the screen. However, each tab character Ctrl-I, or CHR$(9), is expanded to the next eight-character boundary.

5. You cannot type a directory.

Notes: The TYPE command displays on the video screen the characters in the file. TYPE allows you to see what a file contains.

If you try to TYPE some data files and most program files, you will see strange characters on the screen because TYPE is trying to display the machine-language instructions as ASCII characters.

The output of TYPE, as with most other DOS commands, can be redirected to the printer by adding the line

     >PRN

or by typing Ctrl-PrtSc. (Don't forget to do another Ctrl-PrtSc to turn off the printing.)

However, unpredictable things can happen if you print when you TYPE a program file or some data files that contain control characters. As a rule, if what appears on the video display looks like nonsense, it will look like nonsense—or worse— on your print

VER
(Display version number)   V2 - Internal

Purpose:	Shows the DOS version number on the video display
Syntax:	**VER**
Exit Codes:	None
Rules:	None
Notes:	The VER command shows the one-digit version number, followed by a two-digit revision number. The current use of this command is to indicate whether or not you are working with DOS V2.0, V2.1, or an earlier version. If you type the line

VER

you will see a message something like this:

IBM Personal Computer DOS Version 2.00

or

IBM Personal Computer DOS Version 2.10

If you see a Bad command or file name message, you are working with DOS V1.x.

VERIFY
(Set/show disk verification)   V2 - Internal

Purpose: Sets/shows whether the data written to the disk(s) has been checked for proper recording

Syntax: To show the verify status:

    VERIFY

To set the verify status:

    VERIFY ON

or

    VERIFY OFF

Rules:
1. VERIFY accepts only one of two parameters: ON or OFF.
2. Once VERIFY is ON, it remains on until one of the following occurs:

    A. A VERIFY OFF is performed.

    B. A SET VERIFY system call turns it off.

    C. DOS is rebooted.

Notes: VERIFY controls the checking of data just written on the disk to ensure that the data has been correctly recorded. If VERIFY is off, DOS will not check the data. If VERIFY is on, DOS will check the data. VERIFY does not affect any other DOS operation.

Two factors affect the tradeoff between VERIFY ON or OFF. If VERIFY is on, data integrity is assured. If VERIFY is OFF, you will be able to write to the disk faster. It is usually safe to leave VERIFY off if you are not working with critical information (such as a company's accounting figures). It is wise to turn VERIFY on when backing up your hard disk or making critical copies on the floppy disks.

The degree of performance lost in verifying the hard disk is different from floppy diskettes. DOS takes only 8 to 9 percent more time to verify information when writing to the fixed disk. DOS takes 90 percent more time when verifying information written to the floppy disk. This difference comes from most hard disks' fast, built-in routines for data verification. As a result, hard disks verify information at a rate faster than that of floppy disks. Also, DOS must do all the work itself when verifying information written to the floppy disk. These factors explain the tenfold difference in verification speed between the hard disk and the floppy disk.

Message: Must specify ON or OFF

ERROR: You entered a word other than ON or OFF after the VERIFY command.

VOL
(Display volume label)   V2 - Internal

Purpose: Displays the volume label of the disk, if the label exists

Syntax: **VOL** *d:*

              d: is the optional name of the disk drive whose label you wish to display.

Rule: If you do not give a disk drive name, the current disk drive will be used.

Message: Volume in drive d has no label

              INFORMATIONAL: The disk or diskette does not have a volume label.

Appendix A

Known Bugs in DOS V2.0

The following list of known bugs in PC DOS V2.0 is not complete but covers the major problems. It is very possible that users of PC DOS V2.0 may never encounter any of these problems.

DOS Input Redirection

DOS does not always find the true end-of-file marker when redirecting input to a program. For example, your redirected program expects an input of 80 characters. Suppose that only 50 characters are left in the file. DOS will read the 50 characters and "wait" forever for the other 30 characters. In other words, if your file does not have enough input to fulfill a program request, DOS will hang. The only remedy for the situation is to turn your system off, then on again. The system reset sequence does not work.

SORT Filter

SORT sorts the entire file line by line, using the file size shown in the directory. Some programs will fill out the last sector of a text file with end-of-file markers. The directory size of the file will be the true file size plus the padding end-of-file markers.

Because end-of-file markers come before any printable characters, SORT will bubble to the top of the file the line containing the end-of-file markers. When other programs, such as TYPE or other text editors, attempt to use the sorted file, the first item they will encounter in the sorted file is the end-of-file marker. These programs will immediately stop reading the file, assuming that they have reached the end of the file. No useful information will now be obtainable from the file.

This is not a bug in SORT per se but a caution. The fault lies with the text editors, which pad the text file with extra end-of-file markers, and with SORT.

SWITCHAR

Many of the DOS programs written by IBM do not use SWITCHAR, the switch character that can be set in CONFIG.SYS. This is not a bug in DOS. IBM does not document or recommend the resetting of SWITCHAR.

The major problem comes from BACKUP and RESTORE. BACKUP will back up files regardless of the SWITCHAR setting. RESTORE will restore only backup files that were saved while SWITCHAR was set to the slash (/), the normal setting. Otherwise, RESTORE will go through the motions of restoring the files but will not copy any files from the backup diskettes to the hard disk. The only solutions are to alter RESTORE (which is not recommended), edit every backup file to change the new path character (the slash) back to a backslash, or to make sure that SWITCHAR is the slash when you BACKUP.

Sample Hierarchical Directory

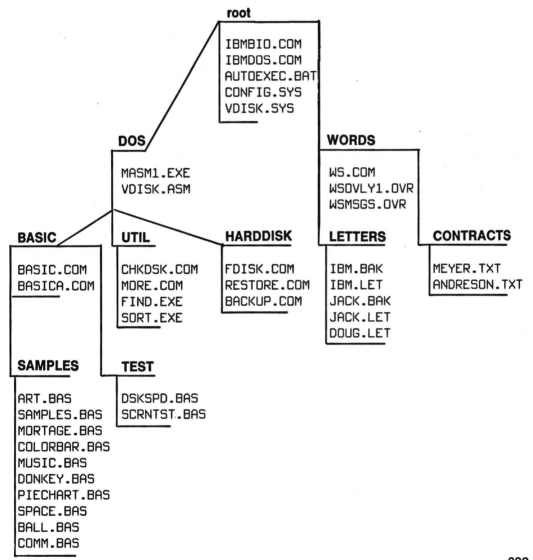

Appendix C
ASCII Codes

The codes for the American Standard Code for Information Interchange, or ASCII, are listed below.

Decimal	Hex	Octal	Binary	ASCII
0	00	000	00000000	(null) NUL
1	01	001	00000001	Ctrl-A SOH
2	02	002	00000010	Ctrl-B STX
3	03	003	00000011	Ctrl-C ETX
4	04	004	00000100	Ctrl-D EOT
5	05	005	00000101	Ctrl-E ENQ
6	06	006	00000110	Ctrl-F ACK
7	07	007	00000111	Ctrl-G (bell) BEL
8	08	010	00001000	Ctrl-H (backspace) BS
9	09	011	00001001	Ctrl-I (tab) horizontal HT
10	0A	012	00001010	Ctrl-J (linefeed) LF
11	0B	013	00001011	Ctrl-K (vertical tabs) VT
12	0C	014	00001100	Ctrl-L (formfeed) FF
13	0D	015	00001101	Ctrl-M (carriage return) CR
14	0E	016	00001110	Ctrl-N SO
15	0F	017	00001111	Ctrl-O SI
16	10	020	00010000	Ctrl-P DLE
17	11	021	00010001	Ctrl-Q DC1
18	12	022	00010010	Ctrl-R DC2
19	13	023	00010011	Ctrl-S DC3
20	14	024	00010100	Ctrl-T DC4
21	15	025	00010101	Ctrl-U NAK
22	16	026	00010110	Ctrl-V SYN

23	17	027	00010111	Ctrl-W ETB
24	18	030	00011000	Ctrl-X CAN
25	19	031	00011001	Ctrl-Y EM
26	1A	032	00011010	Ctrl-Z SUB
27	1B	033	00011011	Escape
28	1C	034	00011100	FS
29	1D	035	00011101	GS
30	1E	036	00011110	RS
31	1F	037	00011111	US
32	20	040	00100000	Space
33	21	041	00100001	!
34	22	042	00100010	"
35	23	043	00100011	#
36	24	044	00100100	$
37	25	045	00100101	%
38	26	046	00100110	&
39	27	047	00100111	'
40	28	050	00101000	(
41	29	051	00101001	)
42	2A	052	00101010	*
43	2B	053	00101011	+
44	2C	054	00101100	,
45	2D	055	00101101	-
46	2E	056	00101110	.
47	2F	057	00101111	/
48	30	060	00110000	0
49	31	061	00110001	1
50	32	062	00110010	2
51	33	063	00110011	3
52	34	064	00110100	4
53	35	065	00110101	5
54	36	066	00110110	6
55	37	067	00110111	7
56	38	070	00111000	8
57	39	071	00111001	9
58	3A	072	00111010	:
59	3B	073	00111011	;
60	3C	074	00111100	<

61	3D	075	00111101	=
62	3E	076	00111110	>
63	3F	077	00111111	?
64	40	100	01000000	@
65	41	101	01000001	A
66	42	102	01000010	B
67	43	103	01000011	C
68	44	104	01000100	D
69	45	105	01000101	E
70	46	106	01000110	F
71	47	107	01000111	G
72	48	110	01001000	H
73	49	111	01001001	I
74	4A	112	01001010	J
75	4B	113	01001011	K
76	4C	114	01001100	L
77	4D	115	01001101	M
78	4E	116	01001110	N
79	4F	117	01001111	O
80	50	120	01010000	P
81	51	121	01010001	Q
82	52	122	01010010	R
83	53	123	01010011	S
84	54	124	01010100	T
85	55	125	01010101	U
86	56	126	01010110	V
87	57	127	01010111	W
88	58	130	01011000	X
89	59	131	01011001	Y
90	5A	132	01011010	Z
91	5B	133	01011011	[
92	5C	134	01011100	\
93	5D	135	01011101	]
94	5E	136	01011110	^
95	5F	137	01011111	—
96	60	140	01100000	
97	61	141	01100001	a
98	62	142	01100010	b

99	63	143	01100011	c
100	64	144	01100100	d
101	65	145	01100101	e
102	66	146	01100110	f
103	67	147	01100111	g
104	68	150	01101000	h
105	69	151	01101001	i
106	6A	152	01101010	j
107	6B	153	01101011	k
108	6C	154	01101100	l
109	6D	155	01101101	m
110	6E	156	01101110	n
111	6F	157	01101111	o
112	70	160	01110000	p
113	71	161	01110001	q
114	72	162	01110010	r
115	73	163	01110011	s
116	74	164	01110100	t
117	75	165	01110101	u
118	76	166	01110110	v
119	77	167	01110111	w
120	78	170	01111000	x
121	79	171	01111001	y
122	7A	172	01111010	z
123	7B	173	01111011	{
124	7C	174	01111100		
125	7D	175	01111101	}
126	7E	176	01111110	~
127	7F	177	01111111	del, rubout

Index

More Computer Knowledge from Que

Que Order Line: 1-800-428-5331

All prices subject to change without notice.

MORE COMPUTER KNOWLEDGE FROM QUE

Improve Your Writing with Word Processing
by David F. Noble, Ph.D., and Virginia Noble, M.L.S.

This innovative book shows you how to use the power of word processing to improve your writing. More than 100 macros, or strings of commands, for popular word-processing programs let you transpose words, phrases, sentences, and paragraphs for analysis and revision. Block-rebuilding macros put revised paragraphs back together. The authors, who have taught university writing courses and are professional editors, present examples by famous writers, "block models" for writing paragraphs, and many practical tips.

IBM PC Expansion & Software Guide, 5th Edition

Que's *IBM PC Expansion & Software Guide* is the leading single source of information about hardware, software, supplies, and services for all IBM Personal Computers, including the XT and the new AT. Each edition of the *Guide* has been a best-seller, and the fifth edition is even bigger and better. Thousands of product descriptions, multiple indexes, easy-to-use format, and many other features make the *Guide* the best resource of its kind. For all users of IBM Personal Computers, this book is an essential investment!

Using 1-2-3
by Geoffrey T. LeBlond and Douglas Ford Cobb

This award-winning book has helped more than 250,000 1-2-3 users take advantage of the program's full power and flexibility. Special emphasis is given to keyboard macros, the data base function, and graphics capability. If 1-2-3 is your first electronic spreadsheet, *Using 1-2-3* offers an introduction to spreadsheeting. Both beginning and experienced users of 1-2-3 will benefit from the detailed, clear explanations and examples this number 1 best-seller provides.

Networking IBM PCs: A Practical Guide
by Michael Durr

This book explains how to select, install, use, and manage a local area network for IBM PCs and PC compatibles. Each of the critical management issues related to networking is discussed, including the risks and benefits of local area networks, security considerations, hardware organization, mainframe accessing, and much more. The author explains how to evaluate a network system before you buy and reviews each of the major network products currently available. If you want to understand the important issue of local area networking, this book is a superb guide.

Item	Title	Price	Quantity	Extension
126	Improve Your Writing with Word Processing	$12.95		
169	IBM PC Expansion & Software Guide, 5th Edition	$21.95		
125	Networking IBM PCs: A Practical Guide	$18.95		
39	Using 1-2-3	$17.95		

Book Subtotal	
Shipping & Handling ($1.75 per item)	
Indiana Residents Add 5% Sales Tax	
GRAND TOTAL	

Method of Payment:

☐ Check   ☐ VISA   ☐ MasterCard   ☐ American Express

Card Number _____ Exp. Date _____

Cardholder Name _____

Ship to _____

Address _____

City _____ State _____ ZIP _____

All prices subject to change without notice.

PCDOSUG-858

FOLD HERE

———

————————————————————

————————————————————

————————————————————

————————————————————

Que Corporation
7999 Knue Road
Indianapolis, IN 46250

_____

_____

_____

_____

Que Publishing, Inc.
7999 Knue Road
Indianapolis, IN 46250